366
RECIPES

MEATS

SUNBURST BOOKS

This edition first published in 1995 by
Sunburst Books, Deacon House, 65 Old Church Street,
London, SW3 5BS.

Copyright © 1995 Sunburst Books

ISBN 1 85778 056 6

Printed and bound in India

CONTENTS

BEEF
MINCE DISHES

SCOTCH MINCE
Serves 4-6

a knob of dripping
1 lb (450 g) lean minced beef
1 small onion; chopped

1 oz (25 g) porridge oats
1 beef stock cube
salt and freshly ground black pepper

Melt the dripping in a saucepan over a low heat, add the beef and fry gently to allow the fat to run out. Increase the heat and fry until brown. Add the onion and oats. Dissolve the stock cube in ¼ pt (450 ml) boiling water and add to the pan, stirring constantly. Season to taste. Cover and simmer for 1 hour or until the beef is tender. Alternatively the mixture may be turned into a casserole and cooked in a 350°F/180°C/Gas Mk 4 oven for 1 hour.

TEVIOT DALE PIE
Serves 4

1 lb (450 g) lean minced beef
1 medium onion, chopped
½ pt (300 ml) beef stock
1 tsp Worcestershire sauce
salt and freshly ground black pepper

8 oz (225 g) self-raising flour
1 oz (25 g) cornflour
3 oz (75 g) shredded suet
about ½ pt (300 ml) milk

Preheat the oven to 350°F/180°C/Gas Mk 4. Place the meat in a large non-stick saucepan and cook in its own fat over a medium heat until just brown. Add the onion and cook for 5 minutes until soft. Pour in the stock and Worcestershire sauce with salt and pepper to taste. Simmer over a low heat for 15-20 minutes. Mix the flour, cornflour and suet in a bowl; gradually add the milk, stirring constantly, to form a thick batter. Season with salt and pepper to taste. Place the meat in a 2 pt (1.1 litre) pie dish and cover with the batter. Bake for 25–30 minutes until the batter is risen and golden brown.

PASTICCIO MACARONIA
Serves 4-6

3 eggs
14 oz (400 g) Cheddar cheese, grated
1½ lb (675 g) beef mince, cooked
¾ pt (450 ml) Béchamel sauce
9 oz (250 g) macaroni
salt and freshly ground black pepper
chopped fresh parsley

Preheat the oven to 350°F/180°C/Gas Mk 4. Beat the eggs and 4 heaped tbsp of the cheese into the Béchamel sauce. Mix 3 tbsp into the mince. Cook the macaroni in boiling salted water until *al dente*, drain and cool slightly. Butter a casserole well and put in half the macaroni. Sprinkle with 3 tbsp cheese and spread the mince over. Add the remaining macaroni, sprinkle with more cheese and pour in the sauce. Top with the remaining cheese and bake for about 45 minutes or until golden brown. Serve with a green salad.

BEEF AND AUBERGINE BAKE
Serves 4

1 lb (450 g) aubergines, sliced
salt and freshly ground black pepper
1 tbsp oil
1 large onion, finely chopped
1 lb (450 g) minced beef
3 green peppers
8 oz (250 g) tomatoes, blanched, skinned, deseeded and sliced

Sprinkle salt over the aubergines and leave for 1 hour. Rinse well, drain and dry on absorbent kitchen paper. Preheat the oven to 375°F/190°C/Gas Mk 5. Heat the oil in a small frying pan and fry the onion until transparent. Remove the onion and mix well with the beef. Season to taste with salt and pepper and form into a large ball. Slice the peppers into rings, reserving the caps with stalks attached. Remove the seeds and white pith. Place the pepper rings around the sides and the bottom of a deep casserole together with three-quarters of the tomato slices. Put a layer of aubergines in the bottom of the casserole. Press the ball of beef into the centre and cover with the remaining tomatoes and aubergines. Place the pepper caps on top. Cover and bake for 1½ hours. Serve at once.

PASTITSIO
Serves 4-6

2 tbsp olive oil
1 medium onion, finely chopped
1 garlic clove, crushed
1 lb (450 g) minced beef
14 oz (400 g) can tomatoes
2 tsp chopped fresh marjoram
   or 1 tsp dried

1 tsp ground allspice
salt and freshly ground black pepper
8 oz (225 g) macaroni
2 eggs
½ pt (300 ml) yoghurt

Preheat the oven to 375°F/190°C/Gas Mk 5. Heat the oil in a heavy-based saucepan, and fry the onion and garlic gently for about 5 minutes until soft and lightly coloured. Add the minced beef in batches and fry until browned, pressing with the back of a wooden spoon to remove lumps. Add the tomatoes, marjoram, half of the allspice, and salt and pepper to taste. Bring to the boil, stirring, then lower the heat, cover and simmer for 20 minutes. Meanwhile, bring a large pan of salted water to the boil. Add the macaroni, boil for 10 minutes and drain well. Put in an ovenproof dish, add the beef and mix thoroughly. Taste and adjust the seasoning. In a bowl, beat the eggs with the yoghurt and remaining allspice. Pour into the dish and bake for 30 minutes.

ORANGE AND CRANBERRY MINCE
Serves 4

1 tbsp oil
1 onion, finely chopped
1 lb (450 g) lean minced beef
1 oz (25 g) plain flour

1 tsp oregano
½ pt (300 ml) stock
juice and grated rind of 1 orange
3 oz (75 g) cranberries

Heat the oil in a frying pan and cook the onion over a low heat until soft. Add the meat, increase the heat and cook until browned. Stir in the flour, oregano, stock, orange juice and rind. Cover and simmer for 20 minutes. Add the cranberries and simmer for a further 15 minutes until the meat is tender and the cranberries are soft but still whole.

CORNISH PASTIES
Makes 4

12 oz (350 g) shortcrust pastry
8 oz (225 g) minced steak
1 small onion, finely diced

4 oz (110 g) potato, finely diced
salt and freshly ground black pepper
egg or milk for brushing

Preheat the oven to 400°F/200°C/Gas Mk 6. Make the pastry and divide into four equal pieces. Mix the meat, onion and potato together in a bowl and season well. Roll the pastry to about ⅛ in (3 mm) thick. Place a quarter of the filling in the centre of each piece, dampen the edges and fold the pastry over, pressing the edges together gently. Prick the tops with a fork and mark the edges with the prongs to decorate. Place on a baking sheet and brush the tops with beaten egg or milk. Bake for 30 to 40 minutes or until the pasties are golden brown.

BEEF AND SPINACH LOAF
Serves 4-6

8 oz (225 g) fresh spinach
  leaves, destalked
12 oz (350 g) minced beef
2 oz (50 g) mushrooms, chopped

2 oz (50 g) fresh breadcrumbs
1 onion, coarsely grated
1 garlic clove, crushed
3 eggs, soft-boiled

Preheat the oven to 375°F/190°C/Gas Mk 5. Blanch the spinach in boiling water for 1 minute and drain well. Grease a 2 lb (1 kg) loaf tin and line the base and sides with the spinach leaves, placing them so that they overhang the sides of the tin. Mix together the beef, mushrooms, breadcrumbs, onion and garlic in a bowl. Place half the mixture in the tin. Make three hollows in the top and put the eggs in. Cover with the remaining beef mixture, flatten the top and fold back the overhanging spinach leaves. Cover with foil and bake for 1 hour.

STUFFED AUBERGINES
Serves 4

4 medium aubergines
oil for frying
4 oz (110 g) cooked minced
  beef

½ pt (300 ml) Béchamel sauce
4 tbsp grated Cheddar cheese

Preheat the oven to 350°F/180°C/Gas Mk 4. Halve the aubergines, blanch for 10 minutes in boiling salted water, then drain and pat dry. Heat a little oil and fry the aubergines until soft. Scoop out the insides, chop finely and include when cooking the mince. Divide the mixture between the aubergine shells and cover with the Béchamel sauce and cheese. Bake until golden on top. Large courgettes may be used instead of aubergines.

BEEF AND RED BEAN SAVOURY
Serves 4

4 oz (110 g) red kidney beans,
  soaked overnight
3 oz (75 g) butter or margarine
1 small onion, thinly sliced
8 oz (225 g) minced beef
2½ oz (60 g) plain flour
7 fl oz (200 ml) beef stock
salt and freshly ground black pepper

8 oz (225 g) can chopped tomatoes
1 tbsp tomato purée
1 tsp chopped fresh mixed herbs
  or ½ tsp dried
9 fl oz (275 ml) milk
2 oz (50 g) Cheddar cheese, grated
¼ tsp made English mustard

Preheat the oven to 400°F/200°C/Gas Mk 6. Drain the beans and put them into a large saucepan. Cover with fresh cold water and bring to the boil. Boil rapidly for a full 10 minutes, then lower the heat and boil gently for about 45 minutes or until tender. Drain. Melt 1 oz (25 g) of the butter in a heavy-based saucepan, add the onion and minced beef and brown over high heat, stirring constantly. Stir in 1½ oz (35 g) of the flour, the stock and season to taste. Bring to the boil and cook for 2-3 minutes until very thick. Transfer to a deep 3 pt (1.5 litre) ovenproof dish. Melt another 1 oz (25 g) of the butter in a saucepan, add the tomatoes and cook for about 10 minutes until soft and broken up. Stir in the beans, tomato purée and herbs and simmer until reduced and thickened. Spread over the meat. Melt the remaining butter in a clean saucepan and add the remaining flour. Cook, stirring for 2 minutes. Remove from the heat and gradually add the milk, stirring after each addition, to prevent lumps forming. Bring to the boil slowly and continue to cook, stirring all the time, until the sauce comes to the boil and thickens. Stir in half the cheese, the mustard and salt and pepper to taste. Pour the sauce over the bean mixture and sprinkle the remaining cheese on top. Bake for about 25 minutes until golden brown on top.

MEAT LOAF WITH ONION SAUCE
Serves 4

2 oz (50 g) butter or margarine
2 medium onions, finely chopped
1 tsp paprika
1 lb (450 g) minced beef
2½ oz (65 g) fresh breadcrumbs
1 garlic clove, crushed
4 tbsp tomato purée

1 tbsp chopped fresh mixed herbs
  or 1 tsp dried
salt and freshly ground pepper
1 egg, beaten
½ oz (10 g) plain flour
½ pt (300 ml) milk

Preheat the oven to 350°F/180°C/Gas Mk 4. Grease a 1 lb (450 g) loaf tin, then line the base with greased greaseproof paper. Melt half the butter in a frying pan, add half of the onions and cook until softened. Add the paprika and cook for 1 minute, stirring, then turn the mixture into a large bowl. Add the beef, breadcrumbs, garlic, tomato purée, herbs and salt and pepper to taste. Stir thoroughly until evenly mixed, then mix in the egg. Spoon the mixture into the loaf tin, level the surface and cover tightly with foil. Stand the tin in a roasting tin and pour in water to a depth of 1 in (2.5 cm). Bake for 1½ hours. Meanwhile, melt the remaining butter in a saucepan. Add the rest of the onion and cook over a low heat, stirring occasionally, for 10 minutes, until soft but not coloured. Add the flour and cook over a low heat, stirring, for 2 minutes. Remove the pan from the heat and gradually add the milk, stirring after each addition to prevent lumps forming. Return to the heat and continue to cook, stirring constantly, until the sauce comes to the boil and thickens. Simmer very gently for a further 2-3 minutes, then add salt and pepper to taste. Turn the meat loaf out onto a warmed serving plate and peel off the lining paper. Serve immediately with the hot onion sauce.

FRIED PIES
Serves 4-6

2 tbsp oil
1 medium onion, finely chopped
½ green pepper, deseeded
  and finely chopped
1 lb (450 g) lean minced steak
½ pt (300 ml) stock
2 tbsp chopped fresh parsley

salt and freshly ground black pepper
2 tbsp plain flour
Worcestershire sauce (optional)
2 hard-boiled eggs, chopped
8 oz (225 g) shortcrust pastry
fat for deep frying

Heat the oil and sauté the onion and green pepper in the hot oil until soft. Stir in the steak and fry until no longer pink, then add the stock, parsley and seasoning to taste. Cover the pan and simmer gently for 30 minutes. Stir in the flour and a dash of Worcestershire sauce, and cook until the mixture thickens. Stir in the egg and leave to cool. Roll out the pastry thinly and cut around a saucer, making about six circles. Put about 3 tbsp of meat mixture on one side of each circle and fold over to make crescent shapes. Dampen the edges and press together. Deep fry until golden; this should take about 3 minutes. Any meat mixture left over may be thinned with a little stock or water, heated and used as a sauce; or liquidised into a gravy.

COTTAGE PIE
Serves 4

2 lb (900 g) potatoes, diced
3 tbsp milk
knob of butter or margarine
salt and freshly ground black pepper
1 tbsp oil

1 large onion, chopped
1 lb (450 g) minced beef
2 tbsp plain flour
½ pt (300 ml) beef stock
2 tbsp chopped fresh parsley

Cook the potatoes in boiling salted water for 15-20 minutes, then drain and mash with the milk, butter, and season to taste. Heat the oil in a frying pan, and fry the onion for about 5 minutes until lightly browned. Add the beef and fry for a further 5-10 minutes until browned, stirring occasionally. Sprinkle with the flour and cook for 2 minutes, then stir in the stock, parsley and salt and pepper to taste. Bring to the boil and simmer for 30 minutes. Meanwhile preheat the oven to 375°F/190°C/Gas Mk 5. Spoon the beef into an ovenproof dish and cover with mashed potatoes. Bake for 25-30 minutes.

CHEESY BEEF FLAN
Serves 4

10 oz (300 g) shortcrust pastry
4 oz (110 g) breadcrumbs
3 oz (75 g) Cheddar cheese, grated
12 oz (350 g) can corned beef, cubed
2 tbsp finely chopped onion

1 egg
6 tbsp milk
1 tbsp Worcestershire sauce
salt and freshly ground black pepper

Preheat the oven to 375°F/190°C/Gas Mk 5. Make the pastry and line an 8 in (20 cm) pie dish with half of it. Mix together the breadcrumbs, cheese, corned beef and onion, and pile into the pastry case. Beat the egg into the milk and add the Worcestershire sauce. Season to taste and pour over the meat mixture. Roll out a pastry lid to fit the pie dish. Moisten the pastry case edge, put on the lid, trim and flute the edge. Bake for 35 minutes or until the pastry is cooked and golden.

MINCED BEEF ROLY POLY
Serves 4-6

12 oz (350 g) self-raising flour
5 oz (150 g) shredded suet
1 lb (450 g) minced beef
2 carrots, grated

1 small onion, grated
½ beef stock cube
½ tsp mixed herbs
salt and freshly ground black pepper

Preheat the oven to 400°F/200°C/Gas Mk 6. Mix the flour and suet and make a pastry, as usual. Roll out to a 10 x 12 in (20 x 30 cm) rectangle. Brown the mince in a little hot oil with the onion and carrot; crumble in the beef stock cube, add the herbs and seasoning. Add a little water if necessary, but keep the mixture firm. Simmer gently until cooked. Leave to cool, then spread over the pastry leaving 1 in (2.5 cm) border. Dampen the edges and roll up. Put on a greased baking tray with the join underneath and bake on the centre shelf for 1 hour or until golden.

BEEF WITH ORANGE AND CHICORY
Serves 4

3 medium oranges
½ oz (10 g) butter
1½ lb (675 g) minced beef
1 garlic clove, finely chopped
4 small chicory heads, thinly sliced

½ tbsp chopped fresh parsley
½ tbsp chopped fresh thyme
8 green olives, stoned and quartered
chicory leaves and orange slices to garnish

Derind and remove pith from two of the oranges and thinly slice the flesh. Squeeze the juice from the third orange. Melt the butter in a large frying pan and add the minced beef, breaking it up. Add the garlic and cook on a high heat, stirring, for 5-7 minutes until the beef is browned. Lower the heat and mix in the chicory, parsley and thyme. Stir in the orange juice and cook for 5-7 minutes. Mix in the olives and sliced oranges. Cook for 1 minute, then garnish with chicory leaves and orange slices and serve.

BOBOTIE
Serves 6

1 slice bread
8 fl oz (250 ml) milk
1 onion, finely chopped
1½ lb (675 g) lean minced beef
1 tbsp curry powder
½ tsp turmeric

2 tsp sugar
3 oz (75 g) raisins
3 tbsp chutney
2 tbsp lemon juice
2 oz (50 g) blanched almonds
2 eggs, beaten

Preheat the oven to 375°F/190°C/Gas Mk 5. Soak the bread in half the milk in a large bowl for 5 minutes. Stir in the onion, beef, spices, sugar, raisins, chutney, lemon juice, almonds and seasoning; mix thoroughly. Grease a 3 pt (1.5 litre) ovenproof dish. Mix the eggs with the remaining milk and pour over the mixture. Bake for 1¼ hours.

STUFFED MARROW
Serves 5-6

1 marrow, about 3 lb (1.4 kg)
butter for greasing
Stuffing:
4 oz (110 g) minced beef
4 oz (110 g) sausage meat
1 medium onion, chopped
1 large egg
2 oz (50 g) fresh breadcrumbs
2 tsp mixed herbs
salt and freshly ground black pepper

Sauce:
½ oz (10 g) butter
1 small onion, chopped
1 tbsp plain flour
good pinch of caster sugar
¼ pt (150 ml) stock
8 oz (225 g) can tomatoes
2 tbsp tomato ketchup

Preheat the oven to 400°F/200°C/Gas Mk 6. Mix stuffing ingredients in a bowl until well combined. Peel the marrow, cut a 3 in (7.5 cm) wide wedge from the top for the lid. Scoop out and discard the seeds from the marrow and lid. Spoon the stuffing into the marrow, pressing down well so that it reaches both ends and fills the centre. Place on a piece of foil and replace the lid. Smear with butter and wrap in foil, sealing the ends firmly. Bake for 1 hour. To make the sauce: heat the butter, fry the onion, and stir in the flour, sugar and seasoning. Gradually add the stock, tomatoes and ketchup, stirring until a thick smooth sauce is obtained. Bring to the boil and simmer for 5 minutes. When the marrow is cooked, remove the foil and lift onto a warmed serving dish. Pour a little sauce around it and put the remainder in a sauce boat. (The sauce may be puréed and reheated.)

BEEF AND BEAN HOT POT
Serves 4

4 oz (110 g) haricot beans, soaked
  overnight in cold water
1 tbsp oil
4 oz (110 g) onion, chopped
12 oz (350 g) minced beef
1 tsp chilli powder
14 oz (400 g) can tomatoes

2 tbsp tomato purée
1 beef stock cube made into
  ½ pt (300 ml) with boiling water
salt and freshly ground black pepper
1 lb (450 g) potatoes, sliced
½ oz (10 g) butter, melted

Preheat the oven to 300°F/150°C/Gas Mk 2. Mix the oil, onion and beef in a bowl. Drain the beans and add together with the chilli powder, tomatoes and the juice, tomato purée, stock, salt and pepper to taste. Pour into a casserole. Arrange the potato slices on the top and brush with the butter. Bake, uncovered, in the centre of the oven for 2 hours until brown.

ITALIAN PIE
Serves 6

2 tbsp oil
1 onion, sliced
1 lb (450 g) lean minced beef
1 garlic clove, crushed
14 oz (400 g) can tomatoes
1 tbsp tomato purée

1 tsp mixed herbs
salt and freshly ground black pepper
6 oz (175 g) short macaroni
2 eggs, beaten
½ pt (300 ml) soured cream or yoghurt
3 oz (75 g) grated cheese

Preheat the oven to 375°F/190°C/Gas Mk 5. Heat the oil and fry the onion until soft, then stir in the beef and fry until browned all through. Add the garlic, tomatoes and juice, tomato purée, herbs and seasoning to taste. Bring to the boil, cover and simmer gently for 20 minutes, stirring from time to time Cook the pasta in boiling salted water for 8-10 minutes or until al dente. Drain. Mix the eggs with the soured cream or yoghurt, add two-thirds of the cheese and stir in the pasta. Put the meat mixture into an ovenproof dish and pour the pasta mixture over the top. Sprinkle with the remaining cheese and bake for 30 minutes until crisp and golden.

BEEF AND PARSNIP BAKE
Serves 4

1 tbsp oil
1 onion, chopped
2 carrots, chopped
1 lb (450 g) minced beef
2 tomatoes, peeled and sliced
¼ pt (150 ml) beef stock

salt and freshly ground black pepper
2 lb (1 kg) parsnips, sliced
2 oz (50 g) butter
2 tbsp milk
2 tbsp fresh white breadcrumbs
1 oz (25 g) cheese, grated

Preheat the oven to 375°F/190°C/Gas Mk 5. Heat the oil in a saucepan and sauté the onion until soft but not brown. Stir in the carrots and beef and cook, stirring, until the beef is lightly browned. Add the tomatoes, stock and seasoning to taste. Bring to the boil, then simmer for 15 minutes. Meanwhile cook the parsnips in boiling salted water for 20-25 minutes until tender. Drain and mash, adding the butter, milk and a generous amount of pepper. Grease an ovenproof dish and spread half the mashed parsnip in the bottom and around the sides. Pile in the beef mixture and spread the remaining mashed parsnip over the top. Sprinkle with a mixture of breadcrumbs and cheese and bake for 30-35 minutes.

BEEF AND MUSHROOM ROULADES
Serves 4

2 oz (50 g) butter or margarine
4 oz (110 g) button mushrooms
12 stuffed olives
4 oz (110 g) onion, chopped
2 tsbp plain flour

6 tbsp fresh white breadcrumbs
12 oz (350 g) minced beef
8 oz (225 g) beef sausage meat
salt and freshly ground black pepper

Heat half the butter and gently sauté the mushrooms, olives, and onion. Stir in the flour and breadcrumbs. Cook for 1-2 minutes, then leave until cold. Mince the beef a second time to give a really fine texture. Mix with the sausage meat and blend thoroughly with fingertips. Season. On a well-floured surface, roll the meat mixture out to about 14 x 9 in (35 x 23 cm). Cut in half lengthways and divide each strip into four squares. Arrange the mushroom mixture over the centre of each square in a neat line. Using a palette knife, wrap the meat around the filling to give a sausage shape. Seal the seam with fingertips and gently rock the roulades backwards and forwards to give a neat shape. Melt the remaining butter in a large frying pan. Fry the roulades for about 20 minutes, seam side uppermost, then turn and continue frying until browned on the other side.

TURKISH MINCE
Serves 4

4 tbsp olive oil
1 large onion, coarsely grated
2 lb (1 kg) lean minced beef
1 green pepper, deseeded and chopped
4 tomatoes, peeled and sliced
1 tsp grated nutmeg
6 peppercorns, crushed
½ garlic clove, crushed

1 tsp each fennel and thyme
1 bay leaf, crushed
2 tbsp tomato purée
½ glass red wine
4 tbsp wholemeal flour
1 chicken stock cube
salt and freshly ground black pepper
8 oz (225 g) Cheddar cheese, grated

Heat the oil in a large heavy-based saucepan and sauté the onions until soft. Add the beef and stir until browned. Add the green pepper and fry, then add the tomatoes. Cook for about 10 minutes, then add the nutmeg, peppercorns, garlic, herbs and tomato purée. Stir well and add the wine, then stir in the flour mixed with a little water. Cook gently for about 5 minutes then add the crumbled stock cube and ½ pt (300 ml) water. Simmer for a further 5 minutes, stirring constantly. Season to taste and add a little more liquid if necessary. Transfer to an earthenware dish and sprinkle with grated cheese. Put under a hot grill until the cheese browns and bubbles.

BEEF AND CARROT BAKE
Serves 4-6

1 lb (450 g) medium potatoes, halved
1 lb (450 g) carrots, thickly sliced
salt and freshly ground black pepper
1 medium onion, chopped
1 lb (450 g) minced beef

5 oz (150 g) can condensed mushroom
* soup*
2 tbsp tomato ketchup
1 beef stock cube

Cook the potatoes and carrots in salted water for 15-20 minutes until just tender. Drain and mash, seasoning to taste. Preheat the oven to 400°F/200°C/Gas Mk 6. Grease a 7 in (18 cm) shallow cake tin and line the base with greased greaseproof paper. Fry the onion and beef in a saucepan, until the beef is brown. Add the soup, ketchup and crumbled stock cube. Stir well, cook for 20 minutes, then skim off surface fat. Spread two-thirds of the mashed carrot mixture over the base and up the side of the cake tin. Pour the meat mixture into the centre and spread the remaining mash over. Place the tin on a baking sheet and bake on the centre shelf for 20-25 minutes until browned. Turn out onto a warmed serving dish.

SPICY BEEF LOAF
Serves 4

1 large onion, finely chopped
1 lb (450 g) finely minced beef
4 oz (110 g) fresh breadcrumbs
3 tbsp soy sauce
1 tbsp tomato purée
1 tsp each turmeric, cumin, coriander
salt and freshly ground black pepper

1 tbsp oil
2 garlic cloves, crushed
14 oz (400 g) can chopped tomatoes
1 tbsp cornflour
¼ pt (150 ml) beef stock
3 pineapple rings, quartered

Preheat the oven to 400°F/200°C/Gas Mk 6. Lightly grease a 1 lb (450 g) loaf tin. Put 2 tsp of onion in a bowl and add the beef, breadcrumbs, soy sauce, tomato purée, spices and seasoning. Mix well and roll into a shape to fit the tin. Place in the tin, cover with foil and bake in a water bath for 30 minutes. Remove the foil and cook for a further 20 minutes. Heat the oil and fry the remaining chopped onion with the garlic for 5 minutes or until soft, then add the tomatoes. Mix the cornflour with a little cold water and stir into the pan; cook gently for 1 minute. Gradually add the beef stock, stirring constantly, and bring to the boil. Simmer for 20 minutes. Turn out the loaf and put a line of pineapple segments down the centre. Serve with the sauce, which may be liquidised or served as it is.

OVEN BAKED MEATBALLS
Serves 4

1 lb (450 g) lean minced beef
2 oz (50 g) semolina
1 tsp ground cinnamon
1 tsp salt
1 garlic clove, crushed
1 large egg, beaten
2 oz (50 g) margarine

1 tbsp oil
4 oz (110 g) onion, sliced
8 oz (225 g) long-grain rice
2 tbsp tomato purée
1 chicken stock cube
2 oz (50 g) Cheddar cheese, grated

Preheat the oven to 350°F/180°C/Gas Mk 4. Mix the beef, semolina, cinnamon, salt, garlic and egg together thoroughly and mash into a smooth purée. Divide into 20 and roll into small balls. Heat the margarine and oil and fry the meatballs for about 10 minutes until browned all over. Remove and keep warm. Add the onion to the pan and sauté until soft. Add the rice and fry for about 3 minutes, stirring. Add 1¼ pt (750 ml) water, the tomato purée and crumbled stock cube. Bring to the boil, stirring. Turn into a casserole and place the meatballs on top. Cover and bake for 35 minutes. Remove the lid and sprinkle over the cheese. Bake, uncovered, for a further 10 minutes.

STEAK AND CASSEROLES

BEEF PAPRIKA
Serves 8

3 lb (1.4 kg) braising steak
3 oz (75 g) butter or margarine
1½ lb (675g) onions, thinly sliced
1 lb (450 g) carrots, thinly sliced
3–4 tbsp paprika

2 tbsp plain flour
1½ pt (900 ml) beef stock
4 tbsp dry white wine
salt and freshly ground black pepper
5 fl oz (150 ml) soured cream

Preheat the oven to 300°F/150°C/Gas Mk 2. Cut the meat into 1½ in (4 cm) pieces. Melt the fat in a frying pan and fry the meat, a little at a time, until browned. Drain and place in a shallow ovenproof dish. Fry the onions and carrots in the fat remaining in the pan for about 5 minutes until lightly browned. Add the paprika and flour and fry for 2 minutes. Gradually stir in the stock and wine; season to taste. Bring to the boil and pour over the meat. Cover tightly and cook for 2 hours (test the beef after 1½ hours) until tender. Pour the soured cream over and serve.

BEEF IN STOUT
Serves 4-6

½ oz (10 g) butter
2 tbsp oil
2 lb (900 g) stewing steak, cut
    into 2 in (5 cm) cubes
4 medium onions, sliced
8 oz (225 g) mushrooms, sliced

salt and freshly ground black pepper
2 tbsp plain flour
½ pt (300 ml) stout
1 bay leaf
1 tsp soft dark brown sugar

Preheat the oven to 350°F/180°C/Gas Mk 4. Melt the butter and oil in a large flameproof casserole, add the meat and cook until brown on all sides. Using a slotted spoon, remove from the casserole. Add the onions and mushrooms to the casserole and cook until soft. Add salt and pepper to taste; gradually stir in the flour. Return the meat to the casserole and pour over the stout. Add the bay leaf and sugar and mix thoroughly. Cover and cook for 1½–2 hours or until meat is tender.

BOILED SALT BEEF
Serves 6-8

2 lb (900 g) salt brisket of beef,
    soaked overnight
cold beef stock
2 onions, quartered

4 carrots, sliced
1 small turnip, chopped
1 tsp black peppercorns
2 tsp dried mixed herbs

Drain the brisket. Place in a large saucepan and cover with the stock. Add the onions, carrots, turnip, peppercorns and herbs. Cover and bring to the boil. Lower the heat and simmer for 1½ hours. Slice the meat and place on a warmed serving dish.

BEEF, BACON AND MUSHROOM CASSEROLE
Serves 4

1 lb (450 g) stewing steak
8 oz (225 g) bacon
plain flour for coating
salt and freshly ground black pepper

2 celery stalks, chopped
3 onions, sliced
8 oz (225 g) button mushrooms
bouquet garni

Preheat the oven to 325°F/170°C/Gas Mk 3. Cut the steak and bacon into 1 in (2. 5 cm) cubes. Coat the meat in seasoned flour. Put it into a casserole with all the remaining ingredients. Pour in some water to almost cover the ingredients. Cover and cook for 2 hours or until the meat is tender. Remove the bouquet garni and serve.

JUGGED BEEF
Serves 4

1½ lb (675 g) shin beef, cubed
2 oz (50 g) plain flour
salt and freshly ground black pepper
oil for frying
4 oz (110 g) streaky bacon, chopped

2 onions stuck with 4 cloves
grated rind of ½ lemon
1 bouquet garni
6 small mushrooms
2 beef stock cubes

Preheat the oven to 300°F/150°C/Gas Mk 2. Roll the meat in seasoned flour. Heat a little oil in a large flameproof casserole and fry the bacon gently. Add more oil as necessary and fry the meat, turning the cubes over so that they brown evenly on all sides. Add the onions, lemon rind, bouquet garni and mushrooms. Dissolve the stock cubes in ¾ pt (450 ml) boiling water and pour into the casserole. Cover and cook in the oven for at least 2-3 hours or until tender. Remove the onions and bouquet garni before serving.

BRAISED STEAK
Serves 4

2 tbsp oil
1½ lb (675 g) braising steak
2 onions, sliced
2 green peppers, deseeded and sliced
1 tsp brown sugar
¼ pt (150 ml) red wine

4 oz (400 g) can chopped tomatoes
1 bay leaf
freshly ground black pepper
Italian seasoning to taste
2 tsp salt

Heat the oil and fry the steak until evenly brown on both sides. Remove from the pan, then fry the onions and peppers gently for 3 minutes. Add the rest of the ingredients, stir well and simmer for a few minutes. Return the steak to the pan and cook slowly for about 1 hour. Leave overnight. Next day transfer to a casserole and reheat in a 300°F/150°C/Gas Mk 2 oven for 45 minutes or until meat is tender.

ALPINE STEAK
Serves 4

4 slices topside of beef, each
    about 6 oz (175 g)
1½ oz (35 g) plain flour
1 tsp salt
¼ tsp pepper
1½ oz (35 g) lard or oil

2 large onions, finely sliced
2 celery stalks, sliced
8 oz (225g) can tomatoes
2 tsp tomato purée
1 tsp Worcestershire sauce
¼ pt (150 ml) beef stock

Preheat the oven to 300°F/150°C/Gas Mk 2. Cut the beef into eight pieces. Mix together the flour, salt and pepper and toss the meat in it, pressing so that most of the flour is used. Heat the fat in a frying pan and fry the meat quickly on all sides until browned. Lift out and place in a casserole. Fry the onions and celery in the fat remaining in the pan, until pale golden brown, then add to the meat. If there is any flour left over stir it into the vegetables and cook for 1 minute. Add the tomatoes, tomato purée, Worcestershire sauce and stock. Cover with a lid or foil and cook in the oven for about 2½ hours or until the meat is tender.

BEEF AND HARICOT BEANS
Serves 4

4 oz (110 g) haricot beans, soaked overnight
1 lb (450 g) braising steak, cubed
4 oz (110 g) lean streaky bacon, chopped
1 large onion, sliced
2 carrots, sliced

2 garlic cloves, crushed
8 oz (225 g) can tomatoes
1 tsp dried mixed herbs
1 pt (600 ml) stock
salt and freshly ground black pepper

Place all the ingredients in a large heavy-based saucepan and bring to the boil. Stir well and cover with a close-fitting lid. Simmer over a low heat for 2-2½ hours until the meat is tender.

GARDENER'S BEEF
Serves 6-8

1 oz (25 g) dripping or 2 tbsp oil
1½ lb (675 g) stewing steak, cut into
    1 in (2.5 cm) cubes
1 oz (25 g) plain flour
2 beef stock cubes
1½ tsp salt
freshly ground black pepper

1 bay leaf
1 large leek, sliced
2 carrots, quartered
1 parsnip, diced
1 turnip, diced
4 potatoes, quartered

Preheat the oven to 325°F/170°C/Gas Mk 3. Melt the dripping in a frying pan and quickly fry the meat to seal in the juices and brown. Stir in the flour, cook for 2 minutes until lightly browned. Dissolve the stock cubes in 1 pt (600 ml) boiling water, pour into the pan and stir until the sauce has thickened. Add the salt, pepper and bay leaf and turn into a large casserole. Cover and cook in the oven for 1 hour. Add the vegetables, return to the oven and continue cooking for a further 1 hour or until vegetables and meat are tender. Taste and adjust the seasoning. Remove the bay leaf.

BEEF BOURGUIGNON
Serves 6

2 lb (900g) chuck steak
2 tbsp oil
3 oz (75 g) streaky bacon,
  coarsely chopped
6 oz (175 g) baby onions
1 tbsp plain flour
1 tsp tomato purée

1 large garlic clove, crushed
½ pt (300 ml) stock
8 fl oz (250 ml) red wine
bouquet garni
salt and freshly ground black pepper
6 oz (175 g) button mushrooms, wiped
chopped fresh parsley

Preheat the oven to 300°F/150°C/Gas Mk 2. Trim the meat and cut into 1 in (2.5 cm) cubes. Heat the oil in a frying pan and brown the meat evenly all over. Remove with a slotted spoon and keep warm. Put the bacon into cold water in a pan with the onions. Bring to the boil and cook for 2 minutes, drain well and add to the remaining fat in the frying pan. Sauté slowly until golden and beginning to soften. Put the bacon with the meat and keep the onions on one side. Stir the flour, tomato purée and garlic into the fat in the frying pan and cook for 1 minute. Slowly stir in the stock and cook until it thickens. Put the meat and bacon in a casserole and pour over the gravy. Put the red wine into a small saucepan and bring to the boil. Pour over the meat, add the bouquet garni and season to taste. Cover and cook in the oven for 1 hour. Remove and stir in the onions and mushrooms. Return to the oven for a further 30 minutes or until the meat is tender. Garnish with chopped parsley.

TOMATO BEEF CASSEROLE
Serves 2

1 oz (25 g) lard or 3 tbsp oil
2 onions, sliced
1 lb (450 g) chuck steak, about
  1 in (2.5 cm) thick
1 oz (25 g) plain flour

½ pt (300 ml) canned chopped tomatoes
pinch dried marjoram
pinch sugar
salt and freshly ground black pepper

Preheat the oven to 300°F/150°C/Gas Mk 2. Heat the fat in a flameproof casserole and fry the onions until pale golden. Coat the meat with the flour, push the onions to the back of the pan and fry the meat coated with flour until evenly browned. Add the tomatoes, marjoram, sugar, and season to taste. Stir in a little water if it is too dry. Cover and cook in the oven for about 2 hours or until the meat is tender. Cut into portions and serve with the sauce poured over.

DORSET JUGGED STEAK
Serves 4

1 oz (25 g) wholemeal flour
1½ lb (700 g) stewing steak,
cut into 1 in (2.5 cm) cubes
1 medium onion, sliced
4 cloves
salt and freshly ground black pepper

2 fl oz (60 ml) port
about ¾ pt (450 ml) beef stock
8 oz (225 g) sausage meat
2 oz (50 g) fresh wholemeal breadcrumbs
2 tbsp chopped fresh parsley
1 tbsp redcurrant jelly

Preheat the oven to 325°F/170°C/Gas Mk 3. Place the flour in a bowl and dip in the meat. Shake off excess flour, then place the meat in an ovenproof casserole. Add the onion, cloves, and season to taste. Pour in the port, followed by enough stock to cover the meat. Cover and cook for 2 hours or until the meat is tender. Meanwhile place the sausage meat, breadcrumbs, parsley, salt and freshly ground black pepper to taste in a bowl and mix thoroughly. Using floured hands, make eight balls from the mixture. About 40 minutes before the end of the cooking time stir the redcurrant jelly into the casserole and put the sausage meat balls on top. Return to the oven, uncovered, until the balls are cooked and slightly brown. Skim off any excess fat and serve at once.

SUSSEX STEW
Serves 4-6

2 tbsp plain flour
1 tsp dried thyme
salt and freshly ground black pepper
2 lb (900 g) stewing steak, in one piece
2 tbsp lard or oil

1 large onion, sliced
½ pt (300 ml) sweet stout
2 tbsp mushroom ketchup
thyme sprigs to garnish

Preheat the oven to 300°F/150°C/Gas Mk 2. Mix the flour with the thyme and salt and pepper and spread out on a large flat plate or sheet of greaseproof paper. Coat the meat in the flour. Melt the fat in a flameproof casserole. Add the onion slices and fry gently for 5 minutes until soft but not coloured. Remove with a slotted spoon and set aside. Add the beef to the casserole, increase the heat and fry quickly until browned on both sides. Return the onion slices to the casserole, then pour in the stout mixed with the mushroom ketchup. Bring slowly to the boil, then cover with a lid and put in the oven for 2-2½ hours or until tender. Taste and adjust the seasoning. Serve garnished with thyme sprigs.

BEEF OLIVES
Serves 4

*4 thin slices topside of beef,
about 1¼ lb (550 g)
1 rounded tbsp plain flour
salt and freshly ground black pepper*

*1 beef stock cube
½ pt (300 ml) boiling water
1 oz (25 g) cooking fat*

*Stuffing:
1 small onion, finely chopped
1 oz (25 g) fresh white breadcrumbs
½ tsp mixed dried herbs*

*1 tsp chopped fresh parsley
salt and freshly ground black pepper
3 tbsp milk*

Put the stuffing ingredients in a bowl and mix well together. Lay the meat on a board, divide the stuffing between each slice and spread over. Roll up each piece and tie with string. Sift the flour, salt and pepper together on a large plate and roll the olives in it until evenly coated all over. Heat the fat and fry the olives until golden brown all over, then remove and keep hot. Dissolve the stock cube in the boiling water. Add any remaining flour to the fat in the frying pan and cook for about 1 minute. Gradually add the stock, stirring until a smooth sauce is obtained. Replace the beef olives, bring to the boil, cover, reduce the heat and simmer for 1½ hours or until tender. Arrange on a warmed serving dish. Check the gravy seasoning, then strain it over the beef olives. Serve with mashed potatoes and green vegetables.

TOPSIDE POT ROAST
Serves 4-6

*1 tbsp oil
2½ lb (1.1 kg) topside of beef
salt and freshly ground black pepper*

*1 beef stock cube
1 lb (450 g) carrots, sliced
1½ lb (675 g) potatoes, cut into chunks*

Heat the oil in a large saucepan and fry the beef until browned on all sides. Add ½ pt (300 ml) water, season and break in the stock cube. Bring to the boil, skim if necessary, then cover, and simmer for 50 minutes. Add the vegetables to the pan and simmer for a further 30 minutes or until the meat is tender. Place the beef on a warmed serving dish and arrange the vegetables around it. Strain the stock into a jug and serve with the meat.

BRAISED BEEF WITH CHESTNUTS AND CELERY
Serves 4-6

18 fresh chestnuts, skins split
½ oz (10 g) butter
1 tbsp oil
2 bacon rashers, derinded and chopped
2 lb (900 g) stewing steak, cubed
1 medium onion, chopped
1 tbsp plain flour

½ pt (300 ml) brown ale
½ pt (300 ml) beef stock
pinch freshly grated nutmeg
grated rind and juice of 1 orange
salt and freshly ground black pepper
3 celery stalks, chopped

Preheat the oven to 325°F/170°C/Gas Mk 3. Place the chestnuts in a saucepan of water and simmer for 7-8 minutes. While still warm, peel off the thick outer skin and thin inner skin. Melt the butter and oil in a flameproof casserole. Add the bacon and beef in batches and cook, stirring occasionally, until brown. Using a slotted spoon, remove the meat and set aside. Fry the onion in the casserole until soft. Drain off most of the fat from and replace the meat, gradually stirring in the flour. Cook for 1-2 minutes. Stir in the ale, stock, nutmeg, orange juice and rind; season to taste. Bring to the boil, stir to loosen any sediment on the bottom of the dish, then add the chestnuts. Seal the casserole with foil and bake for 45 minutes. Stir in the celery and bake for another hour until the meat is tender.

BEEF FLORENTINE
Serves 4-6

salt and freshly ground black pepper
1 tsp dried oregano
2 lb (900 g) braising steak,
  cut in ¾ in (2 cm) slices
2 tbsp oil
1 large onion, diced
1 garlic clove, crushed

2 tsp brown sugar
2 fl oz (60 ml) red wine vinegar
1 beef stock cube, crumbled
2½ oz (60 g) tomato purée
1 bay leaf
boiled rice to serve
sliced stuffed olives to garnish

Preheat the oven to 300°F/150°C/Gas Mk 2. Put salt, pepper and oregano onto a chopping board and coat the steaks in it well. Heat the oil and sauté the onion and garlic until softened, then add the meat and cook briskly until brown on both sides, sprinkling with brown sugar to hasten the process. Place the meat and onion in a warmed casserole, then add the remaining ingredients and enough hot water to just cover the meat. Cook slowly for 1½-2 hours until the meat is tender. Serve with plain boiled rice and scatter sliced stuffed olives over the top.

BRAZILIAN-STYLE BEEF
Serves 4-6

3 tbsp oil
2 lb (900 g) skirt steak, cut into strips
3 onions, sliced into rings
1 garlic clove, crushed
1 oz (25 g) plain flour
¼ pt (150 ml) black coffee

¼ pt (150 ml) beef stock or red wine
14 oz (400 g) can tomatoes, chopped
salt and freshly ground black pepper
pinch grated nutmeg
2 tsp soft light brown sugar

Preheat the oven to 325°F/170°C/Gas Mk 3. Heat the oil in a frying pan and fry the meat quickly, then lower the heat, add the onions and garlic and cook until soft. Add the flour and stir for 1 minute. Gradually mix in the coffee and stock or wine, then add the tomatoes. Add salt and pepper to taste, nutmeg and brown sugar. Bring to the boil, transfer to a casserole, cover and cook in the oven for 1½-2 hours or until the meat is tender.

CORNED BEEF AND POTATO HASH
Serves 2

6 oz (175 g) potato, cubed
4 oz (110 g) carrot, diced
1 tbsp oil
1 medium onion, chopped
½ tsp made mustard

1 tsp vinegar
1 tsp Worcestershire sauce
3 tbsp tomato ketchup
¼ lb (110 g) corned beef, cut in one slice

Cook the potato and carrot in just enough boiling salted water to cover until just tender. Do not overcook. Drain well. Heat the oil and fry the onion until soft but not brown, then stir in the mustard, vinegar, Worcestershire sauce and tomato ketchup. Cut the corned beef into ½ in (1 cm) cubes and add to the pan together with the potatoes and carrots. Stir gently but well. Cover the pan with a lid and simmer over a low heat for about 5 minutes until completely heated through. Serve immediately.

BEEF IN WHISKY SAUCE
Serves 6

1 oz (25 g) butter
1½ lb (700 g) sirloin steak,
    cut into strips
1 large onion, finely chopped

3 tbsp whisky liqueur
3 fl oz (90 ml) double cream
salt and freshly ground black pepper

Place the butter in a frying pan and heat until melted. Add the beef strips together with the onion and cook for 5-10 minutes until beef has browned. Pour in the liqueur and cream and heat gently to reduce liquid slightly. Season to taste and serve at once.

BEEF ITALIANO
Serves 4

3 tbsp oil
1½ lb (700 g) chuck steak, cubed
14 oz (400 g) can chopped tomatoes
1 onion, sliced
½ red pepper, deseeded and
  finely sliced

¼ tsp ground mace
salt and freshly ground black pepper
1 beef stock cube
4 oz (110 g) spaghetti, broken into pieces
4 oz (110 g) grated cheese

Preheat the oven to 300°F/150°C/Gas Mk 2. Heat the oil and fry the meat until browned evenly all over. Put into a casserole with the tomatoes, onion, red pepper, mace and seasoning. Melt the stock cube in ¼ pt (150 ml) hot water and pour into the casserole. Cook gently for 1½ hours, then stir in the spaghetti. Cook for a further 30 minutes until the beef and spaghetti are both tender. Sprinkle with grated cheese and serve.

TOCANA
Serves 4

4 oz (110 g) lard
1½ lb (675 g) chuck steak, cubed
2 lb (900 g) onions, sliced
1 red and 1 yellow pepper,
  deseeded and sliced

1 tbsp wine vinegar
14 oz (400 g) can chopped tomatoes
salt and freshly ground black pepper
soured cream (optional)
chopped fresh parsley

Heat the lard and brown the meat on all sides. Place in a flameproof casserole or large saucepan. Sauté the onions until lightly browned and add to the meat. Fry the pepper strips until softened and add to the casserole. Put the casserole back on the heat and stir in the vinegar. Add the tomatoes, season to taste, cover and cook for a few minutes, stirring occasionally. Add enough water to barely cover the ingredients and simmer very gently until the meat is tender, stirring and adding more water if necessary. Stir in a few spoonfuls of soured cream if liked, then sprinkle with chopped parsley. This dish is usually served with pickled cucumbers or large gherkins.

BELGIAN BEEF
Serves 4-6

1½ oz (35 g) butter or dripping
 or 3tbsp oil
1 large onion, finely chopped
1 garlic clove, crushed
2 lb (900 g) chuck steak, cut
 into 1 in (2.5 cm) cubes
¾pt (450 ml) stout

2 tsp Dijon mustard
2 tsp brown sugar
2 tsp malt vinegar
1 tsp salt
1 bay leaf
pinch dried thyme
2 oz (50 g) white breadcrumbs

Heat the fat in a large saucepan and fry the onion and garlic until soft. Add the meat and fry until browned all over. Stir in all the remaining ingredients except the breadcrumbs. Bring to the boil, stirring constantly. Cover tightly, then simmer very gently for 2 hours. Remove the bay leaf, stir in the breadcrumbs and serve.

BRISKET OF BEEF WITH BARLEY
Serves 4-6

1 oz (25 g) lard or 2 tbsp oil
3 lb (1.4 kg) boned and rolled brisket
2 medium onions, roughly chopped
1 beef stock cube

1 oz (25 g) pearl barley
salt and freshly ground black pepper
1 lb (450 g) carrots, cut into fingers
4 oz (110 g) frozen peas

Heat the fat in a large saucepan and brown the meat all over. Lift the meat out, add the onions and fry for about 5 minutes. Stir in ½ pt (300 ml) water and the stock cube, bring to the boil and stir until dissolved. Return the meat to the pan, cover and simmer for 2 hours. Add the barley, season with salt and pepper to taste and cook for a further 40 minutes. Add the carrots, cook for a further 20 minutes; add the peas and cook for a further 5 minutes. Lift the meat onto a warm serving dish and surround with the vegetables.

BEEF IN BEER
Serves 4

1½ oz (35 g) lard or 3 tbsp oil
1½ lb (675 g) stewing steak, cut into
 strips ½ in (1 cm) thick
8 oz (225 g) onions, sliced
2 large carrots, sliced
1½ oz (35 g) plain flour

¾pt (450 ml) pale or brown ale
1½ tsp salt
freshly ground black pepper
1 rounded tbsp demerara sugar
1½ tsp made English mustard

Melt the dripping in a saucepan, add the meat and brown quickly. Lift out with a slotted spoon and keep on one side. Add the onions and carrots to the pan and fry until golden brown. Stir in the flour and cook for 1 minute. Pour in the ale and bring to the boil, stirring constantly, until thickened. Add the remaining ingredients and the meat to the pan. Stir well to mix, cover and simmer very gently for 3-4 hours or until the meat is tender. Taste and adjust the seasoning. Turn into a warm serving dish.

CHILLI BEEF WITH VEGETABLES
Serves 4-6

1½ lb (675 g) chuck steak	12 small onions
1 oz (25 g) plain flour	2 carrots, sliced
salt and freshly ground black pepper	1 parsnip or 1 turnip, sliced
1–2 tsp chilli powder	1 lb (450 g) potatoes, sliced
2 tbsp oil	1 pt (600 ml) beef stock

Preheat the oven to 325°F/170°C/Gas Mk 3. Remove excess fat and cut the meat into 1 in (2.5 cm) cubes. Season the flour with salt, pepper and chilli powder to taste. Coat the meat in the flour. Heat the oil in a saucepan and fry the meat until browned. Add the onions, carrots, parsnip or turnip, potatoes and stock. Bring to the boil, stirring occasionally. Pour the mixture into a casserole and cook in the oven for 2 hours or until both meat and vegetables are tender.

BAR ROOM BEEF
Serves 6

3 lb (1.4 kg) brisket, boned and rolled	¼ pt (150 ml) red wine
8 oz (225 g) streaky bacon	1 tbsp treacle
1 lb (450 g) onions, finely sliced	salt and freshly ground black pepper
½ pt (300 ml) brown ale	1 bay leaf
½ pt (300 ml) stock	cornflour (optional)

Preheat the oven to 250°F/120°C/Gas Mk 1/2. Lay the slices of bacon in the base of a deep casserole and put the meat on top. Put the onions around the meat. Mix the ale, stock, wine and treacle together and pour over. Season well, cover and cook for at least 3 hours or until the meat is tender right through. Remove from the casserole and place on a warmed serving dish surrounded by the onions. Discard the bacon. The gravy may be thickened with a little cornflour if desired.

STEAK AND KIDNEY PIE
Serves 4-6

2 lb (900 g) skirt beef
8 oz (225 g) ox kidney
1 oz (25 g) plain flour
1 oz (25 g) dripping or 2–3 tbsp oil
1 large onion, chopped

1 beef stock cube
salt and freshly ground black pepper
4 oz (110 g) mushrooms, sliced
7½ oz (210 g) packet puff pastry, thawed
milk or beaten egg, for brushing

Cut the steak and kidney into 1 in (2.5 cm) cubes, put in a polythene bag with the flour and toss until well coated. Melt the fat in a saucepan, fry the meat and onion until browned. Dissolve the stock cube in ½ pt (300 ml) hot water. Stir into the pan. Season to taste, partially cover the pan and simmer for 1½ hours or until the meat is almost tender. Stir in the mushrooms and continue cooking for a further 30 minutes or until the meat is really tender. Taste and adjust the seasoning. Turn the mixture into a 1½ pt (900 ml) pie dish and allow to become quite cold. Place a pie funnel in the centre. Preheat the oven to 425°F/220°C/Gas Mk 7. Roll out the pastry on a lightly floured surface and cover the pie with it. Seal and crimp the edges, make a small slit in the centre to allow the steam to escape and use any pastry trimmings to decorate the top. Brush with milk or beaten egg and cook in the oven for 30-35 minutes or until the pastry is risen and golden brown and the meat is hot through. If the pastry becomes brown cover it with foil.

BEEF AND CHEESE PIE
Serves 4

1½ lb (700 g) shin beef
plain flour for coating
salt and freshly ground black pepper
2 tbsp oil
4 oz (110 g) carrots, sliced
4 oz (110 g) onion, chopped

½ pt (300 ml) stock
2½ lb (1.1 kg) potatoes, cubed
milk
2 oz (50 g) butter
3 oz (75 g) Cheddar cheese, grated
1 pinch mustard powder

Preheat the oven to 325°F/160°C/Gas Mk 3. Trim the meat, cut into cubes and roll in seasoned flour. Heat the oil and fry the meat until browned. Transfer to a casserole. Fry the carrots and onion and add to the casserole. Pour in the stock and season to taste. Cover and cook for 2 hours. Boil the potatoes in salted water, drain and mash well with a little milk and butter. Stir in the cheese and mustard and put on top of the meat. Increase the oven temperature to 200°C/400°F/Mk 6 and bake the dish for about 20 minutes until golden brown.

BEEF STROGANOFF
Serves 4

1½ lb (675 g) rump steak, thinly sliced
3 tbsp plain flour
salt and freshly ground black pepper
2 oz (50 g) butter
1 onion, very finely chopped
8 oz (225 g) mushrooms, wiped and sliced
¼ pt (150 ml) soured cream
2 tsp tomato purée (optional)

Beat the steak with a meat mallet or rolling pin between two sheets of greaseproof paper. Trim off the fat and discard. Cut the meat across the grain into thin strips. Coat the strips in seasoned flour. Melt half the butter in a frying pan, and fry the strips for 5-7 minutes, tossing constantly until golden brown. Add the remaining butter, and fry the onion and mushrooms, stirring, for 3-4 minutes. Stir in the soured cream, and tomato purée if using. Season well and heat through gently, without boiling. Transfer to a warmed serving dish.

STEAK AND KIDNEY STEW
Serves 4

1¼ lb (550 g) steak and kidney
salt and freshly ground black pepper
1 oz (25 g) plain flour
1 oz (25 g) lard
1 onion, finely chopped
1 bay leaf
1 beef stock cube
2 oz (50 g) button mushrooms, wiped

Dust the steak and kidney all over with seasoned flour. Heat the lard in a heavy-based saucepan and fry the steak and kidney until well sealed. Remove from the pan and fry the onion for about 4 minutes. Stir in any remaining seasoned flour and the bay leaf. Return the steak and kidney to the pan. Break the stock cube into ¾ pt (450 ml) boiling water, stirring until dissolved. Gradually add to the pan, stirring until smooth, then add the mushrooms. Cover and cook very slowly for 2-2½ hours or until the meat is tender. Season to taste and remove the bay leaf. Place in a warmed serving dish and served with mashed potatoes and green vegetables.

BEEF PRUNEAUX
Serves 4–6

2 tbsp oil
2 lb (900 g) braising beef
3 rashers streaky bacon
8 oz (225 g) onions, chopped
8 oz (225 g) carrots, chopped

8 oz (225 g) prunes
salt and freshly ground black pepper
½ pt (300 ml) red wine
8 oz (225 g) ribbon pasta
grated Parmesan cheese (optional)

Preheat the oven to 300°F/150°C/Gas Mk 2. Heat the oil and fry the
meat until evenly browned all over. Place the bacon in the base of a
casserole and put the meat on top. Surround with the vegetables and
prunes, season and pour in the wine. Cover and cook in the oven for
about 3 hours or until the meat is tender. Just before serving cook the
pasta in plenty of boiling salted water until al dente, drain and place
on a warmed serving dish. Cut the meat into slices and put in the
centre of the pasta, surrounded by the vegetables and prunes. Serve
with the gravy separately, and a dish of grated Parmesan if desired.

BEEF AND BACON SUET ROLL
Serves 6–8

8 oz (225 g) self-raising flour
salt and freshly ground black pepper
4 oz (110 g) shredded suet
6 fl oz (180 ml) water

6 oz (175 g) skirt steak, chopped
4 oz (110 g) rindless bacon, chopped
1 tbsp chopped fresh parsley

Sift the flour and 1 tsp salt into a bowl, stir in the suet and add
sufficient water to make a soft dough. Place on a floured surface and
knead lightly until smooth. Roll out to a rectangle about 10 x 12 in
(25 x 30 cm). Mix the beef, bacon and parsley together and sprinkle
with pepper. Spread the mixture over the pastry, leaving a narrow rim
around the edges. Dampen the edges and roll up like a Swiss roll,
pressing the pastry together to seal in the filling. Wrap the roll in
greased foil, allowing room for the pastry to expand, and seal the
edges of the foil well. Place in a large saucepan and add boiling water
to reach to halfway up the sides of the parcel. Cover the pan and boil
gently for 2 hours, adding more boiling water if necessary. Remove
the parcel from the saucepan and carefully unwrap the foil. Serve
immediately.

FRENCH COUNTRY RAGOUT
Serves 2

2 tbsp olive oil
1 lb (450 g) braising steak, cubed
2 lamb kidneys, cored and sliced
1 large onion, chopped
2 carrots, sliced
1 green pepper, deseeded and sliced

2 tbsp red wine
2 tbsp Worcestershire sauce
½ pt (300 ml) rich gravy
  made from granules
bouquet garni
1 bay leaf

Heat the oil and fry the beef and kidneys until browned all over. Remove and place in a large saucepan or flameproof casserole. Fry the onion, carrot and green pepper for 3 minutes, turning with a spoon to brown evenly. Add to the meat. Pour in the wine, Worcestershire sauce and gravy; add the bouquet garni and bay leaf. Cover and simmer gently for about 1½–2 hours or until the meat is tender.

BEEF AND WALNUT COBBLER
Serves 4–6

9 oz (250 g) plain flour
salt and freshly ground black pepper
1½ lb (675 g) chuck steak, cubed
4 oz (110 g) margarine
2 onions, sliced
1 green pepper, deseeded and sliced
1 garlic clove, crushed

¾ pt (450 ml) beef stock
2 tbsp tomato purée
pinch bicarbonate of soda
1 tsp cream of tartar
1 egg, beaten
5 tbsp milk
1 oz (25 g) chopped walnuts

Preheat the oven to 425°F/220°C/Gas Mk 7. Season 1 oz (25 g) of the flour and toss the meat in it. Melt half the margarine in a flameproof casserole and sauté the onions, green pepper and garlic for 5 minutes. Remove and set aside. Add the meat to the casserole and cook until browned all over. Replace the vegetables, add salt and pepper to taste, stock and tomato purée. Cover and cook in the oven for 1½ hours. Put the remaining flour and margarine, bicarbonate of soda, cream of tartar, egg and milk in a bowl with a pinch of salt and mix thoroughly to a soft dough. Knead lightly on a floured surface, then cut into 2 in (5 cm) circles. Arrange on top of the meat, brush over with a little milk and sprinkle over the walnuts. Return to the oven for a further 20–25 minutes.

GUINNESS CASSEROLE
Serves 4

2–3 tbsp oil
2 oz (50 g) streaky bacon, derinded
  and cut in strips
1 medium onion, sliced
1 medium carrot, cut into chunks
2 oz (50 g) mushrooms, wiped
  and sliced
4 x 4 oz (110 g) blade steaks
1½ tbsp plain flour
5 fl oz (150 ml) Guinness or stout

½ pt (300 ml) beef stock
1 tsp tomato purée
1 tsp dried marjoram
1 bay leaf
salt and freshly ground black pepper
Caraway dumplings:
6 oz (175 g) self-raising flour
3 oz (75 g) shredded suet
1 tsp caraway seeds

Preheat the oven to 300°F/150°C/Gas Mk 2. Heat 2 tbsp oil in a
frying pan and sauté the bacon and onion for 3 minutes, then add the
carrot and mushrooms and brown evenly. Lift out into a casserole.
Add more oil if necessary and fry the steaks until well sealed and
brown. Add to the vegetables. Stir the flour into the fat remaining in
the pan and cook for 1 minute. Gradually add the beer and stock and
stir until the sauce is smooth. Stir in the tomato purée, herbs and
seasoning to taste. Pour into the casserole and cover the surface with
greaseproof paper. Put on the lid and cook in the oven for 3–3½ hours.
Half an hour before serving, mix the flour, suet and caraway seeds
together, season and bind with enough cold water into a firm dough.
Break into eight and roll into dumplings between the palms of floured
hands. Transfer the meat and vegetables from the casserole to a
warmed serving dish. Cover and keep hot. Bring the gravy to the boil,
drop in the dumplings and boil gently for 20–25 minutes. Pour on top
of the meat and serve with mashed potatoes and green vegetables.

HORSERADISH STEAK
Serves 4

4 tsp horseradish sauce
4 tsp Greek yoghurt
2 tsp paprika
3 tsp chopped fresh thyme
½ tsp each salt and pepper

1 lb (450 g) rump steak, cut into
  very thin strips
1 oz (25 g) butter
6 tsp sherry

Place the horseradish, yoghurt, paprika, thyme, salt and pepper in a
deep bowl and stir until well blended. Add the steak strips and stir
until evenly coated. Cover and leave in a cool place for 1 hour. Heat
the butter in a frying pan. Using a slotted spoon, remove the steak

from the yoghurt mixture, place in the pan and cook for 1–3 minutes only. Remove to a warm serving dish. Pour the yoghurt mixture into the frying pan, add the sherry and bring to the boil, stirring constantly. Pour over the steak and serve immediately.

SCANDINAVIAN HOT POT
Serves 4

2 oz (50 g) butter or margarine
2 medium onions, sliced
4 oz (110 g) celeriac, cubed
4 carrots, cubed
6 oz (175 g) potatoes, sliced
1 tsp salt
¼ tsp freshly ground black pepper

1 tsp fennel seeds
8 oz (225 g) can tomato purée
1 can beer
sugar (optional)
6 oz (175 g) leftover cooked beef
2 large tomatoes, quartered

Heat the butter in a large saucepan and sauté the onion and celeriac gently for about 10 minutes. Add the carrots, potatoes, salt, pepper and fennel seeds; stir well. Stir in the tomato purée and beer. You may like to add a little sugar at this stage. Cover and simmer for about 15 minutes. Cut the cooked beef into strips and add to the pan. Continue simmering gently for another 25 minutes. Then add the tomatoes and continue cooking for another 5 minutes. If the stew is too wet, simmer uncovered for the last 15 minutes.

BEEF HARE
Serves 4

plain flour for coating
salt and freshly ground black pepper
freshly grated nutmeg
2 lb (900 g) chuck steak, cut
  into strips

1 tbsp celery seeds
8 cloves
1 medium onion, quartered
1 small parsnip, grated
¼ pt (150 ml) dry red wine

Preheat the oven to 425°F/220°C/Gas Mk 7. Mix the flour with salt and pepper and plenty of nutmeg. Coat the meat, shaking off any excess flour. Arrange in a deep 1½ pt (900 ml) ovenproof dish, scattering celery seeds between the layers. Stick 2 cloves into each onion quarter and arrange with the grated parsnip on top of the meat. Pour over the wine, cover tightly and leave to marinate for 2 hours. Put in the oven and immediately reduce the temperature to 325°F/ 170°C/Gas Mk 3. Bake for 2¼ hours until the meat is tender.

CITRUS BEEF OLIVES

1 oz (25 g) butter
1 small onion, chopped
4 oz (110 g) fresh white breadcrumbs
rind and juice of 1 lemon
2 oz (50 g) sultanas
1 tbsp chopped fresh parsley
salt and freshly ground black pepper

4 slices ham
8 long thin slices topside of beef
1 tbsp oil
2 tbsp dry sherry
rind and juice of 1 orange
½ pt (300 ml) beef stock
2 tbsp cornflour

Preheat the oven to 325°F/170°C/Gas Mk 3. Heat the butter and
sauté the onion until soft. Stir in the breadcrumbs, lemon rind and
juice, sultanas and parsley and mix well together. Season to taste and
set aside. Cut each slice of ham in half and lay one on top of each slice
of beef. Divide the stuffing between the slices and spread evenly. Roll
up each slice and secure with a wooden cocktail stick. Heat the oil
and fry the olives until brown all over, then transfer to a casserole and
keep warm. Add the sherry, orange rind and juice to the frying pan
and heat gently, stirring in the meat juices. Pour over the olives with
the stock, cover and cook in the oven for 30 minutes until the meat is
tender. Transfer to a hot serving plate with a slotted spoon and
remove the cocktail sticks. Cover and keep warm. Pour the sauce into
a small pan. Mix the cornflour with a little water, then stir into the
sauce. Boil gently, stirring, then reduce the heat and simmer, stirring,
until a smooth thickish sauce is obtained. Serve hot in a sauce boat,
with a little poured over the beef olives.

FIESTA BEEF
Serves 4

4 tbsp oil
1 lb (450 g) beef topside
1 onion, chopped
2 tomatoes, skinned, seeded
  and chopped
1 tbsp tomato purée
1½ pt (900 ml) beef stock

1 bay leaf
salt and freshly ground black pepper
1 tsp chilli powder
5 oz (150 g) sweetcorn kernels
4 oz (110 g) prunes, stoned and sliced
2 peaches, peeled, stoned and sliced
1 orange, peeled and sliced

Heat the oil in a flameproof casserole and brown the meat on all sides.
Add the onion and cook gently for 5 minutes. Stir in the tomatoes,
tomato purée, stock and bay leaf; season well with salt, pepper and
chilli powder. Bring to the boil, cover and simmer gently for 1½ hours.
Add the sweetcorn, prunes, peach and orange slices and cook gently
for another 5 minutes. Serve with rice or creamed potatoes.

FRENCH HOT POT
Serves 6

½ lb (225 g) lima beans, soaked
   overnight, or canned broad beans
4 tbsp oil
1½ lb (675 g) stewing beef, cubed
2 onions, chopped
1 garlic clove, crushed
2 tbsp plain flour

1 tbsp tomato purée
¼ pt (150 ml) white wine
bouquet garni
rosemary sprig
salt and freshly ground black pepper
2 courgettes, wiped and sliced
4 tomatoes, quartered

Preheat the oven to 350°F/180°C/Gas Mk 4. If using dried beans cook them in plenty of unsalted water until tender. Drain and rinse. Fry the meat in the hot oil, turning to brown evenly all over. Add the onion and garlic and fry gently for 2 minutes. Stir in the flour and cook for another 2 minutes, then add the tomato purée and gradually stir in the wine and ½ pt (300 ml) water. Add the bouquet garni and rosemary sprig and season to taste. Bring to the boil, reduce heat and simmer for 10 minutes. Pour into a casserole, add the beans, cover and bake for about 2 hours or until the meat is tender. Add the courgettes and tomatoes and put back in the oven for another 15 minutes.

BEEF AND CELERY CASSEROLE
Serves 4

1–2 tbsp oil
8 oz (225 g) streaky bacon,
   cut into match sticks
1½ lb (675 g) chuck steak,
   trimmed and cubed
2 medium onions, chopped
1 garlic clove, crushed

4 stalks celery, chopped
2–3 tsp plain flour
¼ pt (150 ml) red wine
bouquet garni
salt and freshly ground black pepper
½ pt (300 ml) beef stock

Heat the oil in a flameproof casserole and fry the bacon until brown. Remove and set aside. Fry the beef for 5–7 minutes, turning once, until browned. Remove and set aside with the bacon. Place the onions and garlic in the casserole and cook over low heat until beginning to brown. Remove and set aside. Cook the celery in the casserole, adding more oil if necessary, until it is slightly brown. Sprinkle in the flour and cook, stirring constantly, for a few minutes, then gradually add the wine. Add the beef, bacon, onions and add the bouquet garni. Season to taste and just enough stock to cover the ingredients. Bring slowly to the boil, cover and simmer over low heat for 1½–2 hours until the beef is tender. Serve at once.

CREAMED BEEF CASSEROLE
Serves 4

2 lb (900 g) thinly sliced rump steak
salt and freshly ground black pepper
plain flour
2 tbsp oil
2 oz (50 g) butter
2 large onions, finely chopped
1 tsp mixed herbs

grated rind and juice of 1 lemon
1 tbsp chopped fresh parsley
1½ pt (900 ml) stock
¼ pt (150 ml) yoghurt
4 carrots, diced
pinch sugar
½ oz (10 g) butter

Preheat the oven to 325°F/170°C/Gas Mk 3. Trim the meat and cut
into strips. Toss in well-seasoned flour. Heat the oil and butter
together and fry the meat until browned all over. Transfer to a
casserole. Add the onions to the frying pan together with the herbs,
lemon juice and parsley. Cook gently until the onions are transparent.
Tip the remaining seasoned flour into the pan, stir in well and cook
for 1 minute. Gradually stir in the stock and bring to the boil, then
simmer for about 3 minutes, stirring, until smooth. Pour the sauce
over the meat, cover tightly and cook in the oven for 1 hour or until
tender. Stir well and add the yoghurt. Return to the oven to reheat for
10 minutes. Cook the carrots in boiling salted water until just tender,
then drain and reheat with a pinch of sugar and the butter. Serve with
the carrots and some mashed potato and green vegetables.

CREOLE CASSEROLE
Serves 4

2 tbsp oil
1 medium onion, chopped
2 garlic cloves, crushed
1½ lb (675 g) lean braising steak, cubed
2 tbsp plain flour
¾ pt (450 ml) beef stock

1 small sweet potato, cubed
1 red pepper, deseeded and sliced
1 sweetcorn cob, trimmed and
   cut into chunks
2 bay leaves
salt and freshly ground black pepper

Heat the oil in a large flameproof casserole and fry the onion and
garlic for about 3 minutes until softened. Add the steak and fry for
5–10 minutes, stirring frequently, until well browned. Stir in the flour
and cook for 1 minute. Gradually add the stock, stirring constantly,
until the sauce is smooth. Bring to the boil, cover and simmer for
1 hour, stirring frequently. Add the sweet potato, red pepper, corn
and bay leaves, then cover and simmer for a further 30 minutes or
until tender. Remove the bay leaves and season to taste.

ENTRECOTE MACON
Serves 4

½ oz (10 g) butter
1 tbsp finely chopped onion
4 x 4 oz (110 g) entrecote or rump steak, cut ¾ in (2 cm) thick
1 tsp plain flour
½ pt (300 ml) red wine
4 tomatoes, peeled, deseeded and chopped
½ tsp tomato purée
2 garlic cloves crushed with ½ tsp salt
1 tbsp sherry
1 bay leaf
salt and freshly ground black pepper

Heat the butter and sauté the onion until soft and golden. Remove to a plate. Add the steaks to the pan and seal on a high heat for about 30 seconds each side. Push to one side , lower the heat and add the flour. Cook, stirring, for about 2 minutes. Gradually stir in the wine and tomatoes and keep stirring until a good consistency is obtained. Add the remaining ingredients and season to taste. Cover and simmer gently for 20 minutes or until the steak is tender. Remove to a warmed plate, remove the bay leaf and pour the sauce over.

BEEF POCKETS WITH MUSHROOMS
Serves 6

4 thick-cut steaks, each weighing about 6 oz (175 g)
salt and freshly ground black pepper
½ oz (10 g) butter
6 oz (175 g) mushrooms, finely chopped
1 garlic clove, crushed
1 large onion, finely chopped
1 tbsp chopped fresh parsley
1 tbsp ginger wine
1 tbsp fresh wholemeal breadcrumbs
1 tbsp double cream

Make a horizontal cut in each steak but do not cut all the way through. Sprinkle with salt and pepper to taste. Heat the butter in a saucepan, add the mushrooms, garlic and onion and cook gently for 5 minutes until soft. Remove from the heat and add the parsley, ginger wine, breadcrumbs and cream, mixing thoroughly. Stuff the steak pockets with the mixture place under a hot grill and cook to taste. Serve at once.

BOEUF À L'ORANGE
Serves 4

2 tbsp oil
1½ lb (675 g) stewing steak, cubed
12 spring onions, chopped
1 tbsp plain flour
4 fl oz (125 ml) red wine
juice of 1 orange
bouquet garni

1 garlic clove, crushed
1 pt (600 ml) stock
salt and freshly ground black pepper
5 celery stalks, sliced
2 oz (50 g) walnuts, halved
1 oz (25 g) butter
2 tbsp shredded orange rind, blanched

Heat the oil and fry the meat, turning over to brown on all sides. Remove and keep hot. Fry the onions gently in the oil until golden. Stir in the flour and cook, stirring, for 2 minutes. Add the wine, orange juice, bouquet garni, garlic and stock and bring to the boil. Add the meat and season to taste. Immediately lower the heat, cover and cook very gently for 2 hours or until the meat is tender. Stir occasionally to prevent sticking. Fry the celery and walnuts in butter and add to the stew about 15 minutes before the end of the cooking time. Serve garnished with orange shreds.

LEAN BEEF CURRY
Serves 2

1 tsp turmeric
2 tsp mild chilli powder
4 tsp ground coriander
1 tsp garam masala
1 large onion, roughly chopped
6 garlic cloves, chopped
5 oz (150 g) yoghurt

oil for frying
12 oz (350 g) lean boneless beef, cubed
spicy boiled rice, to serve
few cloves
few cardamom pods
2 oz (50 g) frozen peas
1 tomato, skinned, deseeded and chopped

Mix the spices with 3 tbsp water. Put the onion, garlic, spice mix and yoghurt in a liquidiser or food processor and process until the onion is finely chopped. Put a very little oil in a heavy or non-stick frying pan and arrange the meat in a single layer on the base. Cover with the yoghurt mixture. Add ¼ pt (150 ml) water, bring to the boil, then cover and simmer very gently for 30 minutes. If the meat is still not tender, simmer for another 15 minutes, adding more water if necessary. Boil the rice with some cloves and cardamom pods. Just before serving, boil the frozen peas for a few minutes until soft and stir into the rice with the chopped tomato.

ELIZABETHAN SPICED BEEF
Serves 4–6

6 lb (2.7 kg) topside of beef
1 tsp each ginger, cinnamon,
  nutmeg and allspice
2 garlic cloves, crushed
2 large onions, chopped
2 celery stalks, sliced
3 carrots, chopped
½ pt (300 ml) red wine vinegar

½ pt (300 ml) red wine
½ pt (300 ml) water
1 tbsp soft brown sugar
1 tbsp Worcestershire sauce
2 bay leaves
4 juniper berries, crushed
salt and freshly ground black pepper

Preheat the oven to 300°F/150°C/Gas Mk 2. Mix all the spices together and rub into the meat. Put into a deep bowl and surround with the vegetables. Pour over the vinegar, wine and water. If there is insufficient to cover the meat add more of each in equal quantities. Stir in the sugar, Worcestershire sauce, bay leaves and juniper berries and seasoning. Marinate for 3 hours or longer in a cool place. Drain the meat and put in a casserole. Strain off the vegetables and put around the meat. Simmer the marinade for 15 minutes and season to taste. Pour enough into the casserole to come halfway up the meat. Cover closely and cook for 1½ hours. Then turn the meat over, adding more stock if necessary, and continue to cook for another 1½ hours. Allow to cool in the stock. Serve sliced, as a cold buffet dish. The remaining stock and vegetables make a good soup with dumplings.

BENDOR STEAK
Serves 6

1 lb (450 g) fillet steak
¼ pt (150 ml) oil
1 tsp white pepper
½ tsp cayenne pepper
1 tsp dried rosemary
½ tsp celery salt

2½ fl oz (75 ml) brandy
1 tbsp plain flour
2 tbsp grated cheese
1 tsp paprika
1 oz (25 g) butter
rosemary sprig, to garnish

Remove any fat from the steak and cut the meat into finger-length strips. Put into a shallow dish. Mix together the oil, pepper, cayenne, rosemary, celery salt and brandy. Pour over the steak and marinate for 30 minutes. Mix together the flour, cheese and paprika. Remove the steak strips from the marinade and coat with the flour mixture. Grill for 5–6 minutes, browning all sides. Pile onto a warmed serving dish and keep hot. Melt the butter in a small saucepan and add the marinade. Stir well and bring to the boil briefly. Garnish the meat with the rosemary sprig and serve with the marinade sauce.

STEAMED STEAK AND KIDNEY PUDDING
Serves 4

1 lb (450 g) stewing steak
4 oz (110 g) ox kidney
1 rounded tbsp plain flour
salt and freshly ground black pepper
1 medium onion, finely chopped
¼ pt (150 ml) stock

Suet pastry:
8 oz (225 g) self-raising flour
1 tsp salt
4 oz (110 g) shredded suet
cold water to mix

Grease a 1½ pt (900 ml) pudding bowl and a double thickness of greaseproof paper to cover, making a pleat down the middle to allow for expansion. Cut the steak into 1 in (2.5 cm) cubes; remove the core from the kidney and cut the meat into small pieces. Sift the flour and seasoning together on a large plate and coat all the pieces evenly. Make the pastry: put the flour and salt in a bowl and stir in the suet. Mix with enough cold water to form a soft but not sticky dough. Cut off one-third of the pastry and roll out the remainder on a floured board. Line the bowl, fill with the meat and onion in alternate layers, add sufficient stock to come half way up the meat. Roll out the remaining pastry as a lid to fit the top of the bowl and dampen the pastry edge. Cover the meat, pressing the edges firmly together. Cover with the greased greaseproof paper and tie down securely with string, making a loop of string as a handle for easy removal from the pan. Put a saucepan of water on to boil with a steamer on top. Steam for 3–3½ hours, refilling the saucepan with boiling water when necessary. Remove the cover and turn out onto a warmed serving plate.

BEEF KEBABS WITH HORSERADISH DIP
Serves 4

6 tbsp whipping cream
¼ pt (150 ml) soured cream
2 tbsp grated horseradish
1 tsp white wine vinegar
½ tsp sugar
salt and freshly ground black pepper
1 lb (450 g) minced beef
1 small onion, grated
1 oz (25 g) fresh breadcrumbs

2 tbsp chopped fresh coriander or parsley
2 tsp ground cumin
¼ tsp cayenne pepper
¼ tsp salt
1 egg, beaten
8 cherry tomatoes
12 small bay leaves
oil for brushing
chopped coriander, leaves to garnish

First make the dip: whip the creams together and fold in the horseradish, vinegar and sugar. Add salt and pepper to taste, spoon into a serving bowl and chill in the refrigerator. Put the minced beef in a bowl and add the onion, breadcrumbs, coriander or parsley, cumin, cayenne and salt. Mix with your hands until evenly combined, then bind with the egg. With wetted hands, form the mixture into 16 balls. Thread four on each of four oiled kebab skewers, alternating with tomatoes and bay leaves. Brush with oil, then grill under a preheated moderate grill for 10 minutes. Turn frequently so that they cook evenly and brush with more oil. Put the kebabs on individual plates, garnish with coriander leaves and serve the horseradish dip separately.

CARBONNADE DE BOEUF
Serves 8

3 lb (1.4 kg) lean blade of beef
6 tbsp oil
3 onions, sliced
3 garlic cloves, crushed
pinch nutmeg
salt and freshly ground black pepper

2 tbsp plain flour
¼ pt (150 ml) beef stock
14 fl oz (400 ml) stout
1 tbsp malt vinegar
bouquet garni
1 tbsp sugar

Topping:
1 French stick
4 oz (110 g) butter

1 garlic clove, crushed
1 tbsp Dijon mustard

Preheat the oven to 375°F/190°C/Gas Mk 5. Cut the beef into slices about ½ in (1 cm) thick, 3 in (7.5 cm) long and 1½ in (4 cm) wide. Heat the oil in a frying pan and brown the meat on both sides, then remove from the pan and drain on absorbent paper. Place in a casserole. Add the onions to the pan and fry very gently until golden. Add the garlic, nutmeg and seasoning; sprinkle in the flour. Cook for 2 minutes, stirring, and then gradually add the stock, stout and vinegar, stirring until the sauce comes to the boil. Pour over the meat and add the bouquet garni. Cover and bake for about 2 hours or until the meat is tender. Cut the French stick into ½ in (1 cm) slices diagonally. Cream the butter, garlic and mustard together and spread thickly over one side of each slice. When the Carbonnade is cooked, remove the bouquet garni and stir in the sugar. Cover the top with the slices of bread, buttered sides up. Make sure each slice is well soaked in the gravy, then return to the oven, uncovered, and bake for 30 minutes so that the bread is crisp and golden. Serve from the casserole.

BEEF PROVENÇALE
Serves 4–6

3 tbsp olive oil
2 lb (900 g) braising steak, cut
 into 1 in (2.5 cm) cubes
6 oz (175 g) rindless streaky bacon,
 chopped
8 oz (225 g) baby onions
8 oz (225 g) carrots, sliced
2 tbsp tomato purée
3 garlic cloves, crushed
½ pt (300 ml) red wine

½ pt (300 ml) beef stock
bouquet garni
pinch of dried thyme
salt and freshly ground black pepper
14 oz (400 g) can chopped tomatoes
4 oz (110 g) black olives, stoned
1 oz (25 g) butter
1 oz (25 g) plain flour
triangles of fried bread to garnish

Preheat the oven to 300°F/150°C/Gas Mk 2. Heat the oil in a
flameproof casserole dish and add the beef. Fry until brown on all
sides and remove. Add the bacon, onions and carrots and sauté for
5 minutes. Stir in the tomato purée, garlic, wine, stock, bouquet garni,
thyme and salt and pepper to taste; bring to the boil. Return the meat
to the casserole, cover and cook in the oven for 1½ hours. Mix in the
tomatoes and olives and cook for ½–1 hour. Mix the butter with the
flour and gradually stir into the casserole, a little at a time. Heat
through but do not boil. Garnish with the fried bread and serve.

BEEF GOULASH WITH YOGHURT
Serves 4

3 tbsp oil
1–1½ lb (450–675 g) stewing beef,
 cubed
1 large onion, chopped
1 garlic clove, crushed
2 tbsp paprika
½ tsp caraway seeds
14 oz (400 g) can tomatoes

¾ pt (450 ml) beef stock
1 red pepper, deseeded and
 cut into strips
1 lb (450 g) potatoes, sliced
4 oz (110 g) button mushrooms
freshly ground black pepper
¼ pt (150 ml) yoghurt

Preheat the oven to 300°F/150°C/Gas Mk 2. Heat the oil in a
flameproof casserole and brown the meat on all sides. Add the onion,
garlic, paprika and caraway seeds and cook for 2–3 minutes, stirring
constantly. Add the tomatoes and stock and bring to the boil. Cover
and cook in the oven for 2–3 hours until meat is tender, adding the
red pepper and potatoes for the last 45 minutes and the mushrooms
for the last 10 minutes. Season with pepper to taste. Serve with the
yoghurt swirled over the top.

ROMAN BEEF
Serves 4–6

1½ lb (675 g) piece fillet steak
4 strips bacon fat
3 fl oz (90 ml) oil
1 carrot, chopped
1 onion, chopped
2 celery stalks, chopped

¼ pt (150 ml) white wine
8 fl oz (250 ml) water
1 stock cube
bouquet garni
¼ tsp cornflour

Preheat the oven to 400°F/200°C/Gas Mk 6. Remove any tough skin from the fillet. Lay bacon fat strips down the sides of it and secure with string tied at intervals of about 1 in (2.5 cm). Heat the oil in a large frying pan and brown the meat on all sides for 8 minutes to seal in the juices. Transfer to a roasting tin and add the carrot, onion and celery. Cook for 20 minutes for pink beef, 40 minutes for very well done. Remove and discard the bacon fat, string and vegetables. Place the fillet on a serving dish and keep warm. Add the wine, ¼ pt (150 ml) water, stock cube and bouquet garni to the meat and vegetable juices in the roasting pan and simmer for 15 minutes. Mix the cornflour with the remaining water and add to the wine stock. Boil for about 3 minutes until thick, then pour over the beef to serve.

SANDRINGHAM BEEF
Serves 4–6

½ oz (10 g) lard
3 lb (1.4 kg) brisket
3 large onions, quartered
3 large carrots, quartered
2 tsp mustard powder
2 tbsp vinegar
3 tbsp tomato purée

2 tbsp brown sugar
1 tsp mixed herbs
1 medium onion, chopped
2 tbsp oil
salt and freshly ground black pepper
2 tbsp cornflour

Heat the lard in a large heatproof casserole and brown the meat all over. Add the quartered onions and carrots and turn over in the fat. Mix the mustard with a little vinegar, then beat with the remaining vinegar, tomato purée, sugar, herbs, chopped onion and oil. Pour over the meat and vegetables, season and cover tightly. Bring to the boil, then reduce the heat and simmer very gently for about 3 hours or until the meat is tender. Remove the joint to a serving dish and surround with the vegetables. Bring the juices in the casserole back to the boil and stir in the cornflour mixed to a smooth paste with a little water. Cook until thickened and pour over the meat.

BOILED BEEF AND PEASE PUDDING
Serves 4

3 lb (1.4 kg) brisket of beef or silverside, boned and rolled
6 small onions
6 small carrots
chopped fresh parsley

Pease pudding:
8 oz (225 g) yellow split peas, soaked overnight
1 small onion
1 oz (25 g) butter
½ tsp each salt and freshly ground black pepper

Dumplings:
4 oz (110 g) self-raising flour
½ tsp salt
1½ oz (35 g) shredded suet
cold water to mix

Wash the meat, place in a large saucepan, cover with cold water and slowly bring to the boil. Skim if necessary, cover and simmer gently for 1 hour. Meanwhile drain the split peas, put into a medium saucepan and add the onion and 1 pt (600 ml) cold water. Bring to the boil, cover and simmer for 1 hour or until the peas are tender. Add the onions and carrots to the meat in the saucepan and cook gently for another hour or until the meat is tender. Lift out onto a warmed serving dish and keep hot. Remove the onion from the peas and add it to the other vegetables. Drain the peas and purée in a liquidiser or rub through a sieve. Put into a clean saucepan, add the butter, salt and pepper and beat together. Keep warm. Sift the flour and salt into a bowl, stir in the suet and add sufficient cold water to make a soft but not sticky dough.. Place on a floured surface and divide into 6 pieces. Roll each piece into a ball between floured hands. Bring the liquor in the saucepan back to boiling point and drop in the dumplings. Cover, lower the heat and simmer for 15 minutes. Remove from the pan and add to the meat and vegetables. Sprinkle with chopped parsley. Serve the pease pudding, gently reheated, in a separate dish and the liquor from the saucepan in a gravy boat.

ROAST BEEF
Serves 6–8

CUTS TO USE: *sirloin, topside, ribs, rump, brisket.*

QUANTITY: *With bone: 8–12 oz (225–350 g) per portion*
No bone: 4–6 oz (110–175 g) per portion

OVEN: *High: 400–425°F/200C–220°C/Gas Mk 6–7*
Moderate: 350–375°F/180–190°C/Gas Mk 4–5
For rare beef 15 minutes per lb/30 minutes per kg
For well done 30 minutes per lb/ 60 minutes per kg

Low: 325°F/170°C/Gas Mk 3
45 minutes per lb/ 90 minutes per kg

Place the meat on a rack or straight into a roasting tin and sprinkle with flour and dry mustard mixed together. Rub well into the fat. If the meat is very lean, add a little dripping or oil to the tin. Roast according to the times above. Serve with mustard or horseradish sauce, gravy, Yorkshire puddings, pork forcemeat balls and boiled or grilled bacon, and with roast potatoes and vegetables. Many cooks like to cook roast beef in a high oven for 15 minutes and then reduce the temperature to moderate.

SPICED STEAK
Serves 8

6 peppercorns
1 bay leaf
sprig of rosemary
small bunch each of thyme,
    marjoram and parsley
few slices of onion
6 cloves

a few juniper berries
salt
2 tbsp each tarragon vinegar and oil
stock
2 lb (900 g) trimmed steak
oil for frying

Crush the peppercorns with a pestle in a mortar and add the herbs. Pound a little to extract the juices. Mix remaining ingredients together (except steak and frying oil) and pour into a shallow dish. Cut the steak into eight pieces and lay in the marinade for at least 12 hours, turning occasionally. Put on a rack to drain. Put a little oil into a hot frying pan and fry the steaks lightly on each side. Pour in the marinade and a little stock and simmer gently until the steak is tender. Lift out and keep hot. Skim the stock and strain into a small saucepan. Reduce by boiling rapidly and pour over the steak.

GLAZED BOILED BEEF
Serves 6

3½ lb (1.6 kg) boned and
  rolled salted silverside or brisket
1 large onion, sliced
2 large carrots, sliced

2 celery stalks, sliced
8 black peppercorns
1 bay leaf

Glaze:
12 cloves
3 oz (75 g) soft brown sugar
½ tsp dry mustard

1 tsp cinnamon
2 tbsp thin honey
2 tsp lemon juice

Put the joint in a large bowl, cover with cold water and soak for several hours or overnight. Rinse well in cold water and place in a large saucepan. Add the vegetables, peppercorns and bay leaf. Pour in cold water to cover. Bring slowly to the boil, remove any scum from the surface, then reduce the heat as low as possible. Cover and simmer for 3–4 hours until tender. Allow the meat to cool in the cooking liquid. Preheat the oven to 350°F/180°C/Gas Mk 4. Drain the beef well and place in a small roasting pan. Press the cloves into the fat. Mix together the sugar, mustard, cinnamon, honey and lemon juice and spoon over the meat. Bake in the centre of the oven for about 45 minutes, basting occasionally during cooking. Serve hot.

HUNGARIAN BEEF AND CARAWAY RICE
Serves 6

2 tbsp oil
2 lb (900 g) stewing beef, cubed
3 celery stalks, chopped
1 large onion, sliced
½ beef stock cube
1 lb (450 g) can pineapple
  pieces with juice
1 tbsp chopped fresh parsley

good pinch sugar
1 tbsp tomato purée
few drops Worcestershire sauce
salt and freshly ground black pepper
12 oz (350 g) long-grain rice
1 oz (25 g) butter
2 tsp caraway seeds

Preheat the oven to 350°F/180°C/Gas Mk 4. Heat the oil and brown the meat cubes. Remove to a casserole. Add the celery and onion to the oil and cook for 3 minutes, stirring, then add to the casserole. Bring some water to the boil and dissolve the stock cube. Drain the pineapple and add the juice to the stock. Put in the parsley, sugar, tomato purée, Worcestershire sauce and season to taste. Pour over the meat, cover the casserole and cook in a preheated oven for 1½ hours.

Add more stock if necessary. Add pineapple pieces 15 minutes before the end of cooking time. Wash the rice thoroughly under cold running water and then cook in boiling salted water for about 12 minutes or until cooked. Drain and return to the pan. Stir in the butter and caraway seeds. Place the rice in a ring around the outside of a large warmed serving dish and pile the stew in the centre.

BOILED BEEF WITH BARLEY WINE
Serves 6

1 oz (25 g) butter
1 tbsp oil
3 lb (1.4 kg) boned rolled brisket beef
1 tbsp coarse-grained mustard
1 onion, sliced
3 carrots
2 medium parsnips
3 celery stalks
2 tbsp plain flour
6 fl oz (180 ml) bottle barley wine
¾ pt (450 ml) beef stock
1 tbsp Worcestershire sauce
salt and freshly ground black pepper

Dumplings:
8 oz (225 g) self-raising flour
4 oz (110 g) shredded suet
cold water to mix

Heat the butter and oil in a 7 pt (3.5 litre) flameproof casserole and fry the meat for 5 minutes, turning until browned on all sides. Lift out with a slotted spoon and spread with the mustard. Set aside. Add the onion to the casserole and fry for 5 minutes until soft. Cut the carrots, parsnips and celery into sticks about 2½ in (6 cm) long. Add to the casserole and cook for 5 minutes, stirring occasionally. Sprinkle the flour over, stir well and cook for 1 minute. Add the barley wine, beef stock, Worcestershire sauce and seasoning and mix well. Return the beef to the casserole and bring the liquid to the boil. Cover and simmer gently for 1½ hours. Meanwhile make the dumplings: put the flour and suet in a bowl with seasoning. Add 8–10 tbsp water and mix to a soft but not sticky dough. Shape into 12 even-sized balls and add to the casserole. Cover and cook for 30 minutes until well risen. Transfer the beef to a serving plate, discard the string and carve into thin slices. Serve with the dumplings, vegetables and gravy.

ENTRECOTE BEARNAISE
Serves 4

1½ lb (675 g) sirloin steak in one piece
salt and freshly ground black pepper
1 oz (25 g) butter
1 tbsp oil

Sauce:
¼ onion, finely chopped
6 tbsp tarragon or wine vinegar
1 tsp finely chopped tarragon
or ¼ tsp dried

3 egg yolks
4½ oz (125 g) butter
chopped fresh parsley, to garnish

Trim the steak and if necessary beat until 1 in (2.5 cm) thick. Season on both sides. Heat the butter and oil and fry the steak for 5–10 minutes each side. Make the sauce: Put the onion in a small pan with the vinegar and tarragon. Bring to the boil and keep boiling steadily until reduced to 1 tablespoonful. Cool slightly. Separate the eggs, putting the yolks in a basin and fitting this over a saucepan of gently simmering (not boiling) water. Beat in the reduced vinegar mixture. Stir continuously over the water until slightly thickened. Beat in the butter a little at a time and season to taste. (If the sauce curdles, quickly place it in a bowl of iced water and stir until smooth again.) .Place the steak in a warmed serving dish, pour the pan juices over it and sprinkle with parsley. Serve the sauce separately.

BOILED BEEF AND CARROTS
Serves 4–6

2½ lb (1.1 kg) salted brisket
or silverside of beef
6 cloves
10 black peppercorns

bouquet garni including celery leaves
2 bay leaves
4 medium onions, quartered
1½ lb (675 g) carrots, sliced

Dumplings:
9 oz (250 g) plain flour
1 tsp baking powder
4 allspice berries, crushed
4 juniper berries, crushed

6 black peppercorns, crushed
4 tbsp chopped fresh parsley
pinch of salt
4 oz (110 g) shredded suet

Soak the beef overnight. Put it into a large saucepan with fresh water to cover, then add the cloves, peppercorns, bouquet garni, bay leaves and onions. Set the pan over a moderate heat and bring the water to the boil. Skim, then cover and simmer for 1 hour. Meanwhile make the dumplings: sift the flour and baking powder into a mixing bowl and add the spices, parsley and salt. Mix in the suet. Make a well in the centre, pour in 4 fl oz (125 ml) cold water and mix to a stiff dough. Divide into 16 pieces and form into balls. When the beef has cooked for 1 hour skim any fat off the liquid. Add the dumplings and cook for a further 10 minutes, then add the carrots. Cook for a further 20 minutes until the carrots are tender. Take out the beef, carve into fairly thick slices and arrange on a large heated serving dish surrounded by the carrots, onions and dumplings. Pour a little of the cooking liquid over the meat and serve the rest separately in a sauceboat.

MEAT PUDDING
Serves 4–6

Suet crust pastry:
12 oz (350 g) plain flour
6 oz (175 g) shredded suet
salt and freshly ground black pepper

1½ lb (675 g) chuck steak	*2 tsp mixed herbs*
1 heaped tbsp plain flour	*1 medium onion, sliced*
salt and freshly ground black pepper	*¼ pt (150 ml) beef stock*

Make the pastry, roll out and cut off one-third for the lid. Butter a medium-sized pudding bowl (a plastic bowl with a lid can also be used) and line with pastry. Cut the meat into fairly small cubes, removing any skin or gristle. Mix flour with seasoning and herbs and coat meat in it. Layer meat in the pudding basin with the onion. Pour in enough stock to come almost to the top of the meat. Dampen the edge of the dough and press the pastry lid on top. Place a piece of buttered greaseproof paper loosely. on top and cover with a doubled piece of foil with a pleat down the centre to allow for expansion. Secure with string, making a handle on the top to facilitate lifting the hot bowl out. Place in a steamer over boiling water, or on an old saucer set upside down in a large saucepan of boiling water. If using the latter method do be careful not to let the water get up to the brim of the basin. Simmer for 3–4 hours.

SALT BEEF AND DUMPLINGS
Serves 4–6

3 lb (1.4 kg) salt beef
1 tsp thyme
1 bay leaf
salt and freshly ground black pepper

3 large carrots, sliced
3 large onions, chopped
1 turnip, chopped

Dumplings:
4 oz (110 g) plain flour
1 tsp baking powder

1½ oz (35 g) shredded suet
cold water to mix

Some salt beef might need to be steeped in cold water; ask your butcher. Place the meat in a deep saucepan and cover it with cold water. Bring to the boil slowly and skim off any froth on top. Add the herbs and seasoning, cover the pan and simmer for an hour. Add the vegetables, cover and cook for another hour, gently simmering, until tender. Remove any frothy scum that appears on the surface during cooking. Combine the flour, baking powder and seasoning. Rub in the suet and mix to a stiffish dough with a little cold water. Roll between floured hands into eight small balls. Remove the meat from the saucepan and keep hot. Drop the dumplings into the pan, cover and cook gently for 25 minutes. Slice the meat and serve surrounded by the vegetables and dumplings.

BEEF ROLLS BELLAGIO
Serves 4

1½ lb (675 g) topside, cut into 4 slices
salt and freshly ground black pepper
2 tbsp lard or oil
1 large onion, finely chopped
1 large garlic clove, crushed
4 celery stalks, finely chopped
4 oz (110 g) fresh white breadcrumbs
1 oz (25 g) butter

1 tbsp olive oil
14 oz (400 g) can tomatoes, chopped
2 tbsp tomato purée
1 tsp dried basil
1 green pepper, deseeded and chopped
1 tsp sugar
1 tbsp wine vinegar

Beat each slice of beef between sheets of greaseproof paper with a meat bat until flat. Cut each piece in half to make eight slices. Season well with pepper. Prepare the stuffing: heat the dripping in a saucepan and gently fry half the onion with the garlic and celery for 5–8 minutes until softened. Stir in the breadcrumbs and season to taste with salt and pepper. Spread each slice of beef with some stuffing, tuck the edges in to neaten and roll up firmly from the shorter edge. Tie securely with string. Heat the butter and oil in a flameproof casserole and sauté the beef rolls, turning them until browned all over. Mix the chopped tomatoes and their juices, tomato purée, basil, green pepper and remaining chopped onion. Add the sugar and vinegar. Season well and pour over the prepared meat. Cover with a lid and simmer gently for 1½ hours or until the meat is tender. Remove with a slotted spoon and cut off the string. Arrange the rolls on a hot serving dish and coat with the sauce.

SPICY BEEF AND PEPPER HOT POT
Serves 4

2 tbsp oil
1 large onion, chopped
1 green pepper, deseeded and chopped
2 green chilli peppers, deseeded and chopped
1½ lb (675 g) stewing steak and kidney, cubed
1 tbsp cornflour
1 tbsp brown sugar
2 tbsp tomato purée
½ tsp paprika
14 oz (400 g) can tomatoes
2 tsp Worcestershire sauce
½ tsp mixed herbs
½ pt (300 ml) beef stock
salt and freshly ground black pepper

Preheat the oven to 350°F/180°C/Gas Mk 4. Heat the oil in a large frying pan. Add the onion, pepper and chillies and fry until soft. Add the meat and fry until evenly browned. Stir in the cornflour and mix well. Add the remaining ingredients and season to taste. Cook and stir until the sauce thickens. Transfer to a casserole and cook for 1–1½ hours in the oven. Serve with boiled rice.

VEAL

VEAL BLANQUETTE WITH CELERIAC
Serves 4

*1½ lb (675 g) pie veal
cut into ¾ in (2 cm) squares
12 oz (350 g) celeriac, roughly chopped
4 celery stalks, roughly chopped
bouquet garni made with
thyme, parsley and lemon zest
8 oz (225 g) carrots, sliced
1 large onion, thinly sliced*

*1 pt (600 ml) veal or chicken stock
pinch ground mace
salt and freshly ground black pepper
1 oz (25 g) butter
3 tbsp plain flour
2 medium egg yolks
1 oz (25 g) grated Parmesan cheese
chopped fresh parsley, to garnish*

Put the veal, celeriac, celery and bouquet garni into a large saucepan with the carrots and onion. Pour in the stock and add the mace, salt and pepper. Bring to the boil over a medium heat, then cover and simmer for 1 hour. Strain off and reserve the stock. Discard bouquet garni. Return the veal and vegetables to the saucepan. Melt the butter in a medium saucepan, stir in the flour and cook for 30 seconds. Stir in ¾ pt (450 ml) of the reserved stock and bring to the boil, stirring. Simmer for 2 minutes and remove from the heat. Beat the eggs yolks with the cheese and gradually add about 6 tbsp of the hot sauce. Stir this mixture back into the rest of the sauce and reheat very gently so the mixture thickens. Mix into the veal and vegetables and let the blanquette stand for 1 hour to let the flavours blend. Just before serving, reheat gently, without boiling, and sprinkle with parsley.

VEAL CUTLETS WITH APPLES AND PORT
Serves 6

*4 fl oz (125 ml) clear honey,
warmed until just liquid
4 fl oz (125 ml) tawny port
pinch dried mixed herbs
pinch freshly grated nutmeg
2 oz (50 g) unsalted butter*

*6 best-end veal cutlets or small
leg steaks about ¾ in (2 cm) thick
salt and white pepper
1 lb (450 g) crisp eating apples, sliced
3 tbsp lemon juice*

Mix the honey with the port, herbs and nutmeg. Heat the butter in a large deep frying pan with a lid over moderately high heat. Add the chops and brown quickly on each side. Sprinkle with salt and pepper and reduce the heat to low. Pour in the port mixture, cover and simmer for 4 minutes. Add the apples and sprinkle with salt and pepper. Spoon some of the sauce over the apples. Cover and simmer for 5 minutes. Stir the lemon juice into the sauce and simmer, uncovered, for 3 minutes. Turn into a warmed serving dish.

VEAL CUTLETS WITH CIDER
Serves 4

4 tbsp oil	*¼ pt (150 ml) dry cider*
4 veal cutlets	*¼ pt (150 ml) water*
2 medium onions, chopped	*salt and freshly ground black pepper*
2 tbsp plain flour	*chopped fresh parsley, to garnish*

Heat the oil in a frying pan, add the cutlets and fry for 10 minutes until brown. Remove and keep warm. Add the onions to the pan and cook until golden brown. Add the flour and stir for 1–2 minutes. Add the cider and water and stir until thickened. Boil for 2 minutes, then season to taste. Return the cutlets to the pan and simmer for 3 minutes. Place on a warmed serving dish and garnish with parsley.

SAUTÉ OF VEAL AND CUCUMBER
Serves 4

1 medium cucumber, peeled	*2 tbsp plain flour*
salt and freshly ground black pepper	*2 tsp paprika*
3 oz (75 g) butter	*¼ pt (150 ml) soured cream*
1 medium onion, chopped	*chopped fresh parsley, to garnish*
4 x 4 oz (110 g) veal escalopes	

Slice the cucumber in half lengthways, scoop out the seeds and cut the flesh into sticks about 1 in (2.5 cm) long and ½ in (1 cm) wide. Sprinkle with salt and leave for at least 30 minutes. Melt the butter in a frying pan, add the onion and cook gently until soft. Meanwhile beat out each escalope thinly. In a bowl mix together the flour, paprika and salt and pepper to taste; dip each escalope into this mixture. Turn the heat up to medium, put the escalopes in the pan and cook until well browned on both sides. Remove and keep warm on a serving dish. Dry the cucumber sticks with kitchen paper and add to the pan. Cook until lightly browned, stirring occasionally. Remove and place beside the escalopes. Spoon over the cream and garnish with parsley.

VEAL IN TOMATO AND WINE SAUCE
Serves 4

1 oz (25 g) butter
2 tbsp olive oil
3 onions, chopped
2 carrots, chopped
1–2 celery stalks, trimmed
  and chopped
1 garlic clove, crushed
4 pieces shin veal,
  2 lb (900 g) total weight
plain flour for coating

salt and freshly ground black pepper
½ pt (300 ml) dry white wine
14 oz (400 g) can tomatoes
¼ pt (150 ml) chicken stock
2 strips lemon peel
1 bay leaf
1 tbsp chopped fresh parsley
½ tsp dried basil
¼ tsp dried thyme

Preheat the oven to 350°F/180°C/Gas Mk 4. Melt the butter and oil in a large frying pan. Add the vegetables and garlic and fry gently for 5 minutes until lightly coloured. Transfer the vegetables to a large flameproof casserole which will hold the meat in one layer. Coat the veal in seasoned flour. Add to the frying pan and fry over moderate heat until browned on all sides. Place on top of the vegetables. Pour the wine into the frying pan and bring to boiling point, stirring constantly with a wooden spoon. Add the remaining ingredients and simmer, stirring, until the tomatoes are broken down. Add seasoning to taste, then pour over the veal in the casserole. Cover and cook in the oven for about 2 hours or until the veal is tender. Check the seasoning before serving.

VEAL AND BEAN SAVOURY
Serves 4

8 oz (225 g) haricot beans,
  soaked overnight
2 tbsp oil
1–1½ lb (450–675 g) stewing veal
1 large onion, chopped
1 tbsp plain flour

salt and freshly ground black pepper
½ tsp oregano
½ tsp grated nutmeg
8 oz (225 g) tomatoes,
  peeled and quartered
½ pt (300 ml) stock

Drain the beans. Heat the oil in a large saucepan and brown the meat on all sides. Stir in the onion and cook until soft. Stir in the flour, salt and pepper to taste, oregano, nutmeg and tomatoes. Add the stock and then the beans. Cover and simmer over a low heat for 1½–2 hours until the meat is tender.

VEAL CHOPS DIJONNAISE
Serves 4

4 x 6–7 oz (175–200 g) veal chops
3 tbsp capers, drained and crushed
2 tbsp olive oil
2 tbsp lemon juice
2 tbsp Dijon mustard

2 tsp chopped fresh tarragon or
 1 tsp dried
freshly ground black pepper
tarragon sprigs

Lay the chops in a shallow dish. Place the capers, oil, lemon juice, mustard, tarragon and some pepper in a bowl and whisk together. Brush the mixture over both sides of the chops, cover and marinate for 2 hours. Grill the chops for 10 minutes, basting frequently with the marinade sauce. Turn over and grill for a further 10 minutes, basting in the same way. Place in a warmed serving dish and pour over the cooking juices from the grill pan. Garnish with tarragon sprigs if available.

VEAL ESCALOPES BÉCHAMEL
Serves 6

2 oz (50 g) butter
1½ lb (675 g) veal escalopes
2 spring onions, thickly sliced
6 oz (175 g)mushrooms, thinly sliced

Béchamel sauce:
¼ pt (150 ml) milk
½ small onion studded
 with cloves
½ oz (10 g) butter

3 tomatoes, peeled, seeded
 and cut into strips
¼ pt (150 ml) chicken stock
½ tsp oregano

½ oz (10 g) plain flour
salt and white pepper
pinch each nutmeg and thyme

Make the sauce: bring the milk to the boil with the onion. Remove from the heat and leave to cool, covered, to infuse the onion flavour. Melt the butter and stir in the flour. Cook, stirring, over a low heat for 1 minute. Gradually stir in the milk, add seasoning and simmer for 5 minutes. Set aside. Heat the butter in a large frying pan and fry the escalopes quickly over a high heat on both sides until cooked through. Remove and keep hot. Add the spring onions to the pan and fry gently for 2 minutes, then add the mushrooms and tomatoes and cook for 5 minutes. Add the stock and oregano, bring to the boil and cook gently for 5 minutes. Add the sauce and cook until the liquid is reduced by a quarter. Check the seasoning and pour over the escalopes. Serve with rice.

VEAL BREAST WITH PEAS AND CARROTS
Serves 4–6

3 lb (1.4 kg) breast of veal
4 tbsp olive oil
bouquet garni
salt and freshly ground black pepper
2 lb (900 g) fresh peas, shelled

1 lb (450 g) button onions
1 lb (450 g) small new carrots
1 tsp sugar
2 oz (50 g) butter

Remove the bones and skin from the veal and cut the meat into small cubes. Heat the oil in a heavy saucepan and brown the veal. Add the bouquet garni, salt, pepper and boiling water to almost cover the meat. Cover and simmer gently for 1½ hours. Add the vegetables to the casserole with the sugar. Continue to simmer slowly until they are tender. Remove the bouquet garni and stir in the butter.

ROAST VEAL

CUTS TO USE: loin, leg, shoulder, boned and rolled,
stuffed breast

QUANTITY: With bone: 8–12 oz (225–350 g) per person
No bone: 4–6 oz (110–175 g) per person

OVEN: Moderate: 350–375°F/180–190°C/Gas Mk 4 or 5
With bone: 20 minutes per lb/40 minutes per kilo
No bone: 30 minutes per lb/60 minutes per kilo

Slow: 325°F/170°C/Gas Mk 3
With bone: 30 minutes per lb/60 minutes per kilo
No bone: 40 minutes per lb/80 minutes per kilo

Place the meat on a rack or in a roasting tin and sprinkle with flour. As veal is very lean the joint should be covered with strips of streaky bacon and a little dripping added to the pan. Cover with foil and remove this 20 minutes before the end of cooking time. The joint should be basted frequently. Serve with pork forcemeat balls and boiled or grilled bacon, roast potatoes and vegetables.

VEAL STIFADO
Serves 4

2 tbsp olive oil
1¼ lb (500 g) pie veal, diced
1 garlic clove, crushed
1 lb (450 g) button onions, blanched
1 tbsp plain flour
1 tsp ground cinnamon
1 tbsp red wine vinegar

¼ pt (150 ml) red wine
3 tbsp tomato purée
¼ pt (150 ml) water
½ tsp oregano
salt and freshly ground black pepper

Preheat the oven to 350°F/180°C/Gas Mk 4. Heat the oil in a flameproof casserole. Add the veal, garlic and onions and cook over moderate heat for 2–3 minutes. Stir in the flour and cook for 1 minute, then add the cinnamon, vinegar, wine, tomato purée, water, oregano, and seasoning to taste. Bring to the boil, stirring well. Cover and cook in the oven for 1½ hours until the veal and onions are tender.

VEAL CHOPS WITH GRAPES
Serves 4

¾ oz (20 g) butter
1 tbsp oil
1 small onion, finely chopped
1 garlic clove, crushed
4 veal chops, trimmed of excess fat
¼ pt (150 ml) orange juice

grated zest of half an orange
½ tsp dried rosemary, crumbled
salt and freshly ground black pepper
8 oz (225 g) white grapes, deseeded
½ oz (10 g) butter, softened
1 tsp plain flour

Heat the butter and oil in a frying pan over medium heat, add the onion and garlic and cook for 3–4 minutes, stirring occasionally, until soft but not brown. Remove and set aside. Add the chops and cook for 5 minutes on each side. Pour over the orange juice, then add the orange zest, rosemary and seasoning to taste; stir well. Return the onion and garlic to the pan, cover, bring to the boil, then simmer for 10 minutes. Add the grapes, return to the boil, cover and simmer for 5 minutes. Mix the butter and flour together. Add to the frying pan in small pieces, increase the heat to medium and stir continuously until the sauce is thick and glossy. Check the seasoning, place the chops on a warmed serving dish and pour over the sauce.

VEAL PAUPIETTES
Serves 6

4 oz (110 g) sausage meat
4 oz (110 g) ham, minced
1 egg
salt and freshly ground black pepper
6 x 4 oz (110 g) veal escalopes
2 oz (50 g) plain flour
4 tbsp oil

2 oz (50 g) margarine
4 oz (110 g) bacon rashers, chopped
1 lb (450 g) carrots, sliced
6 fl oz (180 ml) white wine
8 oz (225 g) spring onions or shallots
½ pt (300 ml) stock
1 tbsp chopped fresh parsley

Mix the sausage meat, ham, egg and seasoning to a smooth paste, then chill. Beat the escalopes until thin. Spread filling on each one, roll up and tie with string. Dust with seasoned flour. Heat half the oil in a pan and brown the paupiettes for 4 minutes, covered with a lid. Remove to a casserole. Add the margarine and remaining oil to the pan and fry the bacon for 1 minute. Sauté the carrot slices gently for 3 minutes, then add both to the veal. Pour in the wine, bring to the boil, cover and simmer for 1 hour or until the meat is tender. Meanwhile boil the shallots in stock for 2 minutes. Remove the string and place the paupiettes on a warmed serving dish surrounded by the bacon, carrots and onions. Reduce the sauce by fast boiling to ½ pt (300 ml), pour over the paupiettes and sprinkle with chopped parsley.

VEAL IN GINGER CREAM SAUCE
Serves 4

3 oz (75 g) butter
1 small onion, finely chopped
2 green peppers, deseeded
    and thinly sliced
8 oz (225 g) button mushrooms,
    thinly sliced
1 lb (450 g) veal escalopes,
    cut into very thin strips

salt and freshly ground black pepper
3 oz (75 g) preserved ginger,
    well drained and very thinly sliced
¼ pt (150 ml) double cream
1 orange, thinly sliced, to garnish

Place half the butter in a heavy-based pan over moderate heat, add the onion and peppers and cook for 2 minutes, stirring occasionally. Add the mushrooms and stir until well coated with the butter. Cook for 1 minute, then remove the vegetables and keep warm. Heat the remaining butter in the pan, add the veal and cook, stirring frequently, for 4–5 minutes until meat is just cooked. Return the vegetables, season to taste and stir in the ginger. Pour in the cream, stir well and lower the heat to simmering point. Transfer to a warmed serving dish and garnish with orange slices.

JELLIED VEAL RING
Serves 4–6

1 lb (450 g) lean veal, cubed
4 oz (110 g) bacon, chopped
2 hard-boiled eggs, sliced
1 tbsp chopped fresh parsley

1 pt (600 ml) rich chicken or
 veal stock
1 oz (25 g) gelatine
watercress and lemon slices, to garnish

Preheat the oven to 325°F/170°C/Gas Mk 3. Mix the veal and bacon
and put into water. Bring to the boil, drain and rinse with cold water.
Put a layer of egg slices in the base of a ring mould rinsed out with
cold water. Arrange the meat and remaining egg in layers. Sprinkle
with parsley and season well. Pour 12 fl oz (350 ml) of the stock over
the meat. Cover with foil and cook in the oven for about 1½ hours,
then cool. Dissolve the gelatine in the remaining stock over a low
heat. Pour into the ring mould, leave to get cold, then refrigerate until
required. Turn out and decorate with watercress and slices of lemon.

VEAL RAGOUT
Serves 6

2 tbsp oil
2 lb (900 g) stewing veal, cubed
3 tbsp plain flour
1 garlic clove, finely chopped
1½ pt (900 ml) chicken stock
2 tbsp tomato purée
1 tbsp finely chopped fresh parsley
1 tbsp fresh thyme leaves
 or ½ tsp dried thyme

1 bay leaf, crushed
salt and freshly ground black pepper
1½ oz (35 g) butter
3 medium onions, quartered
4 medium carrots, cut in
 1 in (2.5 cm) pieces
1 tbsp sugar
6 medium new potatoes, halved
2 tbsp finely chopped chives, to garnish

Heat oil in a large flameproof casserole over moderate heat. Add the
veal and cook for 10 minutes to brown on all sides. Sprinkle with the
flour and continue to cook, stirring frequently, for 5 minutes until the
flour is brown. Add the garlic and cook for 30 seconds. Pour in the
chicken stock and stir well. Add the tomato purée, parsley, thyme,
bay leaf and seasoning to taste. Cover and simmer for 30 minutes. In a
large frying pan, melt the butter and cook the onions and carrots for
5 minutes stirring frequently. Sprinkle with sugar and cook for
another 5 minutes, stirring constantly. Transfer to the casserole, cover
and cook gently for 30 minutes. Add the potatoes and cook for a
further 30 minutes. Check the seasoning and garnish with chives.

VEAL ESCALOPES IN MARSALA
Serves 4

4 veal escalopes
2 oz (50 g) butter
4 fl oz (125 ml) Marsala
6 fl oz (180 ml) gravy or thickened stock
pinch cayenne pepper

Place the escalopes between dampened greaseproof paper and beat with a meat mallet or rolling pin until ⅛ in (3 mm) thick. Heat the butter in a frying pan and fry until well browned. Transfer to a warmed serving dish and keep hot. Add the Marsala to the pan and boil for 5 minutes, stirring well. Add the gravy or stock and cayenne, mix well and pour over the veal.

VEAL WITH CAPERS
Serves 4

4 veal escalopes, flattened
seasoned flour
2 oz (50 g) butter

juice of ½ lemon
2 tbsp capers, chopped

Dip the veal into the seasoned flour and coat well. Heat the butter in a frying pan, lay in the veal and cook over low heat for about 10 minutes, turning once. Remove and place on a warmed serving dish. Stir the lemon juice and capers into the frying pan, heat through and pour over the veal.

WIENER SCHNITZEL
Serves 4

4 veal escalopes
1½ oz (35 g) seasoned flour
1 egg, beaten

2 oz (50 g) fine dried breadcrumbs
2 oz (50 g) butter
4 slices lemon

Place the escalopes between dampened greaseproof paper and beat with a meat mallet or rolling pin until very thin. Coat veal with seasoned flour, then dip in beaten egg and breadcrumbs until thoroughly coated. Melt the butter in a large frying pan. Add the veal and fry over a moderate heat until golden brown on both sides, turning once during cooking. Transfer to a warmed serving dish and serve immediately, garnished with lemon slices. Accompany with new potatoes tossed in parsley and a green salad.

VEAL FRICASSÉE
Serves 4

1 oz (25 g) butter
1 tbsp oil
1–1½ lb (450–675 g) stewing veal, cubed
8 oz (225 g) back bacon, cut
  in two thick slices and cubed
½ small onion, finely chopped

½ pt (300 ml) veal stock or water
salt and freshly ground black pepper
¾ oz (20 g) plain flour
¾ oz (20 g) butter, softened
1–2 tbsp lemon juice
fresh parsley, to garnish

Preheat the oven to 350°F/180°C/Gas Mk 4. Melt the butter and oil in a frying pan, and brown the veal and bacon on all sides. Remove and place in a large casserole. Add the onion to the frying pan, cook until soft, then add to the meat. Pour over the stock or water, add salt and pepper to taste, cover and cook in the oven for 1½ hours. Strain the liquid into a small pan, keeping the meat hot in the casserole. Knead together the flour and butter and break into very small pieces. Drop these into the liquid, stir well to thicken, bring to the boil and cook for 2–3 minutes. Add the lemon juice and check the seasoning. Place the meat on a warmed serving dish and pour over the sauce. Garnish with parsley.

SALTIMBOCCA
Serves 4

8 thin slices of tender veal
  from the leg
8 thin slices of ham
8 small fresh sage leaves or dried sage
salt and freshly ground black pepper

1½ oz (35 g) butter
6 fl oz (180 ml) Marsala or
  sweet white wine
8 slices bread
olive oil for frying

Preheat the oven to 350°F/180°C/Gas Mk 4. Beat out the veal slices between greaseproof paper. Place a thin slice of ham on each veal slice, and then a sage leaf or small pinch of dried sage. Season with salt and pepper. Roll each slice up tightly and fasten securely with toothpicks. Heat the butter and brown the rolls all over for about 5 minutes. Add the Marsala or white wine and a little salt and pepper. Cover and cook gently in the oven for about 15 minutes. Cut the bread into rounds and fry until golden brown and crisp. Place each roll on a fried bread crouton and serve around a dish of spinach.

MOROCCAN VEAL
Serves 4

1¼ lb (500 g) topside of veal, trimmed
and cut in ¾ in (2 cm) cubes
½ large onion, finely chopped
2½ tsp paprika
1½ tsp ginger
½ tsp cinnamon
salt and freshly ground black pepper

4 oz (110 g) dried apricots
4 oz (110 g) prunes
1 oz (25 g) pine nuts
¾ pt (450 ml) unsalted stock
¼ tsp saffron threads
coriander sprigs, to garnish

Preheat the oven to 325°F/170°C/Gas Mk 3. Mix together the veal, onion, paprika, ginger and cinnamon with pepper and salt to taste in a large bowl, making sure the meat is well coated. Add the dried fruit and pine nuts, then transfer to a flameproof casserole. Bring the stock to the boil and stir in the saffron. Pour over the meat mixture, cover and cook in the oven for 2 hours. Serve garnished with coriander sprigs.

VEAL CORDON BLEU
Serves 4

4 thick veal cutlets
4 oz (110 g) minced cooked ham
4 oz (110 g) Gruyére cheese, grated
garlic salt and freshly ground black pepper
1 oz (25 g) butter
1½ oz (35 g) plain flour
2–3 tbsp oil
8 fl oz (250 ml) white wine
4 fl oz (125 ml) chicken stock
2 tbsp chopped fresh parsley and tarragon

Preheat the oven to 350°F/180°C/Gas Mk 4. Cut a pocket in each cutlet from the boneless side of the meat but be careful not to cut right through to the outside. Mix the ham and cheese together, seasoning with garlic salt and pepper. Melt ½ oz (10 g) of the butter and stir in. Spoon this mixture carefully into the pockets and seal the openings with toothpicks. Dust well with seasoned flour. Heat the oil with the remaining butter, fry the cutlets until golden brown on each side, then place in an ovenproof dish. Add the stock and wine to the juices in the pan and bring to the boil. Stir in the herbs and pour over the cutlets. Cook in the oven for about 30 minutes or until the veal is tender. Remove the toothpicks.

VEAL ESCALOPES IN MUSTARD CREAM
Serves 4

8 veal escalopes or 4 veal steaks, beaten thin
seasoned flour
1 tbsp oil
1 oz (25 g) butter
4 fl oz (125 ml) single cream
4 tsp Dijon mustard
salt and white pepper

Dust the veal lightly with seasoned flour. In a heavy frying pan, heat the oil and butter. Cook the veal in batches until lightly browned on both sides, transferring to a hot serving dish as they are done. Keep warm. Pour the cream into the pan, stir in the mustard and cook, scraping and stirring to remove all the pan sediments, until the sauce is coffee-coloured and fairly thick. Season and spoon over the escalopes.

VEAL ENVELOPES
Serves 4

4 slices veal
2–3 tbsp oil
1 oz (25 g) butter
2 oz (50 g) mushrooms, chopped
1 small onion, chopped

squeeze of lemon juice
4 tbsp white wine
salt and freshly ground black pepper
1 tbsp double cream

Preheat the oven to 375°F/190°C/Gas Mk 5. Flatten the veal slices by beating with a rolling pin on a wet chopping board. Cut out four circles of greaseproof paper about 2 in (5 cm) larger than each slice. Brush both sides of the veal slices with oil and lay in the centre of the paper circles. Melt the butter and sauté the mushrooms and onion until soft. Add the lemon juice, white wine and seasoning and cook for a few minutes more to reduce the liquid. Stir in the cream. Remove from the heat and place a quarter of the mushroom mixture in the centre of each piece of veal. Fold the paper circle over in the shape of a Cornish pasty and fold and pinch the edges together to make a tight seal. Grease a shallow baking dish well, put in the envelopes and cook for 30 minutes, when the paper will have puffed up. Serve from the envelopes to retain all the juices.

VEAL CURRY
Serves 4

1 oz (25 g) butter
2 medium onions, finely chopped
1 garlic clove, chopped
2 tsp curry powder
1 tsp curry paste
1 lb (450 g) lean veal, diced
a few pickled gherkins
2 tsp chutney
juice of ½ lemon
salt and freshly ground black pepper

Heat the butter and sauté the onion and garlic for about 8 minutes, then stir in the curry powder and paste. Cook for a further 4 minutes, stirring. Add the veal, turn it over in the paste and fry until browned all over. Add the gherkins, chutney and lemon juice and season to taste. Cover and cook very slowly for 2 hours, stirring from time to time until all the juices have been absorbed and the curry is fairly dry. Serve on hot boiled rice with wedges of lemon around the edge.

VEAL SCALOPPINI WITH GORGONZOLA
Serves 4–6

12 small thin veal slices, 1½ oz (35 g) each
3 tbsp olive oil
4 fl oz (125 ml) brandy
1½ tsp plain flour, plus extra for dredging
3 oz (75 g) chilled unsalted butter, diced
4 oz (110 g) Gorgonzola cheese, derinded and chopped
4 fl oz (125 ml) double cream

Beat the veal slices until very thin and dredge well with flour. Heat 1 tbsp oil in a large frying pan. Over fairly high heat, fry four scaloppini for 30 seconds on each side until just cooked through. Remove to a warmed serving platter and keep warm while you cook the remainder. Reduce the heat to low, add the brandy and sprinkle with 1½ tsp flour. Scrape up any crusty bits and boil rapidly until the sauce is reduced by half. Add the butter and cook, stirring, until it melts, then immediately stir in the cheese and cream. Cook, stirring, until the cheese is fully melted. Coat the scaloppini with the sauce.

HUNGARIAN VEAL
Serves 4

1½ lb (675 g) boned shoulder of veal,
  cubed
3 oz (75 g) plain flour
1 tsp paprika
1 tsp salt
¼ tsp freshly ground black pepper

2–3 tbsp oil
1 onion, sliced
1 garlic clove, crushed
¼ pt (150 ml) soured cream
1 tsp caraway seeds
1 tbsp chopped fresh parsley

Preheat the oven to 350°F/180°C/Gas Mk 4. Mix the flour with the paprika, salt and pepper and dust the veal until each piece is well covered. Reserve the remaining seasoned flour. Heat the oil and fry the veal gently until golden brown, then put in a casserole and keep warm. Sauté the onion and garlic until soft but not browned and stir in the remaining flour. Add ½ pt (300 ml) hot water and bring to the boil. Pour over the meat and stir. Cover and cook in the oven for 40 minutes or until the meat is tender. Stir in the soured cream and caraway seeds, and sprinkle with parsley. Serve with buttered noodles.

VEAL AND LIVER GRATIN
Serves 4

1 tbsp oil
1½ oz (35 g) butter
1 large onion, chopped
1 lb (450 g) minced veal
8 oz (225 g) chicken livers,
  trimmed and chopped

1 tbsp tomato purée
½ tsp dried thyme
salt and freshly ground black pepper
1 tbsp cornflour
2 lb (900 g) potatoes
tomato slices, to garnish

In a large saucepan, melt the oil and ½ oz (10 g) of the butter. Add the onion and cook for 10 minutes until soft. Add the veal and sauté for 5 minutes. Stir in the livers, tomato purée, thyme and seasoning to taste. Mix the cornflour with 1 tbsp water, then stir into the pan and heat for about 10 minutes until thick. Meanwhile cook the potatoes in salted boiling water until just tender and firm enough to cut into slices. Arrange layers of the meat mixture and sliced potato in a deep heatproof dish, finishing with potato. Melt the remaining butter and sprinkle on the top. Place under a hot grill and cook until golden. Serve garnished with sliced tomato.

VEAL CARMELLA
Serves 6–8

3 tbsp oil
2 lb (900 g) leg of veal
4 oz (110 g) streaky bacon
1 lb (450 g) spring onions,
  sliced diagonally
8 oz (225 g) carrots, cut into fingers

8 oz (225 g) button mushrooms
salt and freshly ground black pepper
½ pt (300 ml) light beer
¼ pt (150 ml) chicken stock
1 tsp dried thyme
2 tbsp clear honey

Preheat the oven to 350°F/180°C/Gas Mk 4. Heat the oil in a large
saucepan and brown the veal all over. Lay the bacon over the veal and
place in an ovenproof dish. Arrange the vegetables around it and
season well. Mix the beer and stock and pour half over the joint.
Sprinkle with the thyme, cover and bake for 45 minutes. Heat the
remaining stock and beer with the honey and pour over the joint.
Raise the heat to 400°F/200°C/Gas Mk 6 and return to the oven,
uncovered, for 30 minutes. Baste at least twice. Put the meat on a
warmed serving dish surrounded by the vegetables; serve the gravy
separately.

ORIENTAL VEAL
Serves 4–6

½ oz (10 g) cornflour
salt and freshly ground black pepper
1 tsp ginger
1 lb (450 g) leg of veal, well
  beaten and cut into strips
4 tbsp oil
1 onion, sliced

¼ pt (150 ml) stock
1 tbsp soy sauce
1 tbsp sherry
½ red pepper, deseeded
  and cut into strips
2 oz (50 g) mushrooms, sliced

Season the cornflour with salt and pepper to taste, add the ginger and
use to coat the meat strips. Heat the oil in a frying pan, and cook the
meat for 7–10 minutes until tender. Remove and keep warm. Place the
onion, stock, soy sauce and sherry in a saucepan, and boil for
3–5 minutes. Add the red pepper and cook for 2–3 minutes. Add the
mushrooms and cook for 1–2 minutes. Blend the remaining seasoned
cornflour with some water and add to the pan, stirring until
thickened. Place in a warmed serving dish with the veal strips on top.

BRAISED VEAL IN MUSHROOM SAUCE
Serves 6

3 oz (75 g) butter
2½ lb (1.1 kg) boned and
   rolled leg or shoulder of veal
2 spring onions, chopped
2 onions, chopped
1 thyme sprig
1 bay leaf

salt and freshly ground black pepper
¾ pt (450 ml) cider
8 oz (225 g) mushrooms, chopped
1 egg yolk
4 fl oz (125 ml) single cream
2 tbsp chopped fresh parsley

Heat 2 oz (50 g) of the butter and fry the veal until brown on all
sides. Remove, then fry the spring onions and onions until softened.
Return the meat to the pan and add the thyme, bay leaf, salt and
pepper to taste and the cider. Bring to the boil, cover and cook over a
low heat for 1½ hours. Then fry the mushrooms in the remaining
butter for 3–4 minutes, add to the pan and cook for 10 minutes.
Remove the veal to a serving dish. and keep warm. Discard the thyme
and bay leaf. Beat the egg yolk with the cream, whisk into the
cooking liquid and cook gently until thickened. Cover the meat with
the sauce and sprinkle with parsley.

VEAL ITALIANO
Serves 6

2 lb (900 g) breast of veal,
   boned and rolled
6 oz (175 g) mozzarella cheese, sliced
6 oz (175 g) ham, sliced

few fresh sage leaves or
   pinch dried sage
salt and freshly ground black pepper
4 tbsp oil

Sauce:
½ oz (10 g) butter
½ oz (10 g) plain flour
¼ pt (150 ml) chicken stock
½ pt (300 ml) milk

pinch salt, nutmeg and pepper
juice of 1 lemon
2 oz (50 g) sweetcorn

Preheat the oven to 400°F/200°C/Gas Mk 6. Make the sauce: melt the
butter and stir in the flour, cook for a few minutes, then stir in the
chicken stock. Cook for 5 minutes, then add the milk, seasoning and
lemon juice. Simmer for another 5 minutes and stir in the sweetcorn.
Unroll the meat and cover with the cheese, ham and sage. Season
well, roll up and tie with string. Brush with oil and roast for 1 hour.
Add ½ pt (300 ml) water and cook for another 30 minutes, basting at
least twice. Place on a warmed serving dish and remove the string.
Slice the meat and serve with the gently reheated sauce.

VEAL CUTLETS BONNE FEMME
Serves 4

4 x 8 oz (225 g) veal cutlets
salt and freshly ground black pepper
2 oz (50 g) plain flour
4 oz (110 g) butter with 1 tbsp oil
8 oz (225 g) boiled cold potatoes,
* thinly sliced*

4 oz (110 g) spring onions
4 fl oz (125 ml) sherry
1 tbsp plain flour
3 tbsp chopped fresh parsley

Preheat the oven to 400°F/200°C/Gas Mk 6. Dust the cutlets with seasoned flour. Heat the butter and oil in a frying pan and fry the cutlets on both sides for a few minutes. Place in an ovenproof dish. Fry the potatoes in the same pan until golden brown, remove and keep warm. Then fry the onions for 2 minutes or until soft. Remove and keep warm. Drain the frying pan, pour in the sherry and stir in 1 tbsp flour; bring to the boil, stirring constantly. Arrange the cutlets on a serving dish surrounded by fried potatoes and onions. Cover with the sauce and sprinkle with parsley.

VEAL AND PORK LOAF
Serves 4–6

4 bacon rashers
8 oz (225 g) raw minced pork
8 oz (225 g) raw minced veal
2 slices stale white bread without crusts
2 tbsp finely chopped onion

salt and freshly ground black pepper
½ tsp chopped sage
1 large egg, beaten
2–3 tbsp dry white breadcrumbs

Sauce:
1½ oz (35 g) butter plus 1 tbsp oil
1 onion, chopped
10–12 medium mushrooms, chopped

½ oz (10 g) plain flour
1 tsp Worcestershire sauce
½ pt (300 ml) fresh or soured cream

Preheat the oven to 375°F/190°C/Gas Mk 5. Finely dice two of the bacon rashers and mix with the pork and veal. Soak the bread in cold water to soften. Squeeze dry and mix into the meat with the onion, seasoning and sage. Mix in the egg thoroughly. Butter a loaf tin, put in the meat and sprinkle over the breadcrumbs. Cover with the remaining bacon. Bake for about 1½ hours, removing the bacon slices for the last 30 minutes. Make the sauce: Heat the butter and oil and sauté the onion and mushrooms for a few minutes until soft. Stir in the flour and Worcestershire sauce, mix well and simmer for a few minutes. Just before serving, stir in the cream and reheat gently.

VEAL WITH NOODLES
Serves 4–6

3 tbsp oil
1½ lb (675 g) shoulder veal, cubed
8 oz (225 g) veal kidney,
    sliced into 2 in (5 cm) pieces
1 large onion, chopped
3 carrots, sliced
2 celery stalks, chopped
¼ pt (150 ml) white wine
¼ pt (150 ml) chicken stock

1 garlic clove, crushed
salt and freshly ground black pepper
1 tbsp cornflour
8 oz (225 g) noodles
2 oz (50 g) butter
4 tbsp cream
large pinch paprika
2 oz (50 g) grated Parmesan cheese
chopped fresh parsley, to garnish

Heat the oil and fry the veal and kidney, to brown all over. Add the vegetables, cover and cook very gently for 15 minutes. Add the wine, stock, garlic and seasoning. Simmer for 1½ hours or until the meat is tender. Add the cornflour mixed with a little water and cook gently for 5 minutes until thickened. Cook the noodles in boiling salted water for 8–10 minutes. Drain, stir in the butter and dust with pepper. Stir the cream and paprika into the meat mixture, bring back to the boil and pour into the centre of a serving dish. Surround with the buttered noodles and sprinkle with Parmesan and parsley.

VEAL STEAKS À LA FRANCAISE
Serves 6

2 lb (900 g) loin of veal, cut in 6 steaks
4 oz (110 g) butter
salt and freshly ground black pepper
½ pt (300 ml) dry white wine
1¾ lb (800 g) potatoes
8 oz (225 g) baby onions

4 fl oz (125 ml) single cream
2 slices cooked ham, diced
8 oz (225 g) cooked mushrooms, diced
6 cooked artichoke hearts
chopped fresh parsley

Preheat the oven to 400°F/200°C/Gas Mk 6. Spread the steaks with half the butter and season with salt and pepper. Put in an ovenproof dish and bake for 30 minutes, turning once and basting occasionally with a little of the wine. Cut out potato balls with a melon baller. Heat the remaining butter and fry them gently together with the baby onions for about 10 minutes or until cooked. Lift out onto absorbent paper and keep warm. Drain the meat cooking liquid into a pan and bring to the boil. Stir in the cream and simmer gently for about 4 minutes. Season to taste. Mix the ham and mushrooms with the artichoke hearts, arrange around the meat and heat in the oven for 12 minutes. Garnish with the potato balls and onions, pour the sauce over the steaks and sprinkle with parsley.

PAPRIKA VEAL WITH YOGHURT
Serves 6

2 tbsp oil
2 green peppers, deseeded and diced
2 oz (50 g) butter
1½ lb (675 g) shoulder veal,
  thickly sliced
2 large onions, quartered

salt and freshly ground black pepper
2 tsp paprika
8 fl oz (250 ml) chicken stock
4 large tomatoes, peeled,
  seeded and chopped
½ pt (300 ml) yoghurt

Heat the oil in a frying pan and fry the peppers gently for about 10 minutes; set aside. Heat the butter in another frying pan and sauté the veal until lightly browned. Remove, add the onions and fry until golden brown. Replace the meat, season to taste and stir in the paprika; cook for about 1 minute. Pour in the stock and bring to the boil. Lower the heat, cover and simmer for 20 minutes or until the meat is tender. Add the tomatoes to the green peppers and cook over a low heat for about 10 minutes, stirring frequently. Remove the veal and onion from the pan and place in a warmed serving dish. Strain the liquid from the peppers and tomatoes into the meat liquor and place them around the meat. Stir the yoghurt into the liquor over a gentle heat and beat with a whisk. Pour over the veal.

SPICED VEAL AND PEPPERS
Serves 4

1 tbsp oil
2 onions, thinly sliced
2 small red peppers, deseeded
  and thinly sliced
1 garlic clove, crushed
½ tsp ginger
½ tsp turmeric
½ tsp cumin

½ tsp chilli powder
¼ tsp ground cloves
8 oz (225 g) can tomatoes
½ pt (300 ml) yoghurt
1¼ lb (550 g) pie veal,
  trimmed and cubed
salt and freshly ground black pepper

Heat the oil in a large saucepan, and cook the onions, peppers, garlic and spices for 1 minute. Stir in the tomatoes. Lower the heat and gradually add the yoghurt, stirring constantly. Add the veal with salt and pepper to taste. Cover and simmer gently for 30 minutes. Uncover and simmer for 30 minutes more to reduce the liquid and until the meat is tender, stirring occasionally.

TERRINE MAISON
Serves 4–6

12 oz (350 g) raw minced veal
4 oz (110 g) pork sausage meat
8 oz (225 g) lamb liver,
  finely minced
1 onion, finely chopped
1 large hard-boiled egg,
  coarsely chopped
3–4 tbsp fresh white breadcrumbs
½ tsp chopped thyme

1 tbsp chopped fresh parsley
pinch mace
salt and freshly ground black pepper
12 bacon rashers
1 bay leaf
5–7 tbsp flour
¼ pt (150 ml) jellied stock
½ oz (10 g) gelatine powder
cucumber and tomato slices, to garnish

Preheat the oven to 325°F/170°C/Gas Mk 3. Mix the meats together.
Add the onion, egg, breadcrumbs, thyme, pasrley and mace; season
generously. Line a long loaf tin or casserole with some of the bacon
rashers. Put in half the mixture and lay more bacon rashers over. Fill
with the remaining mixture and flatten. Press the centre down a little
and lay on the bay leaf. Cover with foil or the lid and seal with a stiff
paste made from 7 tbsp flour mixed with 6 tbsp water, to prevent
steam from escaping. Bake for about 1–1½ hours. Remove the bay leaf
and cover with greaseproof paper and a heavy weight. Leave
overnight. Dissolve gelatine in a little stock, then stir into remaining
stock. Leave to set. Turn out meat onto a serving dish and spoon the
setting stock. Garnish with cucumber and tomato slices.

VEAL CHOPS WITH MUSHROOMS
Serves 4

4 veal loin chops, trimmed
½ tsp salt
1 tsp paprika
2 oz (50 g) butter
6–8 mushrooms, sliced
2 tsp plain flour

4 tbsp single cream
few drops lemon juice
2 tbsp dry white wine or 1 tbsp brandy
2 tbsp chopped fresh parsley
4 slices Gruyére cheese

Sprinkle the veal chops on both sides with salt and paprika. Heat half
the butter in a frying pan and sauté the chops until lightly browned.
Place on a heatproof platter. Sauté the mushrooms in the same pan,
adding more butter if necessary. When lightly browned stir in the
flour, cook for 30 seconds, then add the cream, lemon juice and wine
or brandy. Simmer for about 4 minutes. Spoon the parsley over the
chops. Place a slice of cheese, cut to fit, over each chop. Grill until the
cheese is melted but not browned.

LAMB

NECK OF LAMB WITH APRICOTS
Serves 4

1 lb (450 g) lean neck of lamb, cut into 1 in (2.5 cm) cubes
2 tbsp oil
3 onions, chopped
1 garlic clove, chopped
2 carrots, chopped
1 pinch cinnamon
1 bay leaf, crushed
lamb stock
salt and freshly ground black pepper
4 oz (110 g) no-soak dried apricots, halved

Preheat the oven to 300°F/150°C/Gas Mk 2. Heat the oil in a casserole and brown the lamb all over. Add the onions, garlic and carrots and cook until the onions are soft and golden. Stir in the cinnamon, bay leaf and just enough stock to cover. Bring to the boil and season to taste. Cover and put in the oven for 2 hours. Add the apricots and simmer for a further 30 minutes. Serve with boiled rice.

LAMB AND OLIVE STEW
Serves 4

1½ lb (675 g) lamb fillet, cubed
6 oz (175 g) onion, chopped
1 stock cube, crumbled
1 large garlic clove, crushed
14 oz (400 g) can tomatoes
10 pimento-stuffed olives
2 tbsp tomato purée
1 tsp sugar
salt and freshly ground black pepper

Preheat the oven to 350°F/180°C/Gas Mk 4. Gently heat the lamb and onion in a large saucepan, so that the fat runs off the meat. Cook for 10 minutes, then add the remaining ingredients. Stir well, heat and pour into a casserole. Cover and cook in the oven for 1½ hours until the meat is tender.

CRISPY LAMB CROQUETTES
Serves 4

1 lb (450 g) shoulder of lamb, minced
1 large onion, finely chopped
2 garlic cloves, crushed
2 tsp tomato purée
1 tsp French mustard
salt and freshly ground black pepper
1 egg, beaten
4 oz (110 g) fresh breadcrumbs
oil for frying
lemon slices and parsley, to garnish

Place the lamb, onion, garlic, tomato purée, mustard, salt and pepper in a mixing bowl and combine thoroughly. Divide into eight and make small sausage-shaped croquettes by rolling between the palms of your hands. Refrigerate for at least 2 hours to firm up. Dip each croquette into the beaten egg and then roll in breadcrumbs, pressing them on firmly. Shallow fry until well browned and cooked through. Garnish with lemon slices and parsley.

MOROCCAN LAMB
Serves 4

oil for frying
1 large onion, chopped
1 garlic clove, crushed
1 lb (450 g) shoulder of lamb, boned and cubed
6 oz (175 g) long-grain rice
1 tbsp tomato purée
½ tsp cinnamon
1 tbsp fresh ginger root, grated
4 oz (110 g) dried apricots, chopped
2 oz (50 g) raisins
salt and freshly ground black pepper

Preheat the oven to 375°F/190°C/Gas Mk 5. Heat a little oil in an ovenproof casserole and fry the onion and garlic. Add a little more oil and brown the cubes of lamb all over. Add all the remaining ingredients, and cook, stirring, for a couple of minutes. Stir in enough water or stock to cover, put on a lid and put in the oven for 1½–2 hours. Check towards the end of cooking time and add more water if it appears to be too dry. Serve with green vegetables or salad.

LAMB IN SPICY SPINACH
Serves 4

4 tbsp oil
1 lb (450 g) boned shoulder of lamb,
 trimmed and cubed
4 onions, sliced
1 in (2.5 cm) fresh ginger root, grated
1 tsp turmeric
½ tsp cayenne pepper

2 tsp cumin
2 tsp coriander
salt and freshly ground black pepper
½ pt (300 ml) lamb stock
1 lb (450 g) potatoes, cut into chunks
4 oz (110 g) frozen leaf spinach,
 thawed and roughly chopped

Heat the oil in a heavy-based saucepan, and fry the lamb over a high heat until well browned. Lift out with a slotted spoon and set aside. Add the onions and cook over a medium heat for 8–10 minutes until soft, stirring occasionally. Stir in the ginger root, spices and seasoning; cook for a further 2 minutes. Return the lamb to the pan, add the stock and bring to the boil. Cover and simmer for 1 hour. Stir in the potatoes and spinach; cook for a further 30 minutes until both meat and potatoes are tender.

LANCASHIRE HOT POT
Serves 4

1 lb (450 g) middle neck of lamb
1 oz (25 g) plain flour
salt and freshly ground black pepper
2 lamb kidneys, cored and sliced

4 onions, sliced
8 oz (225 g) carrots, sliced
1½ lb (675 g) potatoes, sliced
¾ pt (450 ml) beef stock

Preheat the oven to 350°F/180°C/Gas Mk 4. Trim the lamb cutlets and coat them with seasoned flour. Place the cutlets, kidneys, onions, carrots and potatoes in layers in a large casserole, finishing with potatoes. Pour in the stock. Cover the casserole and put in the oven for 2 hours. Remove the lid and cook for a further 30 minutes to brown the potatoes.

LAMB AND APRICOT STEW
Serves 4

8 oz (225 g) dried apricots
5 lb (2.3 kg) leg of lamb, boned
 and trimmed of excess fat
1 tsp oil
1 large onion, chopped

1 tsp ground coriander
1 tsp ground cumin
½ tsp ground cinnamon
1 oz (25 g) ground almonds
salt and freshly ground black pepper

Place the apricots in a bowl together with ½ pt (300 ml) boiling water and leave for 2 hours. Cut the meat into cubes. Drain the apricots well, reserving the liquid. Heat the oil in a large saucepan, and cook the lamb and onion for 10 minutes, stirring frequently, until browned. Add the coriander, cumin, cinnamon, almonds and salt and pepper to taste, then the apricot soaking liquid. Halve the apricots and stir into the mixture. Cover and simmer gently for 1½ hours until the meat is tender, stirring occasionally.

LAMB WITH YOGHURT
Serves 4

1½ lb (675 g) leg of lamb, boned, trimmed and cut into cubes
5 fl oz (150 ml) yoghurt
1 small onion, grated
1 tbsp curry powder or to taste

¼ tsp each ground ginger, cinnamon and cloves
1 tbsp oil
1 tbsp lemon juice
salt and freshly ground black pepper

Arrange the lamb in a shallow dish (put them on skewers if liked). Mix all the remaining ingredients together and pour over the lamb. Marinate for 3–4 hours, turning occasionally. Cook the lamb over a hot heat (or under a hot grill) until tender. Baste frequently with the marinade. Heat any remaining marinade gently and serve as a sauce.

MARINATED LAMB CHOPS
Serves 4

4 lamb chops
2 tbsp olive oil
juice of ½ lemon
½ onion, finely chopped
1 tbsp chopped fresh parsley

¼ tsp thyme
¼ tsp oregano
freshly ground black pepper
lemon wedges and fresh parsley sprigs, to garnish

Combine all ingredients except lamb in a shallow dish. Then put the chops in, spooning the marinade over, and cover the dish. Place in the refrigerator for 2 hours or longer if possible, turning occasionally. Remove the chops from the marinade and cook under a preheated grill for 10–15 minutes, turning halfway through. Brush with the marinade frequently. Serve at once, garnished with lemon wedges and sprigs of parsley.

LAMB AND MUSHROOM BAKE
Serves 4

olive oil for frying
2 lamb fillets, cut in small, thin pieces
24 baby onions, peeled
3 celery stalks, chopped
18 button mushrooms
1 oz (25 g) pearl barley

¼ pt (150 ml) dry white wine
¾ pt (450 ml) chicken or lamb stock
salt and freshly ground black pepper
six medium potatoes, thinly sliced
1 oz (25 g) butter, melted

Preheat the oven to 170°C/325°F/Gas Mk 3. Heat a little oil and fry the lamb until brown all over and well sealed. Remove to a 4 pt (2.4 L) casserole. Brown the onions and add to the meat. Briefly fry the celery, mushrooms and pearl barley; add to the casserole. Mix the wine with the stock and pour over enough to cover the meat. Season with salt and plenty of pepper. Arrange the potato slices in over-lapping circles on top and brush with butter. Season lightly with salt and pepper. Cover and put in the oven for 1½ hours. Remove the lid, increase the temperature to 375°F/190°C/Gas Mk 5 and cook for a further hour or until the potatoes are golden brown.

LAMB NOISETTES WITH AUBERGINE RAGOUT
Serves 4–6

8 noisettes of lamb

Marinade:
1 onion, roughly chopped
1 garlic clove, crushed
1 tsp paprika
1 tsp ground cumin
generous pinch cayenne pepper
freshly ground black pepper

1 pinch powdered saffron
2 tbsp chopped fresh parsley
2 tsp thin honey
2 tbsp lemon juice
2 tbsp olive oil

Aubergine ragout:
14 oz (400 g) aubergines, sliced
salt
olive oil for frying
1 medium onion, finely chopped
1 garlic clove, crushed

3 oz (75 g) raisins
8 oz (225 g) can tomatoes, chopped
2 tbsp pine nuts, chopped
chopped fresh parsley, to garnish

Place all the marinade ingredients in a food processor or liquidiser and process until smooth. Place the noisettes in a shallow dish and pour the marinade over. Cover and leave for at least 2 hours in the refrigerator. Sprinkle the aubergine slices with salt and leave for

30 minutes to draw out excess juice. Rinse and pat dry. Heat about 6 tbsp of oil in a frying pan and fry the slices until golden brown on both sides. Remove and drain on absorbent paper. Heat some more oil in a heavy-based saucepan and fry the onion and garlic until soft, then add the raisins and tomatoes and simmer gently for about 15 minutes, adding a little water if necessary. Add the aubergines, season well and simmer for a further 5 minutes. Add the pine nuts. Grill the noisettes under a preheated high grill for about 4 minutes on each side if preferred slightly pink inside; or more slowly to cook right through. Add any excess marinade to the aubergine ragout and heat through. Serve with the noisettes, garnished with parsley.

LAMB AND PEACH BAKE
Serves 4

2 small packets potato crisps
8 oz (225 g) cooked lamb, cut
*   into ½ in (1 cm) cubes*
8 oz (225 g) frozen peas

2 oz (50 g) cheese, grated
10 oz (300 g) can cream of celery soup
15 oz (425g) can sliced peaches

Preheat the oven to 375°F/190°C/Gas Mk 5. Arrange three-quarters of the crisps in a casserole. Then add the lamb, peas and three-quarters of the cheese in layers. Pour the soup over the top. Cover and bake for 20 minutes. Drain the peach slices and arrange them on top. Sprinkle with the remaining cheese and brown under a hot grill for a few minutes. Sprinkle on the rest of the crisps and serve.

ORANGE CUTLETS
Serves 4

8 lamb cutlets, trimmed
grated rind and juice of 1 large orange
2 tbsp oil
1 garlic clove, crushed

salt and freshly ground black pepper
dash of Worcestershire sauce
1 tbsp demerara sugar
orange slices and watercress, to garnish

Put the chops in a foil-lined grill pan. Mix together the orange rind and juice, oil, garlic, salt and pepper to taste, Worcestershire sauce and sugar. Brush over the lamb generously and cook under a hot grill, brushing frequently with the sauce until browned. Turn over, brush with the sauce and cook until browned and cooked to taste. Arrange on a warmed serving dish and garnish with orange and watercress.

LAMB AND WATERCRESS BAKE
Serves 4

1 lb (450 g) minced lamb
2 large onions, finely chopped
4 oz (110 g) plain flour
2 bunches watercress, trimmed
   and finely chopped
2 tsp dried oregano
½ pt (300 ml) lamb or chicken stock

2 fl oz (60 ml) dry white wine
salt and freshly ground black pepper
1 oz (25 g) butter
1 pt (600 ml) milk
6 oz (175 g) Lancashire cheese, crumbled
8 oz (225 g) oven-ready lasagne verde

Preheat the oven to 375°F/190°C/Gas Mk 5. Place the lamb in a large saucepan and cook gently in its own fat until well browned. Drain away the excess fat. Add the onions and fry for 5 minutes, stirring occasionally. Stir in 2 tbsp of the flour, then add the watercress and oregano. Cook for 2 minutes, then gradually pour in the stock and wine with salt and pepper to taste. Bring to the boil, then simmer for 45 minutes, stirring occasionally. Place the butter, milk and remaining flour in a small saucepan over low heat. Whisk until it thickens, boils and is smooth; simmer for 2 minutes. Remove from the heat and gradually stir in 4 oz (110 g) of the cheese until melted. Add salt and pepper to taste. Place alternate layers of the lamb and uncooked lasagne in a fairly deep ovenproof dish. Pour over the cheese sauce and sprinkle with the remaining cheese. Bake for 40 minutes until brown. Serve at once.

SPICY LAMB
Serves 4

1½ lb (675 g) boneless fillet,
   leg or shoulder of lamb
1½ oz (35 g) plain flour
2 tsp mild curry powder
1½ tsp salt
freshly ground black pepper

2 tbsp oil
2 chicken stock cubes
8 oz (225 g) button onions
8 oz (225 g) small carrots,
   quartered lengthways

Trim any excess fat from the lamb and cut the meat into 1 in (2.5 cm) cubes. Put the flour, curry powder, salt and pepper in a bag, add the lamb and shake well to coat it thoroughly. Heat the oil in a saucepan, and fry the lamb for 2–3 minutes, then stir in the remaining flour. Dissolve the stock cubes in 1 pt (600 ml) boiling water and add to the pan. Bring to the boil, stirring constantly. Add the onions and carrots, cover and simmer very gently for about 1¼ hours or until the lamb and vegetables are tender. Taste and adjust the seasoning. Turn into a warmed dish and serve immediately.

LAMB WITH ONION PURÉE
Serves 4

3 tbsp oil
1 tbsp white wine vinegar
¼ tsp dried sage
1 garlic clove, crushed
4 x 8 oz (225 g) lamb chump chops,
    trimmed of excess fat

2 medium onions, finely chopped
2 tbsp plain flour
½ pt (300 ml) milk
1 clove
2 tbsp single cream
salt and freshly ground black pepper

Whisk together the oil, vinegar, sage and garlic in a bowl. Lay the chops in a shallow dish and pour over the oil and vinegar mixture. Leave in a cool place to marinate for about 1 hour. Remove from the marinade, place under a hot grill and cook for 7–10 minutes on each side. Pour the marinade into a saucepan together with the onions. Cover and cook over low heat for 10–15 minutes until soft. Gradually stir in the flour, then the milk. Add the clove and bring to the boil, stirring from time to time. Lower the heat and simmer for 2 minutes. Remove and discard the clove, transfer the mixture to a liquidiser and purée well. Place the purée in a clean saucepan, add the cream and salt and pepper to taste and heat gently. Arrange the chops on a warmed serving dish and pour over the onion purée. Serve at once.

TARRAGON LAMB BAKE
Serves 4

2 tbsp oil
1 onion, finely chopped
1 lb (450 g) minced lamb
1 lamb stock cube

1 tbsp dried tarragon
salt and freshly ground black pepper
1 tsp cornflour (optional)

Topping:
3 oz (75 g) butter
6 oz (175 g) flour
2 oz (50 g) mature Cheddar cheese, grated

2 tsp dried tarragon
3 oz (75 g) breadcrumbs

Preheat the oven to 400°F/200°C/Gas Mk 6. Heat the oil in a large frying pan, fry the onion until brown and soft. Stir in the lamb and brown. Dissolve the stock cube in ½ pt (300 ml) boiling water and add to the pan with the tarragon and seasoning. Stir in cornflour to thicken, if necessary. Make the topping: rub the butter into the flour,. stir in the cheese, tarragon and breadcrumbs. Spoon the meat mixture into a 1¾ pt (1 L) ovenproof dish. Sprinkle the topping over and bake for 20–25 minutes until golden brown.

MOUSSAKA
Serves 6–8

1–1½ lb (450–675g) minced
  lamb (half a shoulder)
8 oz (225 g) onions, chopped
2 garlic cloves, crushed
1½ oz (35 g) plain flour

1½ tsp salt
freshly ground black pepper
14 oz (400 g) can tomatoes
3 aubergines, cut into ¼ in (5 cm) slices

Sauce:
1½ oz (35) butter
1½ oz (35 g) flour
¾ pt (450 ml) milk
1 tsp made mustard

salt and freshly ground black pepper
pinch grated nutmeg
6 oz (175 g) Cheddar cheese, grated
1 egg, beaten

Butter a large ovenproof casserole. Place the lamb in a large saucepan and cook over low heat to let the fat run out, stirring to prevent it sticking to the pan. Add the onions and garlic, increase the heat and fry for about 15 minutes to brown the meat. Spoon off any excess fat. Add the flour and stir well. Add the salt, pepper and tomatoes. Bring to the boil and simmer for 5 minutes. Preheat the oven to 375°F/190°C/Gas Mk 5. Taste and adjust the seasoning. Blanch the aubergines in a pan of boiling water for 1 minute. Drain in a colander and dry on absorbent paper. Make the sauce: slowly melt the butter in a saucepan, add the flour and cook for a few minutes over moderate heat without colouring. Gradually stir in the milk and bring to the boil, stirring well. Add the mustard, nutmeg, salt, pepper and cheese. Heat until the cheese melts, then remove from the heat. Cool slightly, add the egg and mix well. Arrange half the meat mixture in the bottom of the dish, cover with half the aubergines and season with salt and pepper. Repeat with the rest of the lamb and aubergines. Pour over the cheese sauce. Bake, uncovered, for 45–60 minutes or until golden brown.

LAMB HOT POT
Serves 6

2 lb (900 g) frozen neck of lamb,
  just thawed
3 leeks, sliced
1 small swede, diced
2 tbsp oil

2 tbsp plain flour
2 tbsp pot barley
1 pt (600 ml) beef stock
1½ lb (675 g) potatoes, thinly sliced
1 oz (25 g) butter

Preheat the oven to 325°F/160°C/Gas Mk 3. Fry lamb in a very large flameproof casserole over a low heat for 10 minutes until browned. Remove with a slotted spoon and reserve. Add the leeks, swede and oil and cook, stirring occasionally, for 5 minutes until softened. Sprinkle the flour over and stir well. Add the barley and cook for 1 minute, then gradually stir in the stock. Return the lamb to the casserole, season well and bring to the boil. Arrange overlapping slices of potato on top, seasoning each layer. Dot with butter, cover and cook in the oven for 2½ hours, removing the lid for the last 1 hour.

ZORBA'S LAMB
Serves 4

1 tbsp oil
1 oz (25 g) butter
2 lb (900 g) best end of neck,
  skinned and trimmed
1 medium onion, chopped
2 large garlic cloves, chopped
1 tbsp plain flour

½ pt (300 ml) chicken or lamb stock
14 oz (400 g) can tomatoes, chopped
1 tsp tomato purée
1 tsp sugar, salt and freshly ground
  black pepper
pinch allspice

Sauce:
1–2 tsp arrowroot
4 ripe tomatoes, peeled, chopped
  deseeded and quartered

2 oz (50 g) black olives, halved and stoned
1 heaped tbsp mixed fresh herbs
salt and freshly ground black pepper

Preheat the oven to 180°C/350°F/Gas Mk 4. Heat the oil and butter in a flameproof casserole and brown the lamb on all sides. Remove from the pan, pour off excess fat and fry the onion and garlic in the remainder until soft. Stir in the flour, cook for 1 minute, then slowly add the stock, tomatoes, purée, sugar, salt, pepper and allspice. Bring to the boil and simmer for a few minutes. Put the lamb back in the pan, cover with a lid and cook in the oven for 50–60 minutes. Turn over once or twice during cooking and baste well. Remove and keep hot. Pour the gravy from the lamb through a sieve into a clean saucepan and rub the tomato flesh through as well. Make the sauce: Mix the arrowroot with 2 tbsp water and stir enough into the sauce to thicken it slightly. Add the tomatoes, olives and herbs. Taste and adjust the seasoning. Divide the lamb into cutlets, arrange around the edge of a warmed serving dish and spoon the vegetables in the centre. Pour a little of the sauce over the cutlets and serve the remainder in a separate sauce dish.

SPRING LAMB WITH HOLLANDAISE
Serves 4–6

2 lb (900 g) best end of lamb, chined
seasoned flour
1 egg, beaten
6–9 oz (175–250 g) dried white
   breadcrumbs
1 large cucumber

3–4 tbsp oil
2 oz (50 g) butter
Hollandaise sauce, to serve
1 bunch spring onions
salt and freshly ground black pepper
2 tsp chopped fresh mint

Get the butcher to saw through the end bones about 2½ in (6 cm) of the meat, and divide into plump cutlets. Trim the bones of any fat or skin and dust the cutlets well with seasoned flour. Dip into egg, then into breadcrumbs, pressing them well on. Put on a wire rack until ready to cook. Preheat the oven to 300°F/150°C/Gas Mk 2. Peel the cucumber and quarter lengthways, then cut into 1 in (2.5 cm) pieces. Blanch in boiling water for 3 minutes, strain, refresh under cold water and drain. Heat the oil and half the butter and fry the cutlets very gently, turning once, for 4–5 minutes until golden brown. Lift out onto a rack, place in a baking tray and put in the oven while preparing the garnish. Melt the remaining butter and add the spring onions, still with about 1 in (2.5 cm) of green stalk left on. Cover the pan and cook gently for 4–5 minutes, then add the cucumber, season well and replace the lid. Simmer very gently for about 5 minutes, shaking the pan occasionally, then add the chopped mint. Arrange the cutlets around the edge of a warmed serving plate and place the cucumber mixture in the centre. Serve with a warm Hollandaise sauce

BRAISED LAMB ROLL
Serves 6

2 lb (900 g) boned breast of lamb
4 rashers streaky bacon
1 cooking apple, peeled and sliced
1 tbsp brown sugar
¼ tsp dried thyme
2 tbsp fresh breadcrumbs

1 lb (450 g) potatoes, thinly sliced
2 celery stalks, chopped
1 onion, chopped
1 tsp plain flour
salt and freshly ground black pepper
¼ pt (150 ml) beef stock

Preheat the oven to 375°F/190°C/Gas Mk 5. Put the lamb boned side up on the work surface. Lay the bacon rashers on top, then the apple. Mix together the sugar, thyme and breadcrumbs and sprinkle over the meat. Roll up and secure at 3 in (7 cm) intervals with string. Place the roll in a casserole. Place the potatoes, celery and onion around it, sprinkle with flour, salt and pepper and pour in the stock. Cover and cook in the oven for 45 minutes, then uncover and cook for a further 45 minutes. Serve the meat and vegetables together.

SPANISH LAMB CHOPS
Serves 4

4 lamb chops
1 tbsp olive oil
2 onions, sliced
1 garlic clove, crushed
14 oz (400 g) can tomatoes

1 tbsp tomato purée
1 tsp ground cinnamon
¼ pt (150 ml) chicken stock
1 bay leaf
salt and freshly ground black pepper

Preheat the oven to 350°F/180°C/Gas Mk 4. Trim excess fat from the chops. Heat the oil in a flameproof casserole and fry the chops until brown. Remove and drain on absorbent paper. Fry the onion and garlic until softened. Chop the tomatoes and add to the pan with the tomato purée, cinnamon, stock, bay leaf and salt and pepper. Bring to the boil. Return the chops to the casserole. Cover and cook in the oven for 45 minutes or until just tender.

LAMB IN THE ROUND
Serves 4

6 onions
1 tsp dried rosemary
1 tsp dried parsley

salt and freshly ground black pepper
1 boned shoulder of lamb
2 oz (50 g) margarine

Preheat the oven to 350°F/180°C/Gas Mk 4. Finely chop three of the onions and mix them with the rosemary, parsley and salt and pepper to taste. Stuff the lamb with this mixture. Hold the meat together with a skewer, then tie it into a round shape with string. Weigh the lamb, then place it in a roasting pan. Slice the remaining onions and arrange them round the meat. Melt the margarine and brush it over the meat. Roast for 25 minutes per lb (450 g) plus 25 minutes over. Remove skewer and string and serve.

RACK OF LAMB
Serves 6

2 x 1¼ lb (550 g) racks of lamb
4 garlic cloves, sliced
2 oz (50 g) butter, softened
2 tsp ground cumin

1 tsp ground coriander
2 tsp paprika
salt and freshly ground black pepper
4 rosemary sprigs

Apricot sauce:
1 onion, finely chopped
9 oz (250 g) no-soak dried apricots

1 tbsp caster sugar
5 tbsp white wine vinegar

Preheat the oven to 350°F/180°C/Gas Mk 4. Cut away any skin or fat from the bones of the rack of lamb, exposing a clean bone. Score the fatty side of the lamb in crossing diagonal lines. Make a small cut at each intersection and push in a garlic slice. Mix together the butter, cumin, coriander, paprika, salt and pepper and spread over the fat. Cover and chill for at least 2 hours. Place the racks in a large roasting tin. Tuck small sprigs of rosemary into the cuts already made. Wrap foil around the bones to prevent them from burning. Roast for 55 minutes or until the meat juices run clear on the insertion of a sharp knife point. Place the sauce ingredients in a saucepan with ½ pt (300 ml) water. Simmer gently, covered, for 20–30 minutes until soft, adding more water if necessary. Leave to cool, then purée in a food processor or liquidiser. Return to a clean saucepan and reheat. Carve the racks of lamb and serve with the apricot sauce.

LAMB AND BEAN PIE
Serves 4

8 oz (225 g) red kidney beans,
    soaked overnight
1½ lb (675 g) boneless lamb
1 oz (25 g) plain flour
salt and freshly ground black pepper
2 tbsp oil

2 onions, sliced
1 lb (450 g) carrots, sliced
1 green pepper, deseeded
    and sliced, (optional)
¾ pt (450 ml) beef stock

Preheat the oven to 325°F/160°C/Gas Mk 3. Cut the lamb into 1 in (2.5 cm) pieces. Season the flour and coat the lamb in it. Heat the oil in a saucepan and fry the lamb until lightly browned all over. Put into an ovenproof dish with the onions, carrots, green pepper, drained beans and stock. Cover and cook in the oven for 2 hours.

LEG OF LAMB WITH PINEAPPLE
Serves 6–8

8 oz (225g) canned pineapple rings
4 lb (1.8 kg) leg of lamb
salt and freshly ground black pepper
glacé cherries to garnish

Preheat the oven to 400°F/200°C/Gas Mk 6. Put the lamb in a roasting tin. Pour the pineapple juice over it and sprinkle the skin with plenty of salt and pepper. Roast 1 hour 40 minutes, basting occasionally. When cooked, place on a heated serving dish. Garnish with halved pineapple rings with a cherry in the centre of each ring.

BESWICK LAMB
Serves 6–8

3 lb (1.4 kg) loin of lamb, boned
1 oz (25 g) butter
2 tbsp oil
1 lb (450 g) garden peas
1 mint sprig

6 spring onions
2 fl oz (60 ml) sherry
juice of 1 orange
redcurrant jelly to serve

Stuffing:
2 oz (50 g) butter
2 bacon rashers, derinded and chopped
2 lamb kidneys, cored and chopped
1 onion, finely chopped

4 lb (110 g) mushrooms, finely chopped
salt and freshly ground black pepper
1 tsp tomato purée
2 oz (50 g) fresh breadcrumbs

Preheat the oven to 400°F/200°C/Gas Mk 6. Make the stuffing: heat the butter and fry the bacon and kidneys for 3 minutes, add the onion and continue cooking until soft, then add the mushrooms and cook for a further 2 minutes. Season to taste, and stir in the tomato purée and breadcrumbs until a soft stuffing mixture is obtained. Add a little melted butter if too stiff. Spread the stuffing on the inside of the joint, roll up and tie with string. Place in a roasting tin and brush with butter and oil. Sprinkle with salt. Roast for 1½ hours or until the meat is tender and cooked through. Boil the peas gently in salted water with the sprig of mint and spring onions, until tender. Drain and pile on a warmed serving dish. Carve the meat into slices and arrange around the peas. Pour off excess fat, stir in the sherry and orange juice, boil for 3 minutes and season. Pour into a gravy boat. Serve lamb with gravy and redcurrant jelly separate.

GREEK LAMB
Serves 4–6

4 tbsp olive oil
2 lb (900 g) small new potatoes
2½ lb (1.1 kg) boned lean shoulder
  of lamb, trimmed and cubed
2 large onions, sliced
1 tbsp plain flour
½ pt (300 ml) dry white wine

14 oz (400g) can chopped tomatoes
2 tbsp wine vinegar
2 cinnamon sticks
2 bay leaves
2 tsp chopped fresh thyme or 1 tsp dried
salt and freshly ground black pepper
thyme sprigs to garnish

Heat 2 tbsp of the oil in a large flameproof casserole. Pierce each potato with a sharp knife, add to the casserole and fry over a moderate heat until golden all over. Remove and drain on absorbent paper. Heat the rest of the oil in the casserole, add the lamb and onions and fry over a moderate heat until browned. Sprinkle in the flour and fry for another minute, stirring until absorbed. Pour over the wine and add the tomatoes and vinegar. Bring slowly to the boil, then lower the heat and add the cinnamon, bay leaves, thyme and seasoning to taste. Cover and simmer gently for 1 hour, stirring occasionally. Add the fried potatoes to the casserole and simmer for another hour or until both meat and potatoes are tender. Remove the cinnamon sticks and bay leaves, then taste and adjust the seasoning. Serve garnished with thyme sprigs.

LAMB IN TOMATO SAUCE
Serves 4–6

2 tbsp oil
2 lb (900 g) fillet of lamb
1 onion, sliced
4 tsp plain flour
1¼ lb (800 g) canned tomatoes
2 tbsp tomato purée

pinch granulated sugar
¼ tsp dried or large sprig fresh rosemary
4 tbsp red wine
salt and freshly ground black pepper
lamb stock if necessary

Preheat the oven to 325°F/170°C/Gas Mk 3. Heat the oil in a flameproof casserole and fry the lamb over a high heat until browned on both sides. Remove and set aside. Add the onion to the pan and fry for 5 minutes until soft. Stir in the flour and cook for 1 minute. Add the tomatoes with their juice, tomato purée, sugar, rosemary and wine. Bring to the boil, stirring continuously. Return the meat to the pan and add salt and pepper to taste. Add a little stock, if necessary, to cover the meat. Cover and cook in the oven for about 1¼ hours. Remove fresh rosemary before serving.

SAG GOSHT
Serves 4–6

1–2 garlic cloves, chopped
1 in (2.5 cm) piece fresh ginger
  root, peeled and chopped
1 tbsp mustard seeds
1 tbsp coriander seeds
1 tsp turmeric
½ tsp chilli powder
salt

2½ oz (65 g) butter or ghee
3 medium onions, thinly
  sliced into rings
2 lb (900 g) boneless lamb fillet, cubed
½ pt (300 ml) yoghurt
1 lb (450 g) fresh spinach or
  8 oz (225 g) frozen leaf spinach, thawed

Pound together the garlic, ginger, mustard seeds and coriander. Mix in
the turmeric, chilli powder and 1 tsp salt. Melt 2 oz (50 g) of the
butter or ghee in a flameproof casserole, add two-thirds of the onions
and fry gently for about 10 minutes until softened. Add the spices and
sauté gently for a few minutes. Add the lamb in batches, increase the
heat and fry until well browned on all sides. Return all the lamb to
the casserole and gradually add the yoghurt. Stir after each addition,
cover and cook gently for an hour or until tender. Then add the
spinach, stir well and continue cooking for a further 5 minutes.
Meanwhile melt the remaining butter or ghee in a saucepan, add the
remaining onion and fry, stirring continuously, until golden. Taste the
curry and add more salt if needed. Turn into a warmed serving dish
and sprinkle the golden onion rings over the top. Serve with plain
boiled rice.

IRISH STEW
Serves 4

2 oz (50 g) plain flour
1½ tsp salt
½ tsp pepper
2 lb (900 g) middle neck or
  scrag end of lamb

2 onions, sliced
1½ lb (675 g) potatoes, thinly sliced
1 tbsp chopped fresh parsley, to garnish

Preheat the oven to 325°F/160°C/Gas Mk 3. Sift the flour, salt and
pepper into a bowl. Trim the chops and coat them with the seasoned
flour. Add one third of the onions to the bottom of a casserole, then
add half the chops. Layer with the second third of the onions, then
add the rest of the chops and top with the remaining onion slices.
Add enough water to cover, then cover the casserole and bake for
1¼ hours. Cover the stew with the potato slices and cook, uncovered,
for a further 45 minutes. Serve garnished with chopped parsley.

SPINACH-STUFFED LAMB
Serves 4

2 lb (900 g) boned breast of lamb
4 rashers streaky bacon, derinded
1 oz (25 g) butter or margarine
1 celery stalk, finely chopped
1 onion, finely chopped
8 oz (225 g) packet frozen
  chopped spinach, thawed
2 tbsp fresh breadcrumbs

3 tbsp chopped fresh parsley
finely grated rind of ½ lemon
1 tbsp lemon juice
pinch grated nutmeg
1 egg, beaten
1 tsp plain flour
3 tbsp oil
salt and freshly ground black pepper

Preheat the oven to 375°F/190°C/Gas Mk 5. Put the lamb boned side up on the work surface. Lay the bacon rashers on top. Melt the butter in a small pan and fry the onion and celery until lightly browned. Drain the spinach and place in a bowl with the onion, celery, breadcrumbs, parsley, lemon rind and juice, nutmeg, egg and flour. Mix together well and season. Spread over the lamb, roll up loosely and tie at regular intervals with string. Heat the oil in a roasting tin and put the lamb in. Cook for 1¼ hours or until tender, basting occasionally.

NAVARIN OF LAMB
Serves 6

2 lb (900 g) middle neck of lamb,
  cut into pieces
1 oz (25 g) plain flour
2 oz (50 g) dripping
1 pt (600 ml) water
2 tbsp tomato purée

1 beef stock cube
1 lb (450 g) small young carrots, sliced
8 oz (225 g) button onions, peeled
salt and freshly ground black pepper
12 small new potatoes

Preheat the oven to 325°F/160°C/Gas Mk 3. Trim any excess fat from the lamb and coat the meat in the flour. Heat the dripping in a large frying pan and quickly fry the meat to brown all over. Transfer to a large casserole. Stir any remaining flour into the fat and cook for 2 minutes. Add the water and tomato purée and bring to the boil, stirring constantly. Add the crumbled stock cube and simmer gently to thicken. Add the carrots and onions to the casserole and pour over the sauce. Season well with salt and pepper, cover tightly and cook in the oven for 1 hour. Add the potatoes, ensuring that they are well pushed down into the sauce. Return to the oven and cook for a further 45 minutes or until the meat and vegetables are tender. Taste and adjust the seasoning.

HERBED LAMB STEW
Serves 6

3 lb (1.4 kg) boneless leg of lamb,
  trimmed of fat and cubed
2 tbsp plain flour
salt and freshly ground black pepper
3 streaky bacon rashers,
  derinded and chopped
1 oz (25 g) butter

2 medium onions, chopped
2 medium carrots, sliced
4 oz (110 g) turnip or swede, diced
2 celery stalks, diced
2 tbsp pearl barley
2 tbsp mixed chopped fresh herbs
½ pt (300 ml) beef or lamb stock

Toss the lamb in the flour seasoned with salt and pepper to taste. Dry fry the bacon in a large flameproof casserole, then add the butter and lamb. Fry until browned on all sides. Remove and set aside. Place all the vegetables in the casserole and fry for 5–10 minutes until just beginning to brown. Replace the lamb and bacon in the casserole, stir in the barley and herbs, then pour over the stock. Bring to the boil, cover and simmer gently for 2 hours, stirring from time to time. Alternately cook in the oven at 325°F/170°C/Gas Mk 3.

SHOULDER OF LAMB A LA TURQUE
Serves 4–6

3 lb (1.4 kg) shoulder of lamb, boned
3 oz (75 g) butter

1 tsp dried rosemary
1 garlic clove, thinly sliced

Stuffing:
½ oz (10 g) butter
1 medium onion, finely chopped
4 oz (110 g) chicken or
  lamb liver, finely chopped
1 tbsp chopped fresh parsley and thyme

4 oz (110 g) long-grain rice,
  boiled and dried
1½ oz (35 g) seedless raisins
1 egg, beaten

Make the stuffing: heat the butter and cook the onion and liver gently until softened. Mix with the other stuffing ingredients and bind with a little egg. Wipe the shoulder and season the pocket where the bone has been removed. Preheat the oven to 375°F/190°C/Gas Mk 5. Push in the stuffing and sew up the flaps with a darning needle and strong thread. Spread the skin with the 3 oz (75 g) butter mixed with the dried rosemary. Also spread a little on the base of the roasting tin. Make little incisions in the skin of the shoulder and stuff with slivers of garlic. Roast for about 1½ hours or until cooked.

LAMB WITH CHERRIES
Serves 6–8

8 oz (225 g) streaky bacon rashers,
   derinded and chopped
½ oz (10 g) butter
3 lb (1.4 kg) boneless shoulder
   of lamb, cubed
1 medium onion, sliced
1 medium carrot, sliced

1 celery stalk, sliced
1 garlic clove, finely chopped
1 pt (600 ml) dry red wine
bouquet garni
freshly grated nutmeg
salt and freshly ground black pepper
1 lb (450 g) fresh red cherries, stoned

Preheat the oven to 300°F/150°C/Gas Mk 2. Dry fry the bacon in a frying pan until browned, then add the butter. Stir in the lamb cubes, a few at a time, and cook until browned on all sides. Remove to a casserole. Place the onion, carrot, celery and garlic in the frying pan and cook for 5 minutes until lightly browned. Add to the casserole with the bouquet garni, a pinch of nutmeg, salt and pepper. Cover and put in the oven for 2 hours, then stir in the cherries, cover again and cook for a further 30 minutes until the lamb is tender and the cherries are soft.

BAKED BREAST OF LAMB WITH ONIONS
Serves 4

2 lean breasts of lamb, about
   3 lb (1.4 kg) total
1 carrot, cut into chunks
1 onion, quartered
1 celery stalk, chopped
6 peppercorns

large bouquet garni
6 medium onions, chopped
2 oz (50 g) butter
3 oz (75 g) fresh white breadcrumbs
2 oz (50 g) Cheddar cheese, grated

Soak the lamb overnight in plenty of cold water. Drain and put with the carrot, onion, celery stalk, peppercorns and bouquet garni into a large saucepan. Cover with cold water, add a little salt and bring to the boil. Lower the heat, cover and simmer for 1½ hours or until the bones will easily come away. Remove the bones and lay the meat out on a shallow dish or a plate. Cover and put a weight on top and leave overnight. Strain and reserve stock. Next day preheat the oven to 350°F/180°C/Gas Mk 4. Cut the meat into portions and lay in a shallow ovenproof dish. Melt the butter and fry the chopped onions until soft and golden brown. Take off the heat and stir in the breadcrumbs and two-thirds of the grated cheese; season to taste. Cover the meat with this mixture, pressing it down lightly. Scatter over the remaining cheese. Sprinkle in 3 tbsp reserved stock and bake for about 30 minutes or until brown and crisp.

CHOPS WITH BLACKCURRANT SAUCE

Serves 4

4 x 8 oz (225 g) lamb chump chops
1 medium onion, chopped
1 tbsp chopped fresh rosemary
1 tbsp chopped fresh parsley
grated rind of 1 lemon

½ pt (300 ml) apple and blackcurrant juice
1 tbsp blackcurrant jelly
2 oz (50 g) blackcurrants, destalked
2 tbsp soured cream

Place the chops in a large frying pan and fry gently in their own fat until brown on both sides. Add the onion, rosemary, parsley and lemon rind; cook gently for 2 minutes. Gradually pour in the apple and blackcurrant juice. Cover and simmer for 20–25 minutes until the meat is tender. Using a slotted spoon, remove the chops to a warm serving dish. Keep hot. Place the blackcurrant jelly and blackcurrants in the pan and boil rapidly to reduce by half the amount. Stir in the soured cream, gently reheat then pour the mixture over the chops. Serve at once.

CROWN ROAST OF LAMB

Serves 4–6

2 best end necks of lamb,
   chined, each with 6–8 cutlets
3 oz (75 g) long-grain rice
salt and freshly ground black pepper
1 oz (25 g) butter
1 small onion, finely chopped
2 celery stalks, finely chopped
1 eating apple, finely chopped

1 small garlic clove, crushed
2 tsp curry powder
7 oz (200g) fresh breadcrumbs
1 oz (25 g) sultanas
2 tbsp chopped fresh parsley
1 egg
2 oz (50 g) lard

Preheat the oven to 350°F/180°C/Gas Mk 4. With a sharp knife trim each cutlet bone to a depth of 1 in (2.5 cm). Bend the joints around, fat side inwards, and sew together with strong cotton to form a circle. (The butcher should do this for you.) Cook the rice in plenty of boiling salted water for about 15 minutes. Drain and rinse under cold running water. Heat the butter and fry the onion, celery, apple, garlic and curry powder until softened. Remove from the heat and stir in the breadcrumbs, sultanas, parsley, rice, egg and salt and pepper to taste. Allow to cool, then spoon into the centre of the lamb. Weigh the meat and stuffing. Melt the lard in a roasting tin and stand the lamb joint in it. Roast for 25 minutes per 1 lb (450 g) plus an extra 25 minutes. Cover with foil if the stuffing gets too brown during the cooking time. Transfer to a serving plate and serve with gravy.

LAMB CHOPS WITH LEMON AND MINT
Serves 4

4 large chump chops
 or 8 small loin chops
juice and rind of 1 lemon
2 tbsp olive oil
1 tbsp fresh mint, chopped

salt and freshly ground black pepper
1 garlic clove, crushed
lemon wedges and mint sprigs,
 to garnish

Place the chops flat on a large plate or dish. Mix the lemon, oil, mint, seasoning and garlic together and pour over the chops. Turn them to coat each side in the marinade. Cover and leave to marinate for 2–3 hours. Heat the grill and cook the chops, brushing occasionally with the remaining marinade. Garnish with lemon wedges and sprigs of mint to serve.

LAMB AND LEEK CASSEROLE
Serves 4–6

butter for frying
8 lamb cutlets, trimmed
2 leeks, cleaned and sliced
1 onion, chopped
1 turnip, diced

8 oz (225 g) baby carrots, scraped
1 pt (600 ml) stock or water
salt and freshly ground black pepper
2 mint sprigs
4 oz (110 g) frozen peas

Preheat the oven to 350°F/180°C/Gas Mk 4. Melt the butter in a frying pan and brown the cutlets for 5 minutes. Remove and place in a casserole. Add all the vegetables, together with the stock or water. Add salt and pepper to taste and the mint. Cook in the oven for 1¼ hours, then stir in the peas and cook for a further 15 minutes.

BRAISED LAMB SHANKS
Serves 4

2 tbsp oil
4 lamb shanks
1 onion, sliced
1 garlic clove, crushed
1 carrot, sliced
1 celery stalk, sliced
14 oz (400 g) can tomatoes

1 tsp salt
½ tsp freshly ground black pepper
½ tsp sugar
5 tbsp stock or water
1 tsp Worcestershire sauce
parley, to garnish

Heat the oil in a large heavy-based saucepan. Fry the lamb shanks until browned all over. Remove and drain off most of the fat. Add the onion, garlic, carrot and celery and cook for about 5 minutes or until the onion is soft, stirring frequently. Stir in the tomatoes, salt, pepper, sugar, stock or water and Worcestershire sauce. Return the shanks to the pan, cover and simmer for 1½–2 hours or until the meat is tender. Add more liquid if necessary. Serve garnished with parsley.

LAMB AND MUSHROOM PIE
Serves 4

1 oz (25 g) butter
1 Spanish onion, chopped
4 oz (110 g) mushrooms, chopped
1 lb (450 g) lamb, chopped into
* 1 in (2.5 cm) pieces*

½ pt (300 ml) beef stock
pinch of mace
salt and freshly ground black pepper
4 oz (110 g) frozen puff pastry, thawed
1 egg, beaten

Preheat the oven to 400°F/200°C/Gas Mk 6. Melt the butter in a pan and gently fry the onion and mushrooms until soft. Add the lamb to the pan. Cook for 10 minutes, then add the stock, mace and seasoning to taste. Cover and simmer for 20 minutes. Pile the mixture into a pie dish and cover with the pastry. Brush with egg and bake for 15 minutes, then lower the temperature to 350°F/180°C/Gas Mk 4 and bake for a further 15 minutes.

LAMB CHOPS WITH QUINCES ON RICE
Serves 4

4 tbsp oil
4 lamb chops
1 medium onion, finely chopped
1 garlic clove, finely chopped
10 oz (300 g) brown rice

4 quinces, peeled, cored and chopped
1 tsp ground cumin
½ pt (300 ml) dry cider
½ pt (300 ml) chicken stock
salt and freshly ground black pepper

Heat the oil in a large flameproof casserole over medium heat. Add the chops and brown quickly on both side, then remove and set aside. Lower the heat, and fry the onion and garlic until soft but not brown. Add the rice, quinces and cumin and cook for 1 minute, stirring constantly. Pour in the cider and stock and bring to the boil. Season to taste, then place the chops deep down in the rice. Cover and cook over the lowest possible heat for 45 minutes. Spoon the rice and quinces onto a warmed serving dish and arrange the chops on top.

LAMB BOULANGÉRE
Serves 4–6

1 small leg of lamb, trimmed of fat
2 garlic cloves, thinly sliced
2 rosemary sprigs
1½ lb (675 g) potatoes, thickly sliced
8 oz (225 g) onions, thinly sliced

salt and freshly ground black pepper
1 beef stock cube dissolved in
½ pt (300 ml) hot water
chopped fresh parsley

Preheat the oven to 375°F/190°C/Gas Mk 5. Make several slits all over the lamb with a sharp knife. Press the garlic slivers into the lamb slits and place one sprig of rosemary over the lamb. Mix the potato and onion slices together and put in a shallow heatproof dish. Season with salt and pepper and lay the lamb on top. Pour the stock over the meat and vegetables. Cover with foil and roast for 30 minutes per lb (450 g) plus an extra 30 minutes. After the first hour remove the foil, baste the meat and vegetables and return to the oven. When the meat is cooked untie the rosemary and place a fresh sprig on top. Sprinkle the vegetables with chopped parsley and serve straight from the dish.

CHILLI LAMB COCONUT CURRY
Serves 4

2 oz (50 g) desiccated coconut
   or 1 medium can coconut cream
7 fl oz (200 ml) milk
4 tbsp oil
3 lb (1.4 kg) boned shoulder of
   lamb, trimmed and cubed
4 celery stalks, chopped
1 onion, chopped

8 oz (225 g) cooking apples, chopped
½ tsp chilli powder
1 tsp ground cinnamon
4 tbsp plain flour
¾ pt (450 ml) chicken stock
salt and freshly ground black pepper
chopped fresh parsley, to garnish

Place the coconut and milk together with 7 fl oz (200 ml) of water in a saucepan and bring to the boil. Remove and leave for 30 minutes. If using desiccated coconut, strain into a jug to extract all the juice. Preheat the oven to 350°F/180°C/Gas Mk 4. Heat the oil in a flameproof casserole, add the lamb and brown on all sides. Remove and set aside. Add the celery, onion and apples and brown lightly. Sprinkle in the spices and flour and gradually add the stock, coconut milk and seasoning, stirring constantly Bring to the boil. Remove from the heat, add the lamb, cover and cook in the oven for 1¼ hours. Sprinkle with parsley to serve.

LAMB AND LENTIL HOT POT
Serves 6

3 tbsp oil
8 middle neck lamb chops, about
   2½ lb (1.1 kg) total weight
2 medium onions, thinly sliced
1 tbsp turmeric
1 tsp paprika

1 tsp cinnamon
3 oz (75 g) red lentils
salt and freshly ground black pepper
1 lb (450 g) potatoes, thinly sliced
1 lb (450 g) swede, thinly sliced
½ pt (300 ml) lamb stock

Trim the chops and sauté in hot oil until well browned. Remove from the pan. Add the onions, turmeric, paprika, cinnamon and lentils. Preheat the oven to 350°F/180°C/Gas Mk 4. Fry for a couple of minutes, then add plenty of salt and pepper and spoon into a shallow ovenproof dish. Place the chops on top and arrange the vegetables over the whole dish. Pour over the stock. Cover tightly and cook for about 1½ hours or until the chops are tender. Uncover and cook for a further 30 minutes to brown the top.

LAMB CASSEROLE WITH TURNIPS
Serves 4

4 lb (1.8 kg) breast of lamb
4 tsp plain flour
4 onions, quartered
bouquet garni
1 garlic clove, crushed
8 fl oz (250 ml) stock or water

2 oz (50 g) lard or a mixture
   of butter and oil
2 lb (900 g) white turnips, peeled and
   quartered
salt and freshly ground black pepper
6–8 small potatoes

Preheat the oven to 350°F/180°C/Gas Mk 4. Remove excess fat and bones from the lamb and cut into strips. Cook the strips slowly in a lightly greased heavy frying pan until brown, drain and transfer to a flameproof casserole. Sprinkle the flour over the meat and allow it to brown, then add the onions, bouquet garni, garlic and stock or water. Bring rapidly to the boil then cover and simmer gently. Heat the fat in the pan used to brown the lamb, cook the turnips slowly until lightly browned then add to the casserole. Season generously with salt and pepper, cover and cook in the oven for about 1¼ hours. Add the potatoes to the casserole and cook for a further 20–30 minutes or until tender.

LAMB GOULASH
Serves 4

1½ oz (35 g) lard
1½ lb (675 g) shoulder of
 lamb, boned and cubed
1 packet powdered onion soup
2 tbsp paprika
½ pt (300 ml) dry red wine

¾ pt (450 ml) water
2 celery stalks, cut into strips
1 red pepper, deseeded and sliced
¼ pt (150 ml) soured cream
salt and freshly ground black pepper
400 g (14 oz) can garden peas

Melt the lard in a large saucepan and quickly brown the lamb.
Remove from the heat and stir in the soup mix, paprika, wine and
water. Add the celery and red pepper, return to the heat and bring to
the boil, stirring continuously. Simmer gently for 1 hour until the
meat is tender. Stir in the cream and season to taste. Heat the peas and
serve on a warmed shallow dish, arranging the peas around the lamb
mixture.

LAMB AND ARTICHOKE HEARTS
Serves 4–6

3 oz (75 g) butter
2¼ lb (1 kg) lean leg of lamb
 cut into thin short strips
6 artichoke hearts cooked
 for 30 minutes
2 tsp plain flour

8 fl oz (250 ml) dry white wine or
 dry cider
4 fl oz (125 ml) chicken or lamb stock
salt and freshly ground black pepper
4 tbsp double cream
1 tbsp chopped fresh parsley, to garnish

Melt 2 oz (50 g) of the butter in a frying pan over a moderate heat and
fry the lamb strips, a few at a time, turning frequently, until browned
outside but moist and tender inside. Transfer to a warmed dish with a
slotted spoon. Melt the remaining butter in the pan, lower the heat
and fry the artichoke hearts for 4–5 minutes, turning once. Add to the
meat. Stir the flour into the fat remaining in the pan and gradually
add the wine or cider and stock, stirring constantly. Season to taste,
bring to the boil and simmer for 5–10 minutes until the sauce is
thickened and slightly reduced. Stir in the cream. Return the lamb,
artichokes and any juices to the frying pan and heat gently without
boiling. Serve garnished with parsley.

CURRIED SHEPHERD'S PIE
Serves 4–6

2 lb (900 g) potatoes, peeled
2 oz (50 g) butter or margarine
a little milk
2 tbsp oil
2 onions, chopped

2 tbsp curry powder
1½ lb (675g) shoulder of lamb, minced
1 tbsp cornflour
¼ pt (150 ml) beef stock
salt and freshly ground black pepper

Preheat the oven to 425°F/220°C/Gas Mk 7. Cook the potatoes in boiling salted water until tender. Mash well and beat in the butter or margarine and sufficient milk to give a soft consistency. Heat the oil in a large saucepan and fry the onions for about 3 minutes. Stir in the curry powder and cook for a further 2 minutes. Add the lamb, stirring to brown it all over. Mix the cornflour to a paste with a little of the stock. Add the remainder of the stock to the pan and season. Cover the pan and simmer for 15 minutes. Stir in the cornflour and bring to the boil again. Turn the meat into an ovenproof dish, cover with mashed potato and mark the surface with a fork. Bake for 25–30 minutes or until the potato is well browned.

ROAST LAMB

CUTS TO USE: *Loin, leg, shoulder, boned and rolled,*
stuffed breast, best end of neck

QUANTITY: *Leg: 12 oz (350 g) per portion*
Loin and shoulder: 1 lb (450 g) per portion
Best end and breast: 8 oz (225 g) per portion

OVEN: *Moderate: 350–375°F/180–190°C/Gas Mk 4 or 5*
30 minutes per lb/60 minutes per kg

Slow: 325°F/160°C/Gas Mk 3
45 minutes per lb/90 minutes per kg

Place the meat on rack or in a roasting tin and sprinkle with flour. Rub salt and a little thyme into the skin. The joint should not need basting. Roast according to times above. Serve with mint or onion sauce, roast potatoes and vegetables, or with pork forcemeat balls and boiled or grilled bacon, roast potatoes and vegetables.

LAMB WITH ROSEMARY AND GARLIC
Serves 6–8

4½ lb (2 kg) leg of lamb
2 large garlic cloves, thinly sliced
2 oz (50 g) butter, softened
salt and freshly ground black pepper

1 tbsp chopped fresh rosemary
or 1 tsp dried
rosemary sprigs, to garnish

Score the lamb to a depth of about ½ in (1 cm) in a diamond pattern. Push the garlic slivers into the scored lamb. Mix the butter, salt and pepper to taste, and rosemary and spread all over the lamb. Cover with cling film and refrigerate overnight. Preheat the oven to 350°F/ 180°C/Gas Mk 4. Uncover the lamb and transfer to a roasting tin. Cook for about 2¼ hours, basting occasionally. Pierce the joint with a fine skewer; when cooked the juices should run clear at first, then with a hint of red. Garnish with sprigs of rosemary and serve with gravy made from the meat juices.

LEG OF LAMB WITH FLAGEOLET BEANS
Serves 6–8

4 lb (1.8 kg) leg of lamb
salt and freshly ground black pepper
rosemary sprigs
8 oz (225 g) flageolet beans, soaked overnight
knob of butter

Preheat the oven to 350°F/180°C/Gas Mk 4. Season the lamb with salt and pepper and make small cuts in the skin with a sharp knife. Tuck a small sprig of rosemary into each slit. Put in a roasting tin and bake for 2½ hours or until cooked through and tender. Baste with the juices and keep hot. Drain the beans, place in a large pan and cover with water. Bring to the boil, then simmer for 35–40 minutes or until tender. Drain, season to taste and add a little butter. Spread out on a warmed serving dish and place the leg of lamb on top. Garnish with a rosemary sprig.

LAMB KORMA
Serves 6

2 onions, chopped
1 in (2.5 cm) piece fresh ginger root, peeled
1½ oz (35 g) blanched almonds
2 garlic cloves, crushed
1 tsp each ground cardamom, cloves, cinnamon, cumin and coriander
¼ tsp cayenne pepper
3 tbsp oil or ghee
2 lb (900 g) boned lamb, cubed
½ pt (300 ml) yoghurt
salt and freshly ground black pepper
double cream and rice to serve

Blend the onions, ginger, almonds, garlic with 6 tbsp water to a smooth paste. Add the spices and mix well. Heat the oil or ghee in a heavy-based saucepan and fry the lamb for 5 minutes to brown. Add the paste mixture and fry for about 10 minutes, stirring. Blend in the yoghurt a little at a time and season. Cover and simmer gently for about 1 hour or until the lamb is really tender. Serve on a bed of rice with double cream or thick yoghurt poured over.

CREAMY LAMB AND MUSHROOMS
Serves 2

4 eggs
¼ pt (150 ml) single cream
salt and freshly ground black pepper
8 oz (225 g) cooked lamb
¼ pt (150 ml) beef stock or gravy
1 oz (25 g) margarine
4 oz (110 g) medium mushrooms

Preheat the oven to 375°F/190°C/Gas Mk 5. Lightly grease a small casserole. Beat the eggs in a bowl, then beat in the cream and salt and pepper to taste. Mince or finely chop the lamb and mix it with the stock or gravy. Pile into the casserole. Heat the margarine in a frying pan and gently fry the mushrooms, keeping them whole. Place the mushrooms, stalks uppermost, on top of the meat. Pour over the egg mixture and bake for 25 minutes or until set.

SWEET AND SOUR LAMB WITH APRICOTS
Serves 4

1 oz (25 g) lard
1½ lb (675 g) fillet of lamb, cubed
2 onions, chopped
1 tsp paprika
1 oz (25 g) plain flour
1 beef or lamb stock cube
1 tsp sugar
1 tbsp vinegar
salt and freshly ground black pepper
8 oz (225 g) can apricots, drained and sliced
chopped fresh parsley

Melt the lard in a saucepan, add the lamb and cook for 5 minutes. Add the onions and paprika and cook for a further minute. Gradually stir in the flour and cook for 2 minutes. Dissolve the stock cube in ½ pt (300 ml) water and add to the pan. Stir in the sugar and vinegar with salt and pepper to taste. Bring to the boil, stirring constantly until thick. Cover and simmer for 1 hour. Add the apricots and simmer for 30 minutes until the meat is tender. Place on a warm serving dish and garnish with parsley.

PILAU OF LAMB
Serves 6

2 lb (900 g) boned shoulder of lamb
2 oz (50 g) butter
2 tbsp oil
4 onions, quartered
5 oz (150 g) rice, washed and drained
1¼ pt (750 ml) stock or water
large thyme or oregano sprig
salt and freshly ground black pepper
3 oz (75 g) raisins

Remove any gristle and trim excess fat from the lamb; cut the meat into cubes. Melt the butter and oil in a heavy pot or flameproof casserole, and cook the onions gently until golden brown. Add the rice and cook, stirring, until coated with butter. Add the stock or water, thyme or oregano, 1 tsp of salt and pepper to taste. Bring to the boil, stirring gently. Once the pilau comes to the boil stop stirring, cover and cook over a gentle heat for about 20 minutes, until the rice has absorbed all the liquid with its flavour and the meat is tender. Take off the lid, remove the thyme or oregano sprig, add the raisins and fluff up the rice with a fork. Serve on very hot plates.

LAMB DAUBE
Serves 4

2 tbsp olive oil
1¼ lb (550 g) lamb neck fillet,
    trimmed and cut into thick slices
8 oz (225 g) shallots or
    pickling onions, halved
3 carrots, diagonally sliced
8 oz (225 g) baby turnips, quartered
2 garlic cloves, crushed

2 tbsp plain flour
¼ pt (150 ml) red wine
¼ pt (150 ml) lamb stock
small bunch fresh herbs
    including 1 lavender sprig
salt and freshly ground black pepper
fresh herbs, to garnish

Preheat the oven to 350°F/180°C/Gas Mk 4. Heat the oil in a flameproof casserole, add the lamb and brown on both sides. Remove from the pan with a slotted spoon. Add the vegetables and garlic and fry for 5 minutes until soft. Stir in the flour and cook for 2 minutes, then add the wine, stock, herbs and plenty of seasoning. Bring to the boil, cover and transfer to the oven for 40 minutes. Discard the herbs and spoon onto warm serving plates. Garnish with fresh herbs and serve at once.

LAMB WITH AUBERGINES
Serves 6

2–3 tbsp salt
1 lb (450 g) aubergines, sliced
1 oz (25 g) butter
1½ lb (675 g) boned leg of lamb,
    in large chunks

2 medium onions, chopped
½ tsp ground cumin
salt and freshly ground black pepper
2 tbsp oil
4 medium tomatoes, sliced

Sprinkle salt over the aubergines and stand for 1 hour. Melt the butter in a flameproof casserole dish, add the lamb and fry until well sealed on all sides. Add the onions and cook over low heat for 3–4 minutes. Add 5 fl oz (150 ml) of water, the cumin and seasoning to taste. Bring to the boil, then lower the heat and simmer for 1¼ hours. Rinse the aubergines and dry between layers of absorbent paper. Heat the oil in a frying pan and cook the aubergines until golden on both sides. Remove with slotted spoon and set aside. Fry the tomatoes in the pan, then place on top of the lamb. Lay the aubergines on top and heat through for 5 minutes. Stir once before serving.

SALMAGUNDI
Serves 4

1 oz (25 g) plain flour
1 tsp mustard powder
salt and freshly ground black pepper
1½ lb (675 g) neck of lamb, cubed
4 oz (110 g) lamb liver, chopped
1 oz (25 g) lard

1 medium onion, chopped
1 large cooking apple, sliced
4 oz (110 g) lean bacon, chopped
1 pt (600 ml) stock or water
1 small can butter beans
6–8 pickled onions

Preheat the oven to 350°F/180°C/Gas Mk 4. Mix the flour, mustard and seasoning in a bowl. Coat the lamb and liver. Heat the lard in a pan and lightly fry the meat and onion. Stir in the apple, bacon and stock or water. Transfer the mixture to a casserole dish, cover and cook in the oven for 1½ hours. Add the butter beans and pickled onions and cook for a further 10 minutes.

LAMB AND HAMBURG PARSLEY CASSEROLE
Serves 6

1 oz (25 g) butter
2 lb (900 g) lean lamb (shoulder or leg), cut in 1 in (2.5cm) cubes
1 lb (450 g) Hamburg parsley root, sliced
12 oz (350 g) carrots, sliced
1 large onion, thinly sliced
1 pt (600 ml) chicken stock
zest and juice of 1 small orange
bay leaf
salt and black freshly ground black pepper
3 tbsp chopped Hamburg parsley leaves

Preheat the oven to 350°F/180°C/Gas Mk 4. Melt the butter in a flameproof casserole over high heat. Add the lamb cubes, brown them quickly and remove. Lower the heat and add the parsley root, carrots and onion. Cover and cook gently for 10 minutes, then pour in the stock and bring to the boil. Add the orange juice, lamb, bay leaf and seasoning. Cover and cook in the oven for 1½ hours. Meanwhile cut the orange zest into small thin slivers. Blanch in boiling water for 2 minutes and drain. Turn the lamb, vegetables and sauce into a warmed serving dish. Scatter the orange zest and chopped parsley leaves over the top.

CHESHIRE LAMB CRUMBLE
Serves 4

12 oz (350 g) cooked roast lamb
1 medium onion, chopped
4½ oz (125 g) plain flour
1 tbsp tomato purée
½ pt (300 ml) beef or lamb stock
salt and freshly ground black pepper
2 oz (50 g) butter
2 oz (50 g) Cheshire cheese, grated
½ tsp dried mixed herbs

Preheat the oven to 375°F/190°C/Gas Mk 5. Mince the lamb and onion together. Add 2 tsp of the flour together with the tomato purée, stock and seasoning to taste. Pile into a shallow ovenproof dish. Place the remaining flour in a bowl and rub in the butter until the mixture resembles fine breadcrumbs. Mix in the cheese, herbs and seasoning to taste; arrange on top of the lamb mixture. Bake for about 1 hour.

LAMB EN CROUTE
Serves 4

1 oz (25 g) butter
1 onion, chopped
1 oz (25 g) breadcrumbs
1 egg, beaten
2 tbsp chopped fresh rosemary
salt and freshly ground black pepper

squeeze of lemon juice
12 lamb cutlets, trimmed
two 13 oz (375 g) packets frozen
*   puff pastry, thawed*
beaten egg, to glaze

To make the stuffing: melt the butter and fry the onion until soft. Remove from the heat, stir in the breadcrumbs and bind with the egg. Mix in the rosemary, salt, pepper and lemon juice. Grill or fry the lamb for 3 minutes on each side. Leave to cool. Preheat the oven to 425°F/220°C/Gas Mk 7. Meanwhile roll out each piece of pastry thinly and cut each into six squares. Place a cutlet on each square of pastry so that the bone comes over the edge. Place stuffing on top. Dampen the edges of the pastry, wrap over the cutlets and seal. Place on a dampened baking tray, folded sides downwards. Brush with egg and bake for 15–20 minutes, then reduce the heat to 375°F/190°C/Gas Mk 5 and bake for another 5 minutes until the pastry is golden.

HERB-STUFFED SHOULDER OF LAMB
Serves 4–5

3¼ lb (1.5 kg) shoulder of lamb, boned
1 oz (25 g) butter
7 fl oz (200 ml) dry white wine, or juice of 1 orange

Stuffing:
2 oz (50 g) butter, softened
2 tbsp chopped fresh parsley
1 tbsp chopped fresh mint
1 tbsp snipped fresh chives

1 tsp chopped fresh thyme or marjoram
freshly ground black pepper
3 oz (75 g) fresh white breadcrumbs
1 egg, beaten

Preheat the oven to 400°F/200°C/Gas Mk 6. To make the stuffing: beat the butter with the herbs, seasoning and breadcrumbs until well mixed, then beat in the egg a little at a time. Open out the joint and spread with the stuffing. Roll up and tie; put in a roasting tin. Spread the joint with the butter, grind over some pepper, pour over the wine or orange juice and roast for 1¼ hours, basting often. Halfway through the cooking time, turn the joint over and add a little stock or water to the pan if the liquid has evaporated. Remove the string from the joint and place on a warmed serving dish. Use the juices in the tin to make gravy.

NOISETTES OF LAMB WITH RED WINE SAUCE
Serves 4

12 lamb noisettes
plain flour for coating
1 oz (25 g) butter
4 tbsp oil
2 large onions, sliced
1 garlic clove, finely chopped

8 oz (225 g) button mushrooms
½ pt (300 ml) red wine
¼ pt (150 ml) chicken stock
1 tbsp tomato purée
2 bay leaves
salt and freshly ground black pepper

Lightly coat the lamb with flour. Heat the butter and oil in a large flameproof casserole and brown the noisettes quickly on both sides. Remove and set aside. Fry the onion and garlic for about 5 minutes until golden. Add the mushrooms and fry for another 2–3 minutes. Stir in the wine, stock, tomato purée and bay leaves. Season well, put the noisettes back and bring to the boil, then cover and reduce heat. Simmer gently for about 40 minutes until tender, turning the noisettes once. Lift out of the sauce, remove strings, place on a warmed serving dish and keep warmed. Discard the bay leaves and boil the remaining liquid to reduce. Taste and adjust the seasoning, then pour over the noisettes.

SPANISH LAMB
Serves 8

4 lb (1.8 kg) leg or shoulder of lamb
2 garlic cloves, crushed
1 tsp mixed dried herbs
few rosemary sprigs

4 tbsp sherry
4 tbsp water
12 small onions
6 stuffed green olives, sliced

Preheat the oven to 375°F/190°C/Gas Mk 5. Put the lamb in a roasting tin. Spread the garlic and herbs evenly over the surface and place rosemary sprigs on top and underneath. Pour the sherry over the meat and leave to stand for 3 hours. Add the water to the roasting pan and arrange the onions around the joint. Roast for 1 hour 40 minutes, basting frequently. Put the lamb on a warmed serving dish surrounded by the onions. Stir the olives into the cooking juices and pour over the joint.

TUSCAN LAMB WITH PEAS
Serves 4

2¼ lb (1 kg) leg of lamb
4 garlic cloves, sliced
2–3 sprigs rosemary
2 tbsp oil
salt and freshly ground black pepper

1¼ lb (550 g) ripe tomatoes, skinned,
    seeded and finely chopped
2 tbsp water
1¼ lb (550 g) shelled peas

Make incisions in the lamb with a sharp knife to create 'pockets' and insert slivers of garlic and 1–2 rosemary spikes in each. Rub the meat all over with a little of the oil and season with salt and pepper. Heat the remaining oil in a flameproof casserole and brown the meat all over. Add the tomatoes and the water to the casserole. Bring to the boil, lower the heat, cover and simmer for 45 minutes to 1 hour. Boil the peas in lightly salted water for 10 minutes, or until almost cooked. Drain and add to the meat 10 minutes before the end of the cooking time. Alternatively, cook the peas for 20 minutes until tender. Drain and warm. Transfer the lamb to a warm serving dish, pour over the sauce and garnish with the peas, if cooked separately. Serve immediately.

LAMB AND SPINACH LASAGNE
Serves 4–6

1 lb (450 g) fresh spinach, washed
2 tbsp oil
1 onion, chopped
1 lb (450 g) minced lamb
8oz (225g) can tomatoes
1 garlic clove, crushed
2 tbsp chopped fresh mint
1 tsp cinnamon
freshly grated nutmeg
salt and freshly ground black pepper
2 oz (50 g) butter or margarine
2 oz (50 g) plain flour
1½ pt (900 ml) milk
¼ pt (150 ml) yoghurt
12–15 sheets oven-ready lasagne
6 oz (175 g) Cheddar cheese, grated

Cook the spinach gently for about 4 minutes. Drain well and chop finely. Heat the oil in a large pan and fry the onion for 5 minutes until softened. Add the lamb and brown well, then drain off all the fat. Stir in the spinach with the tomatoes and their juice, garlic, mint and cinnamon. Season with nutmeg, salt and pepper to taste. Bring to the boil and simmer, uncovered for about 30 minutes. Preheat the oven to 350°F/180°C/Gas Mk 4. Leave to cool while making the white sauce. Melt the butter in a saucepan, add the flour and cook gently, stirring, for 1–2 minutes. Remove from the heat and gradually stir in the milk. Bring to the boil, stirring constantly, then simmer for 3 minutes until thick and smooth. Add the yoghurt and season to taste. Spoon one-third of the meat mixture over the base of a rectangular baking dish. Cover with sheets of lasagne and spread over one-third of the white sauce. Repeat these layers twice more, finishing with sauce. Sprinkle the cheese over the top. Stand on a baking sheet and bake for 45–50 minutes or until well browned and bubbling.

PORK

GRECIAN PORK
Serves 4

4 tbsp oil
1 lb (450 g) pork tenderloin
8 oz (225 g) pickling onions
2 garlic cloves, crushed
½ pt (300 ml) red wine

1 tsp salt
freshly ground black pepper
8 oz (225 g) can prunes
¼ oz (15 g) plain flour

Heat the oil in a large frying pan with a lid. Leave the pork in one piece and cook quickly in the hot oil until golden brown. Lift out and set aside. Lower the heat, and cook the onions and garlic for about 5 minutes to brown. Pour in the wine and boil quickly for 1 minute to evaporate the alcohol. Lower the heat, return the pork to the pan and season with salt and pepper. Cover and simmer very slowly for 20 minutes. Meanwhile remove the stones from the prunes and blend the prune juice and flour to a smooth paste. Remove the pan from the heat and cut the pork into slices about 1 in (2.5 cm) thick. Stir the flour and prune juice into the pan and stir quickly to make a smooth red sauce. Add the prunes, return to the boil and simmer very gently for a further 5 minutes. If the sauce has reduced too much add a little water. Taste and adjust the seasoning.

RICH PORK IN BEER
Serves 8

3 tbsp oil
4 pork loin steaks, trimmed of fat
2 small onions, cut into segments
4 carrots, cut into thick sticks
1 bay leaf

2 cloves
½ tsp dried rosemary
freshly ground black pepper
¾ pt (450 ml) can beer or pale ale

Heat the oil in a large frying pan, cook the steaks until brown on both sides. Remove and drain on absorbent paper. Fry the onions and carrots for a few minutes until lightly browned. Drain off excess fat and return the chops to the pan with all the remaining ingredients. Bring to the boil, then reduce heat to a simmer, cover and cook for about 20 minutes or until the pork and carrots are tender. Remove the bay leaf before serving.

PORK AND HARICOT BEANS
Serves 6

*1 lb (450 g) haricot beans,
   soaked overnight
2 rashers streaky bacon
2 lb (900 g) belly pork
1 beef stock cube
1 heaped tbsp tomato purée*

*2 tsp soft dark brown sugar
½ tsp dried sage
fat for frying
1 Spanish onion, chopped
1 garlic clove, chopped
salt and freshly ground black pepper*

Preheat the oven to 325°F/160°C/Gas Mk 3. Drain the beans, reserving the water. Cut the bacon and pork into small cubes. Dissolve the stock cube with the tomato purée, brown sugar and sage in ½ pt (300 ml) boiling water. Heat a little fat in a flameproof casserole and fry the onion and garlic until just softened. Stir in the meat, stock and bean soaking water; season to taste. Cover and bake for 3–4 hours or until the pork is tender and the beans are soft.

KIDNEY-STUFFED PORK CHOPS
Serves 4

*4 loin pork chops, derinded
   and trimmed
1 oz (25 g) butter
1 pig kidney, cored and finely diced*

*1 onion, finely chopped
½ oz (10 g) fresh brown breadcrumbs
½ tsp thyme
salt and freshly ground black pepper*

*Sauce:
1½ tsp plain flour
3 tomatoes, peeled and cut into wedges
1½ tsp tomato purée*

*2 tsp Worcestershire sauce
salt and freshly ground black pepper*

Insert the tip of a sharp knife into the fat side of each chop and cut inwards to make a large pocket. Melt the butter in a saucepan, and cook the kidney and onion quickly for about 5 minutes until golden brown. Heat the grill to moderate. Remove the pan from the heat and stir in the breadcrumbs, thyme, salt and pepper. Cool, then divide into four and pack into the chops. Press to flatten slightly without dislodging the stuffing. Grill for about 10 minutes each side, then remove and keep warmed on a serving dish. Pour the sediment and juices from the grill pan into a small saucepan. Stir in the flour and ¼ pt (150 ml) water; bring to the boil. Add the tomatoes, tomato purée, Worcestershire sauce, salt and pepper and cook for 1 minute, then pour over the meat.

PORK HONGROISE
Serves 4–6

2 tbsp oil
1 oz (25 g) butter
1½ lb (675 g) pork fillet or boned loin
  of pork, cut into 1½ in (3.5 cm) pieces
1 onion, chopped
1 tbsp paprika
½ oz (10 g) plain flour

1 chicken stock cube
5 tbsp sherry
1 tsp tomato purée
salt and freshly ground black pepper
6 oz (175 g) small button mushrooms
½ oz (10 g) cornflour
¼ pt (150 ml) soured cream

Heat the oil and butter in a saucepan, add the pork and fry until just beginning to brown. Remove and drain on absorbent paper. Add the onion and paprika to the pan and fry for 2 minutes. Remove the pan from the heat, stir in the flour and cook for 1 minute. Stir in ½ pt (300 ml) water, crumbled stock cube, sherry and tomato purée, return to the heat and bring to the boil, stirring constantly until the sauce has thickened. Season well and add the meat. Cover and simmer for about 40 minutes or until the pork is tender. At the end of cooking time, add the whole mushrooms. Mix the cornflour to a smooth paste with 2 tbsp water, add to the pan and bring to the boil. Just before serving, stir in the soured cream.

CALYPSO PORK
Serves 4

2 tbsp oil
1 onion, sliced
1 garlic clove, crushed
4 x 8 oz (225 g) pork chops, derinded
2 tbsp rum

3 tbsp guava jelly
1 tsp ground ginger
1 tbsp cornflour
salt and freshly ground black pepper
1 guava, peeled and sliced, to garnish

Preheat the oven to 375°F/190°C/Gas Mk 5. Heat the oil in a frying pan and cook the onion and garlic until soft, Transfer to a casserole. Fry the pork chops for 2 minutes on each side. Pour the rum over the chops, ignite and when the flames have subsided transfer to the casserole. Add the guava jelly and ginger to the frying pan and stir gently over very low heat until the jelly has melted. In a small bowl, mix the cornflour with 6 tbsp water, then pour into the frying pan. Bring to the boil, season to taste, then pour over the chops. Cover and cook in the oven for 45 minutes. Serve garnished with the guava slices.

ROAST PORK

CUTS TO USE: *Leg, loin, spare ribs, hand and spring, blade*

QUANTITY: *With bone: 8–12 oz (225–350 g) per portion*
No bone: 4–6 oz (110–175 g) per portion

OVEN: *Moderate: 350–375°F/180–190°C/Gas Mk 4 or 5*
35 minutes per lb/70 minutes per kg

Score the skin in ¼ in (5 mm) strips and rub salt into the slits. Place the meat on a rack or in a roasting tin and roast according to the recipe you are following using the above times as a guide. Cook pork well; it should not be underdone. Serve with sage and onion stuffing, apple sauce, baked apple rings or cranberry sauce, roast potatoes and vegetables.

SCRUMPY PORK CHOPS
Serves 4

3 tbsp clear honey
¼ pt (150 ml) dry cider
2 tsp white wine vinegar
1 tbsp chopped fresh sage
or 1 tsp dried

1 garlic clove, crushed
4 pork chops
2 large cooking apples,
peeled, cored and chopped

Mix together the honey, cider, vinegar, sage and garlic. Place the chops in a shallow dish and pour over the marinade. Leave in a cool place for 2 hours, turning at least once. Preheat the grill to high. Strain the marinade into a saucepan. Stir the apple into the marinade, cover and cook over a very gentle heat until soft. Grill the chops for 8 minutes each side or until tender. Serve with the hot apple sauce.

GINGERED PORK CHOPS
Serves 2

2 spare rib pork chops
1 tbsp brown sugar
1 tbsp vinegar
1 tsp ground ginger

2 tbsp Worcestershire sauce
salt and freshly ground black pepper
8 oz (225g) can pineapple pieces in syrup
watercress, to garnish

Preheat the oven to 375°F/190°C/Gas Mk 5. Put the chops in a shallow ovenproof dish. Mix together the sugar, vinegar, ground ginger, Worcestershire sauce, seasoning and 2 tbsp pineapple syrup. Pour over the chops and bake, uncovered, for 30 minutes or until almost cooked, basting once. Drain the pineapple, scatter over the chops and continue cooking for 10–15 minutes. Serve garnished with watercress.

CIDER AND CHEESE CHOPS
Serves 4

4 oz (110g) mushrooms, sliced
2 cooking apples, sliced
1 onion, thinly sliced
salt and freshly ground black pepper

4 pork chops
½ pt (300 ml) dry cider
2 oz (50 g) dry breadcrumbs
4 oz (110 g) Cheddar cheese, grated

Preheat the oven to 400°F/200°C/Gas Mk 6. Grease a 3 pt (1.7 litre) shallow ovenproof dish. Place the mushrooms, apples and onion in the dish and season to taste. Arrange the chops on top and pour over the cider. Mix together the breadcrumbs and cheese and sprinkle over the meat. Bake for 1¼–1½ hours.

ORANGE AND PORK CASSEROLE
Serves 4

1½ lb (675 g) pork spare ribs
1 tbsp plain flour
salt and freshly ground black pepper
1 oz (25 g) lard
1 medium onion, chopped

2 oz (50 g) lentils
grated rind and juice of 1 large orange
¾ pt (450 ml) chicken stock
1 small orange, to garnish

Preheat the oven to 350°F/180°C/Gas Mk 4. Cut the meat from the bone and chop into cubes. Toss in seasoned flour until completely coated. Heat the fat and fry the onion until soft and golden, then add the meat and seal on all sides. Transfer to a casserole and stir in any remaining flour together with the lentils, orange rind and juice and the stock. Cover and cook in the oven for 1¼ hours or until both the meat and lentils are tender. Garnish with orange slices.

PORK RAGOUT
Serves 6

2 lb (900 g) belly of pork, boned
oil for frying
2 onions, sliced
8 oz (225 g) baby carrots
1 bay leaf
1 tsp dried sage
1 tbsp plain flour

½ pt (300 ml) stock
14 oz (400 g) can tomatoes
salt and freshly ground black pepper
1 lb (450 g) fresh peas, shelled
6 medium potatoes, quartered
1 tsp sugar

Preheat the oven to 375°F/190°C/Gas Mk 5. Slice the meat into strips; removing any excess fat. Dry fry the meat in a heavy-based frying pan over medium heat until brown on both sides. Transfer to a large ovenproof casserole. Heat a little oil in the frying pan, and fry the onions until soft. Transfer to the casserole with the carrots, bay leaf and sage. Sprinkle the flour into the frying pan and mix with the remaining oil. Cook for 1 minute, stirring constantly. Gradually add the stock and tomatoes and bring to the boil, stirring. Season to taste and pour over the meat and vegetables. Cover and cook in the oven for 1¼ hours. If the casserole is too dry add a further ½ pt (300 ml) stock. Add the peas, potatoes and sugar and cook for a further 45 minutes until the vegetables are tender.

GINGERED APPLE CHOPS
Serves 4

2 tbsp oil
4 pork chops
8 oz (225 g) onions, chopped
1 lb (450 g) small new potatoes
1 lb (450 g) cooking or eating
  apples, cored and thickly sliced

1½ tsp ground ginger
1 tbsp plain flour
8 fl oz (250 ml) dry ginger ale
2 tbsp soy sauce
salt and freshly ground black pepper
1 stock cube, crumbled

Preheat the oven to 375°F/190°C/Gas Mk 5. Heat the oil and fry the chops until brown on both sides. Remove from the pan and add the onions, potatoes and apples and fry briskly for 3 minutes, stirring. Add the ginger and flour and cook, stirring, for 1 minute. Gradually stir in the ginger ale, soy sauce, seasoning and stock cube. Bring to the boil, stirring, and cook for a further minute. Pour the vegetable mixture into a roasting tin, arrange the chops on top and cover with foil. Bake for 40 minutes. Ten minutes before the end remove the foil to allow the chops to crisp on top.

LIKKY PIE
Serves 4

8 oz (225 g) leeks, trimmed
and sliced
salt and freshly ground black pepper
1 lb (450 g) boneless pork,
cut into 1 in (2.5 cm) cubes
¼ pt (150 ml) milk

3 fl oz (90 ml) single cream
2 eggs, lightly beaten
7½ oz (210 g) packet frozen
puff pastry, thawed
plain flour

Preheat the oven to 400°F/200°C/Gas Mk 6. Place the leeks in a saucepan of salted water and boil for 5 minutes. Drain well. Put with the pork in a large pie dish and season to taste. Pour over the milk. Cover with foil and cook in the oven for 1 hour. Mix together the cream and eggs, add to the pie dish and leave to cool. Preheat the oven to 425°F/220°C/Gas Mk 7. Place the pastry on a lightly floured surface and roll out so that it is 2 in (5 cm) wider than the size of the pie dish. Cut a 1 in (2.5 cm) strip from the edge, dampen the rim of the dish and line with it. Moisten the pastry rim, then place the pastry lid over the top. Seal well and flute the edges. Make a small hole in the centre of the pastry lid and use the trimmings to decorate. Bake for 25–30 minutes until golden.

PORK FILLET WITH WINE AND CORIANDER
Serves 6

1½ lb (675 g) pork fillet, trimmed and cut into ½ in (1 cm) slices
½ oz (10 g) butter
1 tbsp oil
1 small green pepper, deseeded and cut into rings
1 medium onion, chopped
½ oz (10 g) plain flour
1 tbsp ground coriander
¼ pt (150 ml) chicken stock
¼ pt (150 ml) dry white wine
salt and white pepper

Using a rolling pin or meat bat, flatten the pork until thin. Heat the butter and oil in a large saucepan and cook the pork until browned on both sides. Add the green pepper and onion and cook for 8–10 minutes until soft. Gradually stir in the flour and coriander and cook for 1 minute. Slowly pour in the stock and wine, stirring constantly until the sauce boils and thickens and is smooth. Season to taste. Simmer for 8–10 minutes until the meat is tender.

PORK SAUSAGE AND BEAN STEW
Serves 4

4 oz (110 g) red kidney beans, soaked overnight
2 medium potatoes, chopped
2 medium onions, chopped
2 medium carrots, chopped
1 large leek, chopped
1½ pt (900 ml) chicken stock
salt and freshly ground black pepper
1 lb (450 g) pork chipolata sausages, browned under the grill
6 oz (175 g) cabbage, shredded

Drain the beans and place in a large saucepan. Add the potatoes, onions, carrots and leeks. Pour in the stock and add salt and pepper to taste. Bring to the boil, stir well, cover and simmer over low heat for 1½ hours. Chop the sausages into 1 in (2.5 cm) lengths. Add the cabbage and sausage to the vegetables and beans and simmer for a further 15 minutes.

HUNGARIAN PORK ROLLS
Serves 4

1 lb (450 g) lean pork meat
2 oz (50 g) smoked streaky bacon
2 onions
3–4 fresh parsley sprigs
oil for frying
salt and freshly ground black pepper
plain flour
1 carrot, leek, celery and turnip, diced
½ pt (300 ml) hot chicken or beef stock

Cut the meat into slices about ½ in (1 cm) thick and flatten with a meat bat or rolling pin. Mince the bacon, one of the onions and the parsley, or chop very finely. Heat a little oil and fry them lightly, stirring to prevent sticking. Season well and spread over the pork slices. Roll up and tie with fine string. Coat in seasoned flour and cook in hot oil, until brown all over. Remove and keep hot. Add the second onion and the other vegetables and brown them lightly. Add 1 tbsp flour and cook for 1 minute, stirring constantly. Gradually stir in the stock. Replace the pork rolls, cover and simmer until tender; about 1 hour.

PORK CHOPS WITH CREAM AND MUSHROOMS
Serves 4

butter for frying
4 pork chops
salt and black freshly ground black pepper
4 oz (110 g) mushrooms, roughly chopped
juice of 1 lemon
1 tbsp plain flour
dried thyme
¼ pt (150 ml) double cream

Preheat the oven to 350°F/180°C/Gas Mk 4. Line a roasting tin with a large sheet of foil with enough at the sides to wrap over. Heat the butter in a frying pan and brown the chops on both sides, lift out with a slotted spoon and place on the foil. Season to taste. Fry mushrooms in the same pan. Add the lemon juice and bring to the boil, then sprinkle in the flour. Stir for 1 minute until the mixture is smooth, then pour over the chops. Sprinkle lightly with thyme, then pour over the double cream. Bring the sides of the foil over and seal well. Bake for 1 hour and serve with the creamy sauce poured over. It will look slightly curdled, but this does not affect the flavour.

BRAISED PORK
Serves 4–6

1 tbsp oil
1 oz (25 g) butter
2¼ lb (1 kg) loin of pork, derinded
2 garlic cloves, chopped
1 large onion, chopped
1 pt (600 ml) milk
5 juniper berries
4 fresh sage sprigs
salt and freshly ground black pepper

Gently heat the oil and butter in a large saucepan. Add the pork, garlic and onion and cook for 15 minutes until the meat is browned on all sides. Add the milk, juniper berries, sage and seasoning to taste. Bring to the boil, cover and simmer gently for 1½–2 hours until tender. Turn and baste occasionally. Remove from the saucepan and place on a warmed dish. Discard the garlic, juniper berries and sage. Liquidise the cooking juices until smooth, adding more salt and pepper if required. Cut the pork into thick slices and pour over a little of the sauce. Serve the remaining sauce separately.

HOT AND SPICY SPARE RIBS
Serves 4

2 lb (900 g) spare ribs
2 garlic cloves, crushed
2 tbsp clear honey
2 tbsp soft dark brown sugar
3 tbsp tomato ketchup

3 tbsp wine vinegar
3 tbsp soy sauce
1 tsp chilli powder
salt and freshly ground black pepper

Preheat the oven to 350°F/180°C/Gas Mk 4. Place the spare ribs in a large roasting tin. Put all the other ingredients in a large jug and whisk together. Pour over the ribs and turn to coat them evenly. Bake, uncovered, for 30 minutes or until the pork is tender and the sauce is thick and syrupy. Serve hot on their own with paper napkins and finger bowls as spare ribs should be eaten with the fingers. They may also be served with boiled rice and stir-fried vegetables.

NORFOLK PORK
Serves 4

4 lean pork chops
1 tbsp plain flour
salt and freshly ground black pepper
12 oz (350 g) onions, chopped

12 oz (350 g) Bramley apples,
  cored and cut into chunks
½ pt (300 ml) cider

Derind and trim excess fat from the pork chops, reserving the fat. Mix the flour with salt and pepper and put it in a plastic bag. Drop in the chops one at a time and shake until thoroughly coated. Preheat the oven to 350°F/180°C/Gas Mk 4. Place the pieces of pork fat in a large frying pan and heat gently until the bottom of the pan is lightly coated. Discard the fat, add the chops and brown on both sides. Lift out onto a plate. Fry the onions gently for 5 minutes. Add the apples and cook for 3–4 minutes, stirring constantly. Season to taste. Place half the onion and apple mixture in a shallow ovenproof dish. Arrange the chops on top, cover with the rest of the onion and apple mixture and pour over the cider. Bake, uncovered, for about 1 hour.

PORK APRICOT KEBABS
Serves 4

14 oz (400 g) can apricot halves
2 green peppers, deseeded
1 lb (450 g) lean boneless pork, cubed
16 bay leaves

salt and freshly ground black pepper
1 tbsp chopped fresh rosemary
2 tbsp oil
1 tsp made English mustard

Drain the apricots, reserving the juice. Cut the peppers to roughly the same size as the pork. Thread pork, apricots, peppers and bay leaves alternately on to eight metal skewers. Mix the apricot syrup with salt and pepper to taste, rosemary, oil and mustard and brush over the kebabs generously. Cook under a hot grill, turning frequently, until the meat is cooked through and well browned. Constantly brush with the syrup liquid. Heat the remaining liquid in a saucepan and boil to reduce. Pour over the kebabs to serve.

PORK STEW
Serves 6

2 lb (900 g) potatoes, thinly sliced
3 lb (1.4 kg) lean pork, diced
1 onion, sliced
1 cooking apple, sliced

2 tbsp chopped fresh sage or 1 tsp dried
salt and freshly ground black pepper
hot chicken stock

Preheat the oven to 375°F/190°C/Gas Mk 5. Lightly butter a casserole and put in a layer of potato. Arrange the pork in layers with the onion, apple and sage, seasoning each layer as you go, and finishing with potato. Pour the stock into the casserole almost to the top, cover and cook for 2 hours or until the pork is tender.

SESAME PORK
Serves 4

2 tbsp vinegar
2 tsp soy sauce
4 tbsp soft brown sugar
¼ pt (150 ml) tomato ketchup

1 tbsp brown sauce
2 tbsp sesame seeds
8 belly pork slices

Mix together the vinegar, soy sauce, sugar, ketchup, brown sauce and sesame seeds. Lay the pork belly slices in a shallow dish and pour over the marinade. Leave in the refrigerator, overnight if possible or for at least 3 hours. Preheat the grill and line the grill pan with foil. Lay in the pork slices and brush with the marinade. Grill for about 15 minutes or until the meat is cooked, turning frequently and brushing constantly with the sauce. Serve hot with garlic bread and a green salad.

RED PEPPER PORK
Serves 4

1 tbsp olive oil
2 red peppers, deseeded and thinly sliced
1 lb (450 g) pork fillet, trimmed and thinly sliced
salt and freshly ground black pepper
1 lb (450 g) tomatoes, chopped
2 tbsp chopped fresh mint

Melt the oil in a heavy frying pan, add the red peppers and sauté for 1 minute. Add the pork and brown over high heat. Season with pepper to taste, cover the pan and reduce to low heat. Cook for 5 minutes, then add the tomatoes. Cover and cook for 10–15 minutes until the meat is tender and the tomato and pepper mixture is reduced. Season with salt and more pepper to taste. Cool for 1 minute, then stir in the mint.

PORK WITH RED CABBAGE
Serves 4

6 oz (175 g) butter beans, soaked overnight
1 lb (450 g) pie pork (boneless stewing pork)
½ oz (10 g) dripping
2 onions, chopped
1 lb (450 g) red cabbage, shredded
1 large cooking apple, cored and sliced
1 tsp salt
4 cloves
vinegar
1 rounded tbsp soft dark brown sugar
chopped fresh parsley, to garnish

Cut the pork into 1 in (2.5 cm) cubes. Melt the dripping in a large saucepan and fry the pork and onions for 5 minutes. Add the butter beans to the pan with the soaking water and bring to the boil. Stir in the cabbage and apple with the salt and cloves. Cover tightly and cook for about 1¼ hours or until the butter beans and pork are tender. Remove the cloves and stir in the vinegar and sugar. Taste and adjust the seasoning. Turn into a warmed serving dish, garnish with chopped fresh parsley and serve very hot.

PORK CHOPS CHARCUTIERE
Serves 6

6 pork chops, trimmed
1 oz (25 g) butter
1 small onion, finely chopped
3 fl oz (90 ml) dry white wine
4 tsp vinegar
1 tbsp tomato purée, optional
salt and freshly ground black pepper
2 tsp mustard
1 gherkin, sliced
1 tbsp chopped fresh parsley

Cook the pork chops in their own fat, then transfer to a serving dish and keep warm. Pour off all but 1 tbsp of the fat, add the butter and cook the onion until soft and golden. Add the wine and vinegar and boil rapidly to reduce the liquid by one quarter. Add the tomato purée and 2 tsp water and cook slowly for 10 minutes. Season to taste and add the mustard, gherkin and parsley. Return the chops to the pan; heat through, but do not the allow the liquid to boil. Serve with the sauce poured over the chops.

PORK IN AN OVERCOAT
Serves 6

leg of pork, parboiled and skinned
2 oz (50 g) butter
3 oz (75 g) breadcrumbs
2 tsp dried sage
1 small onion, finely chopped
salt and freshly ground black pepper
sage and onion stuffing

Preheat the oven to 375°F/190°C/Gas Mk 5. Put the joint in a roasting tin with the butter and roast for 30–35 minutes per lb (60–70 minutes per kg). Mix together the breadcrumbs, sage, onion and seasoning. About 15 minutes before the end of cooking time remove the tin from the oven, baste the joint well and sprinkle the breadcrumb mixture over it. Return to the oven, turn the heat up to 425°F/220°C/Gas Mk 7 and bake until the 'coat' is brown and crisp. Garnish with sage and onion stuffing balls and serve with apple sauce.

SAUSAGE MEAT ROLL
Serves 4

½ oz (10 g) plain flour
salt and freshly ground black pepper
4 hard-boiled eggs, shelled
1½ lb (675 g) pork sausage meat

½ tsp chopped thyme
½ tsp mixed herbs
2 tbsp sage and onion stuffing mix

Put the flour and plenty of salt and pepper in a plastic bag. Dry the eggs thoroughly on absorbent paper. Put in the bag with the seasoned flour and shake well until coated. Mix together the sausage meat and herbs and add a little extra salt and pepper. Sprinkle the work surface with the sage and onion stuffing mix and roll or pat the sausage meat into a rectangle 11 x 8 in (27.5 x 20 cm). Lay the eggs end to end down the centre of the sausage meat. Firmly fold over the sausage meat, pressing well to seal but without stretching it otherwise it will split. Roll to coat well with stuffing mix. Lift it onto a baking sheet and chill in the refrigerator for 1 hour. Preheat the oven to 375°F/190°C/Gas Mk 5. Bake the roll for 30 minutes. Carefully lift off the baking sheet and place on a flat dish. Allow to cool, then chill in the refrigerator before slicing.

PORK, RED PEPPER AND SWEET POTATO STEW
Serves 4

1 oz (25 g) lard
2 lb (900 g) lean hand or
  shoulder of pork, cubed
2 medium onions, chopped
1 garlic clove, finely chopped
2 large red peppers, deseeded
  and coarsely chopped
1 tbsp paprika

⅓ tsp cayenne pepper
14 oz (400 g) can tomatoes
¼ pt (150 ml) dry white wine
¼ pt (150 ml) chicken stock
1½ lb (675 g) sweet potatoes,
  finely diced
6 sage leaves, chopped
salt

Melt the lard in a large saucepan on a high heat. Add the pork, brown quickly and remove from the pan. Lower the heat, add the onions and garlic and cook until soft but not coloured. Add the peppers, cover and cook for 5 minutes. Stir in the paprika and cayenne, add the tomatoes, cover and cook for a further 5 minutes. Pour in the wine and stock and bring to the boil. Add the pork, sweet potatoes and sage and some salt. Cover and cook on a low heat for 45 minutes.

STUFFED CABBAGE LEAVES
Serves 4

12 large cabbage leaves
12 oz (350 g) lean pork
1 medium onion, chopped
1 tbsp oil
3 oz (75 g) long-grain rice,
  cooked and drained

salt and freshly ground black pepper
1 egg, beaten
2 tbsp cornflour
2 tbsp tomato purée
1 chicken stock cube

Heat a large saucepan of water until boiling, then drop in the cabbage leaves four at a time, for about 2 minutes per batch. Lift out, drain well and trim away the thickest part of the stalks. Finely mince the pork with the onion. Heat the oil in a frying pan and fry the meat and onion mixture for 5 minutes, stirring constantly. Add the rice and season well. Remove and stir in the egg. Preheat the oven to 350°F/180°C/Gas Mk 4. Divide the meat mixture into 12 equal portions, place one in the centre of each cabbage leaf and roll up to form parcels, tucking in the ends. Arrange in a single layer in a shallow ovenproof dish. Place the cornflour, tomato purée, crumbled stock cube and ¾ pt (450 ml) water in the frying pan and bring to the boil, stirring, until the sauce has thickened. Pour over the cabbage leaves, cover and bake for 45–60 minutes. Serve straight from the dish.

PORK PRUNEAUX
Serves 4

3 lb (1.4 kg) loin of pork
1 lemon
6–8 prunes, pitted

salt
¼ pt (150 ml) dry cider
cornflour if needed

Preheat the oven to 450°F/230°C/Gas Mk 8. Rub the joint with half a lemon, using all the juice. Make holes in the joint with a large skewer. Cut each prune into four pieces and push one piece into each hole. Bake the joint in a greased roasting tin until brown. Remove from the oven and sprinkle well with salt. Pour the cider around the joint, reduce the oven to 375°F/190°C/Gas Mk 5 and roast for about 1½ hours, basting every 10 minutes. When cooked remove from the tin and keep hot. Thicken the juices with a little cornflour if necessary and serve with the meat.

SPANISH-STYLE RIBS
Serves 4

14 oz (400 g) can chopped tomatoes
2 tbsp red wine vinegar
14 oz (400 g) can pimientos, drained
2 garlic cloves, crushed
2 tsp made English mustard
½ tsp Tabasco sauce
½ tsp dried oregano
3 lb (1.4 kg) pork spare ribs
2 tbsp soft light brown sugar

In a large bowl mix together the tomatoes, vinegar, pimientos, garlic, mustard, Tabasco sauce and oregano. Arrange the spare ribs in a large shallow dish and pour over the marinade. Leave in a cool place (not the refrigerator) for at least 2 hours. Preheat the oven to375°F/190°C/ Gas Mk 5. Lift the ribs out, drain off excess juices, and put in a single layer in a roasting tin. Sprinkle with the sugar. Bake for 1 hour or until the coating is crispy and the meat tender.

PORK IN ONION SAUCE
Serves 4

1 oz (25 g) butter
2 carrots, sliced
3 celery stalks, chopped
1 small green pepper, deseeded and chopped
1 lb (450 g) lean pork, diced
2 x 12 oz (350 g) packets onion sauce mix
1 pt (600 ml) milk
1 bay leaf
salt and freshly ground black pepper

Preheat the oven to 350°F/180°C/Gas Mk 4. Heat the butter in a flameproof casserole dish, add the carrots, celery and green pepper and cook for 2–3 minutes. Add the pork and cook for a further 3–4 minutes, stirring constantly. Make the onion sauce mix using the milk and following the packet instructions. Pour into the pork mixture and add the bay leaf. Thoroughly mix together and bake for 1½ hours. Check the seasoning.

CASSOULET
Serves 4

8 oz (225 g) haricot beans, soaked overnight
8 oz (225 g) salt pork
2 garlic cloves, crushed
2 tbsp oil
1 onion, sliced
bouquet garni
1 tsp salt
½ tsp pepper
4 oz (110 g) pork or garlic sausage
2 tomatoes, skinned and chopped
chopped fresh parsley, to garnish

Preheat the oven to 300°F/150°C/Gas Mk 2. Place the pork and garlic in a saucepan and cover with cold water. Bring to the boil and simmer for 5–7 minutes. Drain and slice the pork. Heat the oil in a flameproof casserole, add the onion and pork and fry until golden brown. Stir in the drained beans, bouquet garni, salt, pepper and boiling water to cover. Cover and cook in oven for 1½ hours. Add the sliced sausage and tomatoes and cook for another hour. Remove the bouquet garni and serve sprinkled with chopped parsley.

SHERPA PORK CURRY
Serves 4

1½ lb (675 g) blade of pork
3 tbsp oil
8 oz (225 g) onions, chopped
3 dried red chillies, halved, deseeded and finely chopped
2 tsp ground cumin
1 tsp ground cinnamon
3 tsp ground coriander
2 garlic cloves, crushed
1 tsp salt and freshly ground black pepper
5 oz (150 g) yoghurt

Chop the pork into small cubes, discarding the skin, bone and any excess fat. Place the oil in a heavy saucepan, add the meat and brown on all sides. Set aside. Brown the onions in the pan. Add the chillies together with the cumin, cinnamon, coriander and garlic and cook for 1 minute. Then add ½ pt (300 ml) water together with the salt, pepper and yoghurt; bring to the boil, stirring constantly. Replace the meat, cover and simmer gently for 1½ hours.

PORK ARGENTEUIL
Serves 4

1 oz (25 g) butter
1 onion, sliced
1 lb (450 g) pork fillet, cut into 16 slices
1 tbsp plain flour
½ tsp chilli powder
salt and freshly ground black pepper
8 oz (225 g) frozen asparagus, cut into 1 in (2.5 cm) pieces
4 oz (110 g) button mushrooms
grated rind and juice of ½ orange
2 firm tomatoes, cut into 6 wedges

Melt the butter in a large frying pan and cook the onion for 3 minutes over a moderate heat. Meanwhile dip the slices of pork in the flour seasoned with chilli, salt and pepper. Move the onion to one side of the pan. Add the pork and cook for 2–3 minutes each side to brown. Sprinkle in any remaining flour. Mix the onions with the meat and add the asparagus. Place the mushrooms on top, cover and cook for 5 minutes. Stir in the orange rind and juice and place the tomato wedges on top. Cover and cook for 2 minutes to warm the tomatoes through.

ORIENTAL PORK CASSEROLE
Serves 4

2 tbsp oil
1 onion, chopped
2 in (5 cm) piece ginger root, peeled and thinly sliced
1½ lb (675 g) pork, trimmed and cubed
1 oz (25 g) seasoned flour
½ pt (300 ml) chicken stock
1 red pepper, deseeded and cut into chunks
4 oz (110 g) button mushrooms, wiped and trimmed
salt and freshly ground black pepper

Heat the oil in a flameproof casserole and fry the onion and ginger until golden. Remove with a slotted spoon. Coat the pork in the flour, add to the casserole and fry until browned on all sides. Return the onion and ginger and pour over the stock. Bring to the boil, stirring, cover and simmer for 1½ hours or until the pork is tender. Add the red pepper and mushrooms and season to taste. Cook for a further 15 minutes.

PORK AND BEETROOT
Serves 4

1 tbsp oil
1 lb (450 g) lean stewing pork, trimmed and cut into cubes
1 lb (450 g) fresh raw beetroot, cubed
1 red onion, sliced
½ pt (300 ml) light beer
2 tbsp malt syrup
8 black peppercorns, crushed
4 allspice berries
1 bay leaf
1 mint sprig
½ tsp salt
1 tbsp potato flour, dissolved in 2 tbsp water

Heat the oil in a large flameproof casserole, add the meat and brown on all sides over high heat. Add the beetroot, onion, beer, malt syrup, peppercorns, allspice, bay leaf, mint and salt. Bring to the boil, then simmer gently for 1–1¼ hours until the pork is tender. Add the potato flour mixture to the casserole and cook for a further few minutes, stirring, until liquid thickens.

GOULASH PENHALIGON
Serves 4

2 tbsp oil
2 rashers bacon, derinded and chopped
1 onion, chopped
1½ lb (675 g) lean pork, cubed
1 tbsp plain flour
2 tbsp paprika
¾ pt (450 ml) beef stock
2–3 tsp caraway seeds
1 tbsp tomato purée
salt and freshly ground black pepper
¼ pt (150 ml) soured cream
1 tbsp chopped fresh parsley

Heat the oil in a large pan, add the bacon and onion and cook for 2 minutes. Add the pork and fry quickly to seal. Mix in the flour, paprika, stock, caraway seeds, tomato purée and seasoning. Cover and simmer gently for 1 hour, then stir in the cream and sprinkle with chopped parsley before serving.

PATÉ-STUFFED PORK FILLET
Serves 4

1 pork fillet
3 bacon rashers

1 tbsp brandy
chopped fresh parsley, to garnish

Paté:
8 oz (225 g) chicken livers
1 bacon rasher, chopped
2–3 mushrooms, finely chopped
1 small onion, finely chopped

1 bay leaf
2 oz (50 g) butter
4 fl oz (125 ml) red wine

Preheat the oven to 400°F/200°C/Gas Mk 6. Make the paté: fry all the ingredients until cooked. Blend until smooth and pour into a greased tin. Cook for 10–15 minutes, then remove from the oven and reduce the temperature to 350°F/180°C/Gas Mk 4. Trim the pork fillet and with a sharp knife cut a pocket through the centre lengthways. Stuff with the paté and cover with the bacon. Tie with string, bringing the bacon round over the cut pocket. Cover with foil and bake for about 45 minutes or until well cooked. Pour off the juices from the pan and add the brandy. Carve the fillet, place on a warmed serving dish and sprinkle with parsley. Strain the juices around it.

PORK AND SESAME MEATBALLS
Serves 4–6 as a snack

4 mushrooms, finely chopped
6–8 canned water chestnuts, finely chopped
1 lb (450 g) minced pork
2 tbsp soy sauce
2 tbsp cornflour
3 spring onions, finely chopped
1 in (2.5 cm) piece fresh ginger root, grated
1 tbsp dry sherry
1 tsp sesame oil
7 tbsp toasted sesame seeds

Preheat the oven to 180°C/350°F/Gas Mk 4. Mix together all the ingredients except the sesame seeds. Shape into walnut-sized balls by rolling heaped teaspoonfuls in the palms of your hands. Roll in the sesame seeds and place on a roasting rack set in a roasting tin. Bake for 20 minutes until golden brown and spoon onto a serving dish. This size meatball is suitable for party food. They can also be made slightly larger, cooked for 30 minutes and served with noodles as a meal.

NORMANDY PORK PIE
Serves 4–6

1 oz (25 g) butter
2 onions, finely chopped
2 garlic cloves, crushed
1 lb (450 g) lean minced pork
8 oz (225g) can chopped tomatoes

2 dessert apples, chopped
2 tsp paprika
2 tsp dried sage
salt and freshly ground black pepper

Topping:
1 lb (450 g) potatoes, diced
1 lb (450 g) parsnips, diced
1 oz (25 g) butter

6 tbsp milk
2 oz (50 g) Cheddar cheese, grated

Melt the butter and sauté the onions and garlic until soft, then add the pork mince and stir until well sealed. Add the tomatoes, apples, paprika, sage and seasoning. Bring to the boil, then simmer gently until the pork is tender; about 15–20 minutes. Put in a heatproof dish and keep hot. Boil the potatoes gently in salted water, adding the parsnips after 5 minutes and cook both until tender. Drain well and mash with the butter, milk and seasoning Spoon over the pork and level off. Sprinkle over the grated cheese and put under a hot grill to brown.

FARMER'S PORK CASSEROLE
Serves 4

1 lb (450 g) pork fillet, trimmed
4 tbsp oil
2 medium carrots, sliced
2 medium onions, sliced
1 small green pepper, deseeded and diced
8 oz (225 g) can tomatoes
1 chicken stock cube dissolved in ½ pt (300 ml) hot water
2 tsp salt and freshly ground black pepper
3 tsp paprika
2 tbsp cornflour

Cut the meat into 1 in (2.5 cm) cubes. Heat the oil in a saucepan, add the meat, carrots, onions and green pepper; fry for 3–4 minutes. Add the tomatoes, stock, salt, pepper and paprika and bring to the boil, stirring constantly. Reduce the heat, cover and simmer gently for 1½ hours or until the pork is tender. Mix the cornflour with 3 tbsp cold water to a smooth paste, add to the pan and stir until the sauce has thickened slightly. Check the seasoning.

JUGGED PORK
Serves 4–6

1¼ lb (550 g) lean pork
1 oz (25 g) bacon fat
1 large onion, sliced
2 cloves

1 bay leaf
1 chicken stock cube
¼ pt (150 ml) red wine
salt and freshly ground black pepper

Forcemeat balls:
2 oz (50 g) fresh white breadcrumbs
1 tsp chopped fresh sage
1 oz (25 g) shredded suet

1 egg, beaten
oil for frying

Cut the meat into 1 in (2.5 cm) cubes. Place the bacon fat in a saucepan and fry the pork with the onion for 3–4 minutes. Add the cloves and bay leaf with ¼ pt (150 ml) water, crumbled stock cube, wine, salt and pepper and bring to the boil. Cover and simmer gently for about 1 hour or until the pork is tender. Meanwhile put the breadcrumbs in a bowl with the sage and suet, season well and add sufficient beaten egg to bind the mixture together. Shape into eight balls and fry in a little hot oil for 4–5 minutes, turning constantly until golden brown all over. Remove from the pan and drain on absorbent paper. Taste the pork and check the seasoning. Turn into a warmed serving dish and arrange the forcemeat balls around the edge.

PORK MEXICANA
Serves 4

2 oz (50 g) kidney beans, soaked
  overnight (or use drained canned beans)
1 tbsp olive oil
1 lb (450 g) pork fillet, trimmed
  and cut into cubes
1 onion, finely chopped
1 garlic clove, crushed

1 tsp chilli powder
¼ tsp ground allspice
1 tbsp tomato purée
½ pt (300 ml) unsalted stock
2 tsp arrowroot
½ tsp salt

Drain the beans, place in a saucepan with plenty of water and bring to the boil. Boil for 10 minutes, then reduce the heat, cover and simmer for 25–30 minutes or until tender. (Canned beans do not need to be cooked.) Drain well. In a large heavy saucepan, heat the oil and cook the pork, onion and garlic for 4–5 minutes, stirring, until the meat is browned all over. Stir in the chilli powder, allspice, tomato purée, and stock. Bring to the boil, cover and simmer for 20 minutes. Stir in the beans. Mix the arrowroot with 2 tbsp cold water, then add to the saucepan. Stir well until the liquid is thick. Season with salt to taste.

PORK AND APPLE CASSEROLE
Serves 4

2 Spanish onions, finely chopped
1 lb (450 g) belly pork, cut in strips
1½ lb (675 g) potatoes, thinly sliced
1 cooking apple, sliced
salt and freshly ground black pepper
stock

14 juniper berries
2 tbsp breadcrumbs
1 tsp rubbed sage
1 egg, beaten
1 dessert apple, sliced
1 tsp oil

Preheat the oven to 375°F/190°C/Gas Mk 5. Lightly butter a
casserole. Reserving 1 tbsp of the onion, put a layer of onion in the
base of the casserole, followed by the pork, potatoes and cooking
apple. Season between each layer. Pour in enough stock to cover, add
the juniper berries, put the lid on and bake for 1 hour or until the
pork is tender. Meanwhile mix together the breadcrumbs, reserved
onion, sage and egg to make a sloppy stuffing-like mixture; add a little
water if necessary. Remove the juniper berries with a spoon. Spread
on top of the hot pot and arrange the dessert apple slices on top.
Sprinkle with oil and return to the oven, uncovered, for about
15 minutes to brown the top.

SPICED PORK WITH DUMPLINGS
Serves 4

1½ lb (675 g) lean belly pork,
   derinded and trimmed
3 tbsp oil
6 oz (175 g) onions, quartered
6 oz (175 g) carrots, quartered
3 tbsp plain flour

4 tsp ground coriander
½ tsp ground cumin
1¼ pt (700 ml) stock
4 oz (110 g) aduki beans, soaked overnight
salt and freshly ground black pepper

Dumplings:
4 oz (110 g) self-raising flour
2 oz (50 g) shredded suet

2 tbsp chopped fresh parsley
cold water to mix

Cut the pork into strips. Heat the oil in a large saucepan and brown
the strips. Add the vegetables and sauté. Stir in the 3 tbsp flour and
spices, cook for 2 minutes, then stir in the stock and drained beans.
Season to taste, bring to the boil, cover and simmer for 1 hour,
stirring occasionally. Sift the self-raising flour with a pinch of salt and
pepper, add suet and parsley. Add enough cold water to bind and
form into 8 even-sized balls. Add to the stew, cover and cook for
15–20 minutes.

PORK CHOPS IN ORANGE PEPPER SAUCE
Serves 6

4 pork loin chops
salt and freshly ground black pepper
1 oz (25 g) sugar
1 oz (25 g) butter
1 garlic clove, chopped
1 oz (25 g) cornflour

½ tsp dried rosemary
3 tbsp lemon juice
3 tbsp orange juice
½ green pepper, deseeded and
  chopped
2 large oranges

Season both sides of the chops with salt, pepper and a little of the sugar. Melt the butter in a frying pan and brown the chops well on both sides with the garlic. Place to one side and discard the garlic. Add the rest of the sugar, cornflour and rosemary to the pan. Stir well and gradually add ½ pt (300 ml) water. Cook, stirring, until glossy. Add the juices and green pepper. Return the chops to the pan and place a thick orange slice on each one. Cover and simmer gently for 40 minutes until tender. Baste occasionally and uncover for the last 10 minutes. Serve garnished with half slices of orange.

PORK À L'ORANGE
Serves 8

3 lb (1.4 kg) loin of pork, boned and
  skinned (keep bones and skin)
salt and freshly ground black pepper
2 small garlic cloves, finely chopped
2 tbsp chopped fresh parsley
1 tsp chopped fresh marjoram
  or ½ tsp dried watercress

2 tbsp oil
7 fl oz (200 ml) chicken stock
juice of 1 large orange
3–4 tbsp Cointreau or Grand Marnier
1 tbsp French mustard
3 tbsp dry white breadcrumbs

Preheat the oven to 325°F/170°C/Gas Mk 3. Lay the loin out flat and sprinkle the inside with salt, pepper, garlic, parsley and marjoram. Roll up and tie with string. Heat the oil in a flameproof casserole and brown the roll all over. Put the skin and bones in the base of the casserole. Add the stock, cover and cook in the oven for 1¼ hours. Pour the orange juice and liqueur over the meat and spread with mustard. Sprinkle with the breadcrumbs and sugar. Return to the oven and cook, uncovered, for 20 minutes or until the juices run clear and the topping is golden brown and crisp. Lift onto a hot serving platter, remove the string and keep warm. Pour off excess fat from the pan and add the orange segments. Heat gently for 3 minutes, lift out with a slotted spoon and arrange around the meat. Garnish with watercress. Serve the gravy separately.

LOIN OF PORK FRUIT BRAISE
Serves 6

16 dried stoned prunes
16 dried apricot halves
½ tsp mixed spice
juice and grated rind of
  ½ orange and ½ lemon
1 pt (600 ml) dry white wine
5 lb (2.3 kg) loin of pork
  (boned weight), rolled and tied

salt and freshly ground black pepper
1 tbsp chopped fresh sage
1 oz (25 g) butter
1 tbsp soft light brown sugar
1 garlic clove, finely chopped
2 cooking apples, sliced
2 tsp cornflour

Place the prunes and apricots in a mixing bowl. Add the spice, orange juice and rind, lemon juice and rind and half the wine. Cover and leave to soak overnight. Rub the pork with salt and pepper and sage. Melt the butter in a flameproof casserole. Add the pork and brown on all sides. Pour in the soaked fruit mixture. Sprinkle over the sugar and garlic and add the remaining wine except for 1 tbsp. Bring to the boil, cover and simmer for 2 hours. Skim off surface fat, add the apple slices, cover and cook for a further 20 minutes. Transfer the meat to a carving board, cut into thick slices and arrange on a warmed serving dish. Keep hot. Mix the cornflour with the reserved wine, stir in a little of the hot liquid from the casserole, mix, then pour back into the casserole and simmer, stirring, for about 5 minutes. Pour the mixture over the meat.

LEMON ROAST PORK
Serves 4

1 tbsp finely chopped fresh oregano
salt and freshly ground black pepper
1½ lb (675 g) boned pork loin,
  trimmed, rolled and tied,
1 tbsp olive oil

2 garlic cloves, finely chopped
8 oz (225 g) can tomatoes
¼ pt (150 ml) red wine
2 tbsp lemon juice

Preheat the oven to 400°F/200°C/Gas Mk 6. Rub the oregano, salt and some pepper into the surface of the pork. Heat the oil in a large shallow flameproof dish or frying pan and put in the pork. Sear on all sides over high heat. Add the garlic, fry for a few seconds, then add the tomatoes, wine and lemon juice. Bake, uncovered, for 1 hour, turning and basting from time to time. Make sure the tomato mixture does not burn by adding water if necessary. Place on a large serving dish and coat with the tomato sauce.

PORK AU GRATIN
Serves 4

1 lb (450 g) potatoes, thinly sliced
8 oz (225 g) onions, thinly sliced
12 oz (350 g) fresh herring fillets
8 oz (225 g) pork fillet or loin,
  trimmed and thinly sliced

salt and freshly ground black pepper
¼ pt (150 ml) skimmed milk
1 egg yolk
4 oz (110 g) soured cream

Preheat the oven to 350°F/180°C/Gas Mk 4. Grease a large ovenproof gratin dish. Place the potatoes, onions, herring fillets and pork slices in layers in the dish beginning and ending with potatoes. Season each layer with salt and pepper to taste. Pour over the milk and bake for 15 minutes. Reduce the temperature to 375°F/190°C/Gas Mk 5 and cook for 1 hour until all the contents are soft. Remove from the oven and carefully drain out all the juice into a bowl. In another bowl, beat together the egg yolk and the soured cream then add 2–3 tbsp of the hot cooking juice. Whisk and add to the remaining hot juice, then add the liquid to the gratin dish. Return to the oven for 15 minutes. Cut in slices and serve hot.

GOULASH SUPREME
Serves 4

1 tbsp olive oil
1 lb (450 g) diced pork
1 small onion, chopped
2 garlic cloves, crushed
2 carrots, cut into chunks
1 lb (450 g) potatoes, cut into chunks
½ red pepper, deseeded and cut
  into strips

4 tsp paprika
14 oz (400 g) can chopped tomatoes
¼ pt (150 ml) chicken stock
½ tsp caraway seeds
salt and freshly ground black pepper
yoghurt and caraway seeds, to garnish

Heat the oil and fry the pork over a high heat until evenly browned. Sauté the onion and garlic until soft. Add the carrots, potatoes, and red pepper and cook for 2 minutes, stirring well. Add the paprika and cook for 1 minute. Add the tomatoes, stock, caraway seeds and season well. Bring to the boil, cover and simmer for 35 minutes, stirring occasionally, until the pork and vegetables are tender. Turn into a serving dish and put a tablespoon or two of the yoghurt on the top; scatter caraway seeds over. Serve the remaining yoghurt separately. Accompany with boiled rice and cabbage.

PORK ESPAGNOLE
Serves 4

2 tbsp olive oil
1 onion, sliced
2 garlic cloves, crushed
1 green pepper, deseeded and chopped
18 oz (500 g) pork tenderloin, cubed
1 tbsp plain flour
¼ tsp cayenne pepper
14 oz (400 g) can chopped tomatoes

7 oz (200g) can pimientos,
  drained and sliced
7 fl oz (200 ml) red wine
3 oz (75 g) stuffed green olives, halved
1 tsp dried marjoram
2 bay leaves
salt and freshly ground black pepper
bay leaves, to garnish

Heat the oil and fry the onion, garlic and green pepper for 5 minutes. Add the pork and fry until browned on all sides. Sprinkle in the flour and cayenne pepper and stir well for 1 minute. Add the tomatoes and pimientos, then stir in the wine. Add the olives, marjoram and bay leaves to the pan. Season well. Bring to the boil, cover and simmer gently for 40 minutes or until the pork is tender. Serve with rice.

PORK AND BEAN CASSEROLE
Serves 6

2 lb (900 g) lean boneless
  shoulder of pork
1½ oz (35 g) plain flour
1 tsp curry powder
salt and freshly ground black pepper
2 tbsp oil

1 large onion, thinly sliced
2 tbsp black treacle
14 oz (400 g) can tomatoes
1 bay leaf
10–12 oz (300–350 g) canned
  butter beans, drained

Preheat the oven to 325°F/170°C/Gas Mk 3. Cut the pork into cubes, removing excess fat. Mix the flour, curry powder and plenty of salt and pepper together in a bowl and toss the pork cubes a few at a time until evenly coated. Heat the oil in a deep flameproof casserole and fry the onion gently for 5 minutes. Raise the heat, add the pork and stir for 2 minutes until the oil has been absorbed and the meat is browning. Dissolve the treacle in ¼ pt (150 ml) boiling water and pour into the casserole with the tomatoes, their juice and the bay leaf. Bring to the boil, cover tightly and immediately transfer to the oven for 1½ hours or until the meat is tender. Stir in the beans, cover and cook for another 30 minutes. Check the seasoning and serve with rice or noodles.

NORMANDY PORK
Serves 4

2½ oz (60 g) butter
1 large onion, finely chopped
4 oz (110 g) pork sausage meat
1 small apple, finely chopped
2 oz (50 g) fresh breadcrumbs
1 tbsp chopped fresh parsley

1 tsp chopped fresh sage
1 egg, lightly beaten
salt and freshly ground black pepper
8 pork escalopes
½ pt (300 ml) cider
2 tbsp plain flour

Preheat the oven to 350°F/180°C/Gas Mk 4. Melt 1 oz (25 g) of the butter in a frying pan. Fry the onion until soft, then transfer to a mixing bowl. Add the sausage meat, apple, breadcrumbs, parsley, sage, egg and seasoning; mix well. Lay the pork escalopes flat and spoon sausage meat mixture onto each one. Roll up and tie with string. Melt 1 oz (25 g) of the remaining butter in the frying pan, add the pork rolls and cook until browned on all sides. Transfer to a flameproof casserole and pour over the cider. Cover and bake for 1 hour or until tender. Transfer to a serving dish, removing string, and keep hot. Put the casserole on top of the cooker and bring the cooking liquid quickly to the boil. Mix the flour and remaining butter to a smooth paste and add in small quantities; simmer, stirring all the time until thickened and smooth. Pour the sauce over the pork rolls and serve.

LEMONY PORK STEAKS
Serves 4

¼ pt (150 ml) dry white wine
2 tbsp oil
2 tbsp soy sauce
2 tbsp lemon juice
1 garlic clove, crushed
salt and freshly ground black pepper

4 x 6 oz (175 g) pork steaks
2 bay leaves
2 tsp cornflour
grated rind and juice of 1 lemon
2 tbsp snipped fresh chives
¼ pt (150 ml) fromage frais

Whisk together the wine, oil, soy sauce, lemon juice and garlic; season well. Lay the pork steaks in a shallow dish and place bay leaves over the top. Pour over the marinade, cover and leave in the refrigerator overnight or for at least 4 hours. Turn the steaks over a couple of times. Line a grill pan with foil and preheat the grill. Remove the steaks from the marinade and lay on the foil. Cook for about 8 minutes on each side, brushing with the marinade four times during the cooking time. Mix the cornflour to a smooth paste with the lemon juice, then stir in the lemon rind, chives, fromage frais and seasoning. Put in a saucepan over a gentle heat and stir until thickened. Pour into a sauceboat and serve with the pork steaks.

PORK WITH MUSTARD AND TARRAGON
Serves 4

1 oz (25 g) butter
4 oz (110 g) onion, sliced
2 garlic cloves, crushed
1 tsp dried tarragon
4 boneless pork loin steaks
1½ oz (35 g) plain flour

2 tsp wholegrain mustard
2 tsp wine vinegar
½ pt (300 ml) vegetable stock
salt and freshly ground black pepper
6 tbsp single cream
tarragon sprigs, to garnish

Preheat the oven to 350°F/180°C/Gas Mk 4. Heat the butter and fry the onion and garlic gently for 5 minutes. Add the tarragon and pork and fry gently for 20 minutes, turning once. Put in a shallow oven-proof dish. Add the flour to the pan and cook, stirring, for 1 minute. Stir in the mustard and vinegar. Remove from the heat and gradually stir in the stock. Return to the heat and cook until the sauce is thick, stirring from time to time. Season to taste and stir in 4 tbsp of the cream. Pour over the pork, cover and bake for 40–50 minutes or until tender. Stir in the remaining cream and garnish with tarragon. Serve with rice and a side salad.

PORK ESCALOPES MIMOSA
Serves 4

18 oz (500g) pork tenderloin, cut into
* ½ in (1 cm) slices*
seasoned flour
1 large egg, beaten with 2 tsp water
3 oz (75 g) dry white breadcrumbs
1 tbsp oil
1 oz (25 g) butter

1 large lemon cut into 8 wedges
trimmed flat-leafed parsley
Mimosa garnish:
1 large hard-boiled egg yolk,
* sieved and white finely chopped*
1 tsp finely grated lemon zest
1 tbsp finely chopped chives

Lay each slice of meat between damp greaseproof paper and beat gently with a rolling pin. Dust with seasoned flour, then dip in the egg and roll in the breadcrumbs until evenly coated. Lay the slices on greaseproof paper and press the coating with a palette knife. Leave in a cold place, covered, for 30 minutes for the coating to firm up. Heat the oil and butter in a large frying pan. When sizzling, fry the escalopes for 3–4 minutes on each side, until cooked and golden brown. Lift out, drain on absorbent paper and keep warm while cooking the remainder. Meanwhile combine the egg yolk, lemon zest and chives. Arrange the escalopes on a warmed serving dish and sprinkle with the garnish. Place lemon wedges in the centre and sprinkle with parsley.

PORK AND PINEAPPLE
Serves 4

2 tbsp oil
1½ lb (675 g) spare rib pork
  chops, trimmed
2 medium onions, chopped
1 garlic clove, crushed
3 celery stalks, sliced
4 oz (110 g) button mushrooms,
  quartered

1 oz (25 g) plain flour
1 pt (600 ml) chicken stock
7 oz (200 ml) can pineapple pieces
1 tbsp tomato purée
1 bay leaf
½ tsp mixed dried herbs
salt and freshly ground black pepper

Heat the oil and fry the chops until golden brown all over. Remove and keep warm. Add the onions, garlic, celery and mushrooms and cook gently for 3 minutes. Stir in the flour and cook for 1 minute. Gradually add the stock, stirring constantly to avoid lumps forming. Add the pineapple and juice with the tomato purée. Stir well. Return the meat to the pan together with the bay leaf and herbs and season to taste. Bring to the boil, cover and simmer gently for 1½ hours or until the pork is tender. Serve with rice or noodles.

PORK FILLETS WITH RED WINE
Serves 6

4 tbsp olive oil
4 oz (110 g) butter
3 lb (1.4 kg) pork fillets,
  cut into thick slices
2 large onions, chopped

salt and freshly ground black pepper
12 fl oz (350 ml) dry red wine
10 oz (300 g) mushrooms, sliced
2 tbsp plain flour
12 fl oz (350 ml) double cream

Preheat the oven to 350°F/180°C/Gas Mk 4. Heat the oil and half the butter in a frying pan and fry the pork slices on both sides to seal and brown. Transfer to a casserole. Add the onions to the frying pan and sauté until soft but not brown. Place on top of the pork, season to taste and pour over the red wine. Put the lid on the casserole and cook for 1–1½ hours or until the pork is tender. Melt the remaining butter in a frying pan and cook the mushrooms for 4 minutes. Add to the casserole and cook for another 10 minutes. Remove the pork slices and keep hot. Gradually mix together the flour and cream to form a smooth paste. Stir in a little of the hot cooking liquid, place the casserole over a low heat and stir in the cream mixture a little at a time until the sauce has thickened. Return the pork slices to the casserole and serve.

PORK AND KIDNEY BAKE
Serves 6

2–3 tsp oil
1½ lb (675 g) onions, thickly sliced
1 lb (450 g) lean pork, cut
  into ½ in (1 cm) strips
4 lamb kidneys, quartered
  and trimmed

2 lb (900 g) potatoes, thinly sliced
¼ pt (150 ml) lager
½ pt (300 ml) stock
½ tsp salt
freshly ground black pepper

Heat the oil in a large frying pan. Fry the onions until lightly browned, stirring frequently. Remove and set aside. Add the pork strips, a few at a time, and fry until well browned. Set aside with the onions. Add the kidney and sear until sealed on all sides. Preheat the oven to 375°F/190°C/Gas Mk 5. In a deep ovenproof dish, place one-third of the onions, a third of the potatoes, all the kidney, another third of the onions, another third of the potatoes, then the pork and a final layer of onions and potatoes. Pour the lager into the frying pan and boil rapidly until almost completely reduced. Stir in the stock, salt and pepper and bring back to the boil. Pour into the dish. Cover with foil and cook in the oven for 2 hours, removing the foil after the first hour to brown the top.

KNACKWURST AND LENTIL CASSEROLE
Serves 6

1 lb (450 g) red lentils
2 pts (1.2 litres) beef or ham stock
1 large onion
bouquet garni
1 oz (25 g) unsalted butter
6 bacon rashers, chopped

2 garlic cloves, chopped
6 knackwurst (German pork sausages),
  cut into 1 in (2.5 cm) thick slices
freshly ground black pepper
4 oz (110 g) Cheddar cheese, grated

Put the lentils, stock, whole onion and bouquet garni in a saucepan. Bring to the boil and simmer for 1 hour or until the lentils are tender. Drain, reserving the cooking liquid. Discard the onion and bouquet garni. Preheat the oven to 350°F/180°C/Gas Mk 4. Melt the butter in a frying pan. Fry the bacon and garlic until the bacon is lightly browned. Add the knackwurst and fry for 5 minutes. Remove from the heat and drain on absorbent paper. Cover the bottom of a baking dish with half the lentils. Add the knackwurst and bacon, sprinkle with pepper and top with the remaining lentils. Pour in the reserved lentil cooking liquid. Sprinkle the cheese on top and bake for 45 minutes or until the cheese is golden brown.

PORK CHOPS IN ORANGE JUICE
Serves 4

2 tbsp plain flour
½ tsp mixed spice
salt and freshly ground black pepper
4 loin pork chops, trimmed
   of rind and fat
½ oz (10 g) butter
2 tbsp oil

1 medium onion, chopped
6 fl oz (180 ml) can frozen
   concentrated orange juice
1 bay leaf
Tabasco sauce
2–3 tbsp shredded orange rind to garnish

Place the flour in a bowl. Add the spice and seasoning. Dip in the chops and coat evenly on both sides. Melt the butter with the oil in a large flameproof casserole. Add the chops and fry over moderate heat until browned on all sides. Remove with a slotted spoon and drain on absorbent paper. Add the onion to the casserole with any flour remaining from the chops and fry gently for 5 minutes until onion is soft but not coloured. Dilute the orange juice with 7 fl oz (200 ml) water and stir into the casserole. Return the chops to the casserole and bring slowly to boiling point. Add the bay leaf and Tabasco sauce to taste. Cover and simmer for 45 minutes until the chops are tender, basting occasionally. A few minutes before the end blanch the orange rind for 1 minute in boiling water. Drain, rinse under cold running water, then dry on absorbent paper. Transfer the chops to a warmed serving dish; check the seasoning of the orange sauce. Pour the sauce over the chops and sprinkle with the blanched orange rind.

TURKISH PORK

Serves 5

2½ lb (1.1 kg) lean blade
   of pork, boned
salt and freshly ground black pepper
oil

1 tbsp plain flour
¼ pt (150 ml) chicken stock
¼ pt (150 ml) dry white wine

Stuffing:
2 oz (50 g) dried apricots, soaked
   overnight, drained and chopped
1 large cooking apple, chopped
1 heaped tbsp sultanas

1½ oz (35 g) fresh white breadcrumbs
juice and finely grated zest of ½ lemon
salt and freshly ground black pepper
1 small egg, beaten

Preheat the oven to 325°F/170°C/Gas Mk 3. Mix all the stuffing ingredients together. Cut a deep pocket horizontally through the blade of pork. Fill with the stuffing and secure with skewers or sew together with thick cotton. Cut slashes in the rind and dust the joint with salt and pepper. Rub thoroughly with oil. Place on a rack in a roasting tin, rind uppermost and roast for 2 hours or until the juices run clear and the meat is tender. Place on a hot serving dish, remove the skewers or cotton and keep warm. Pour off surplus fat from the roasting tin, add the flour and cook for 1 minute, stirring. Stir in the stock and white wine and bring to the boil. Simmer for 5 minutes and season to taste. Pour into a gravy boat and serve separately.

FRUITY PORK FILLETS
Serves 6

8 oz (225 g) packet dried fruit salad, chopped
½ pt (300 ml) medium white wine
½ pt (300 ml) apple or pear juice
4–6 tbsp oil
1 medium onion, finely chopped
2 oz (50 g) chopped walnuts
salt and freshly ground black pepper
2 pork fillets
¼ tsp turmeric
¼ tsp chilli seasoning

Preheat the oven to 375°F/190°C/Gas Mk 5. Place the dried fruit in a bowl with the wine and fruit juice. Cover and marinate overnight or for at least 6 hours. Heat 2–3 tbsp of the oil and sauté the onion gently for 5 minutes. Put the marinated fruit into a sieve and drain, reserving the juice. Mix the fruit with the onion and walnuts; season to taste. Wet the fillets, slice each along its length, not quite through, and open out. Wrap each piece in cling film and flatten slightly with a rolling pin. Spoon the filling mixture down the middle of one and bring the side together to enclose it. Tie with string. Heat the remaining oil in a roasting tin and brown the fillets all over. Pour over the marinade, mixed with the turmeric and chilli seasoning. Place any leftover filling around the fillets and bake for 30 minutes, basting occasionally. Transfer to a serving dish and keep warm. Scrape the bottom of the roasting pan and add a little water. Season to taste and boil to reduce. Strain into a warmed sauceboat. Slice the meat thickly and ladle over a little of the sauce.

PORK AND PINEAPPLE LOAF
Serves 6

3lb (1.4 kg) belly pork
small can pineapple rings in syrup
2 oz (50 g) breadcrumbs
1 oz (25 g) butter
1 small onion, finely chopped
½ tsp dried sage
pinch dried thyme
a little grated lemon rind
1 egg, beaten with 3 tbsp milk
butter and dry breadcrumbs for coating tin

Sauce:
1 oz (25 g) margarine
1 oz (25 g) plain flour
½ pt (300 ml) chicken stock
salt and freshly ground black pepper

Preheat the oven to 350°F/180°C/Gas Mk 4. Mince the pork finely and mix with two finely chopped pineapple rings and the breadcrumbs. Heat the butter and fry the onion until soft but not brown. Add to the mix with the herbs and grated lemon rind. Stir in enough beaten egg to make a fairly firm mixture. Butter and breadcrumb a loaf tin, spoon in the mince mixture and level the top. Cover with foil and bake for 1½ hours in the centre of the oven. Make the sauce: heat the margarine in a small pan, stir in the flour and cook for a few minutes until it starts to colour. Add enough stock to the pineapple syrup to make ½ pt (300 ml) and gently stir into the flour mix. Bring to the boil, stirring, until smooth. Add seasoning to taste and small chunks of pineapple. Turn the pork loaf onto a warmed serving dish and serve with the sauce.

HAM AND BACON

TATWS RHOST (WELSH HOT POT)
Serves 4

1½ lb (675 g) potatoes, peeled and thickly sliced
1 lb (450 g) thickly sliced smoked bacon, derinded
4 tbsp chopped fresh parsley
3 large onions, thinly sliced
salt and freshly ground black pepper
2 tbsp plain flour
½ pt (300 ml) stock or cider

Preheat the oven to 275°F/140°C/Gas Mk 1. Butter a deep casserole and fill with layers of potato, bacon, parsley and onion, seasoning in between each layer and sprinkling very lightly with flour. Finish with a layer of potato. Pour over the stock, cover with buttered foil and then the lid and bake for about 2 hours. Uncover for the last 30 minutes to allow the top to brown.

HAM COOKED IN BEER
Serves 10–15

10 lb (4.5 kg) ham, soaked overnight
1 pt (600 ml) light beer
1 pt (600 ml) dark beer
6 oz (175 g) soft light brown sugar
½ oz (10 g) butter
2 tbsp plain flour

Preheat the oven to 180°C/350°F/Gas Mk 4. Bring the beers and sugar to the boil in a roasting tin, stirring to dissolve the sugar. Remove from the heat. Drain the ham and peel the skin and excess fat; place it in the roasting tin. Baste with the beer mixture. Bake for 2 hours, then transfer to a warmed serving dish and keep hot. Strain the cooking liquid into a saucepan. Mix the butter with the flour to make a paste. Add in small pieces to the cooking liquid, stirring, and bring to the boil. Simmer, stirring, until thickened and smooth. Pour into a warmed sauceboat and serve with the ham.

BACON CHOPS IN GOOSEBERRY SAUCE
Serves 4

1 tbsp soft light brown sugar
1 tsp mustard powder
freshly ground black pepper
4 x 6 oz (175 g) bacon chops
½ oz (10 g) butter

1 large onion, chopped
¼ pt (150 ml) vegetable stock
4 oz (110 g) gooseberries,
   topped and tailed

Mix together the sugar, mustard and pepper. Rub into each side of the
bacon chops. Heat the butter in a large frying pan, and cook the
onion for 2 minutes. Add the chops, half the stock and the
gooseberries. Simmer gently for 15 minutes. Using a slotted spoon,
remove the chops from the pan. Pour the onions and gooseberries
into a liquidiser and purée well. Return the chops and purée mixture
to the pan and add the remaining stock. Cook over a low heat for
10 minutes until the meat is tender.

SOMERSET BACON CHOP
Serves 1

1 tbsp olive oil
1 tbsp granulated sugar
6 oz (175 g) bacon chop,
   rind removed

1 medium cooking apple, quartered
2 tbsp tomato ketchup

Heat the oil in a frying pan, sprinkle in the sugar and heat until
dissolved and golden brown. Add the bacon chop and cook for
1–2 minutes on each side until browned. Remove from the pan. Cut
each apple quarter in half again, then add to the caramel remaining in
the pan. Cook over high heat for 1 minute, turning the slices until
browned. Add the tomato ketchup and 6 tbsp water to the pan. Bring
to the boil, stirring. Put the chop back, cover tightly and cook gently
for 5 minutes until cooked through.

EGG AND BACON PIE
Serves 4

6 oz (175 g) back rashers bacon,
   derinded and chopped
2 oz (50 g) margarine
3 oz (75 g) breadcrumbs
8 oz (225 g) cooked carrots, sliced

2 hard-boiled eggs, sliced
¼ pt (150 ml) stock
freshly ground black pepper
2–3 tomatoes, skinned

Preheat the oven to 400°F/200°C/Gas Mk 6. Gently dry fry the bacon pieces, then drain on absorbent paper. Melt the margarine in the pan and toss the breadcrumbs in it. Grease a pie dish, and fill with the bacon, carrots and eggs in layers. Pour in the stock, season with pepper and cover with the breadcrumbs. Bake, uncovered, for 20 minutes. Lay the sliced tomatoes over the top for the last 5 minutes. As an alternative a layer of shortcrust or puff pastry can be used to top the pie dish.

HAM AND BROAD BEAN SAVOURY
Serves 4

1½ lb (675 g) shelled broad beans
1 tsp olive oil
8 oz (225 g) lean ham, diced
1 tbsp plain flour

4 tbsp dry white wine
freshly ground black pepper
2 tbsp single cream

Boil a saucepan of water, add the beans and simmer for about 5 minutes until soft. Strain, reserving the cooking liquid, and set aside. Heat the oil in a large heavy saucepan, add the ham and fry for 1 minute. Stir in the flour and cook for a further minute stirring constantly. Add the wine and ¼ pt (150 ml) of the reserved bean liquid. Simmer for 2 minutes, adding more liquid if the sauce is too thick. Season with pepper to taste. Stir in the cream and allow the liquid to bubble once. Stir in the beans and warm through.

BOMBAY BACON
Serves 2

1 oz (25 g) lard
1 lb (450 g) bacon joint,
    thawed if frozen, cubed
1 medium onion, sliced
1 tbsp plain flour

1 tbsp curry powder
pinch garam masala
1 apple, peeled and chopped
1 oz (25 g) sultanas
1 tbsp mango chutney

Heat the lard and brown the cubes of bacon lightly; remove and keep warm. Sauté the onion until golden. Stir in the flour, curry powder and garam masala; cook for 1 minute. Gradually stir in about ¾ pt (450 ml) water until a smooth sauce is obtained, then add the bacon and remaining ingredients. Bring to the boil, cover and simmer gently for 1 hour or until the bacon is cooked and tender. Serve with rice.

STEWED KNUCKLE OF HAM WITH VEGETABLES
Serves 4

2 lb (900 g) ham knuckle
bouquet garni
8 small carrots
8 small turnips
5 leeks, sliced
14 oz (400 g) can black-eyed or haricot beans
freshly ground black pepper
chopped fresh parsley

If the ham is likely to be salty, soak in cold water for an hour. Place in a large pan and cover with water. Bring to the boil and simmer for 10 minutes. Discard the water and refill with cold water. Return to the boil and remove any scum which may appear on the surface. Add the bouquet garni, cover and simmer for 1 hour. Add the carrots and turnips, whole if very small, cut in half if larger. Simmer for 15 minutes and then add the leeks, beans and pepper and cook for another 15 minutes or until the bacon joint is tender and cooked through. Sprinkle with parsley to serve.

WHOLE BAKED GAMMON
Serves 30

16 lb (7.2 kg) whole gammon
1 tbsp French mustard
2 tbsp dark marmalade or redcurrant jelly
24 cloves

Soak the gammon in cold water for 2 days, changing the water each day. Preheat the oven to 350°F/180°C/Gas Mk 4. Check the weight of the gammon and calculate the cooking time at 15 minutes per 1 lb (30 minutes per kg) plus an extra 15 minutes. Wrap in aluminium foil and bake in a roasting tin for the calculated time. About 15–20 minutes before the end remove from the oven and open up the foil. Increase the temperature to 425°F/220°C/Gas Mk 7. Strip the rind from the gammon with a sharp knife and score the fat in a criss-cross pattern. Smear the fat with the mustard and then with the marmalade (removing any orange peel) or redcurrant jelly. Push the cloves into the fat distributing them evenly. Return the uncovered joint to the oven to finish cooking. Leave until completely cool; about 12 hours.

DEVONSHIRE SQUAB PIE
Serves 4

6 oz (175 g) shortcrust pastry
10 oz (300 g) smoked bacon rashers, diced
1 lb (450 g) stewing lamb or pork, trimmed of fat and cut into small cubes
8 oz (225 g) cooking apples, sliced
3 oz (75 g) onion, sliced
salt and freshly ground black pepper

Make the pastry in the usual way. Preheat the oven to 450°F/230°C/
Gas Mk 8. Put a layer of bacon in a pie dish, then a layer of onions, a
layer of meat and finally apple. Season well with salt and pepper and
repeat the layers until all is used. Add cold water to come half way up
the dish. Cover with a pastry lid and cut a hole in the centre. Bake for
15 minutes to set the pastry, then reduce the heat to 350°F/180°C/
Gas Mk 4 for the remainder of the time; about 1¼ hours. Cover pastry
with foil to prevent it becoming too brown.

BACON AND POTATO CAKE
Serves 4–6

2 tbsp olive oil
4 rashers smoked bacon, derinded and chopped
1 bunch spring onions, trimmed and finely chopped
1½ lb (675 g) potatoes, thinly sliced
salt and freshly ground black pepper
2 eggs, beaten with 4 tbsp milk
2 tsp chopped chives, to garnish

Heat the oil in a frying pan and fry the bacon until just cooked.
Remove and mix with the chopped spring onions. Line the bottom of
the pan with a layer of overlapping potato slices. Put a layer of bacon
and onions on top, then follow with another layer of potato and
continue until all the ingredients have been used, finishing with
potatoes. Cover the pan with a sheet of lightly buttered foil and put a
plate on top to weigh it down. Cook over a gentle heat for
15 minutes, then remove the foil. Season the egg mixture and slowly
pour over the potato cake. Cover as before and weigh down. Cook
for 15 minutes. Remove the foil and place under a hot grill for about
5 minutes to brown the top. Sprinkle with chopped chives and serve
from the pan.

ROSTI WITH PEPPERS AND BACON
Serves 4

12 oz (350 g) unsmoked streaky bacon
½ oz (10 g) butter
1–2 tbsp olive oil
1 red, 1 green and 1 yellow pepper, deseeded and diced
1 lb (450 g) potatoes, peeled and coarsely grated
½ tsp ground coriander
salt and freshly ground black pepper

Grill the bacon and snip into small pieces. Heat the butter and 1 tbsp oil in a large heavy-based frying pan. Mix together the peppers, potatoes, coriander and seasoning. Press into the pan in an even layer. Cook over a gentle heat for 20 minutes, shaking the pan occasionally to prevent the mixture from sticking. Invert a plate over the pan and turn it over so that the rosti falls onto the plate. Add more oil if needed and slide the rosti back into the pan, uncooked side down. Cook for 15–20 minutes. Serve warm with a green salad.

FIDGET PIE
Serves 4

1½ oz (35 g) butter
8 oz (225 g) onions, chopped
1 lb (450 g) bacon joint, thawed if frozen, cubed
1 tbsp plain flour
¼ pt (150 ml) cider
¼ pt (150 ml) single cream
2 medium apples, thickly sliced
freshly ground black pepper
8 oz (225 g) shortcrust pastry
beaten egg

Preheat the oven to 375°F/190°C/Gas Mk 5. Heat the butter and sauté the onion until soft, then add the bacon and stir in the flour. Cook for 1 minute, stirring. Gradually add the cider, stirring until well mixed in and smooth. Bring to the boil, cover and simmer for 30 minutes. Stir in the cream, apple and pepper to taste. Pour into a 1½ pt (900 ml) pie dish. Roll out the pastry and cut a lid to fit the dish. Brush with the beaten egg and bake for 45 minutes or until the pastry is cooked and golden brown.

HAM FLORENTINE
Serves 2

4 oz (110 g) packet frozen spinach, thawed
1 tsp made English mustard
½ oz (10 g) butter
salt and freshly ground black pepper
2 slices ham, each 3–4 oz (75–110 g)
2 tbsp milk
5½ oz (160 g) can condensed celery soup
2 tbsp grated Cheddar cheese

Preheat the oven to 350°F/180°C/Gas Mk 4. Cook the spinach according to the packet instructions and drain well. Beat the mustard and butter together and then beat into the spinach; season to taste. Halve the spinach mixture and spread one half on each ham slice, roll up and transfer to a shallow ovenproof dish. Mix the milk with the celery soup and pour over the ham rolls. Cover and bake for 15 minutes. Remove the lid, sprinkle with the grated cheese and bake for another 15 minutes or until the cheese is golden.

HAM CANNELLONI
Serves 4

½ pt (300 ml) pancake batter
1 oz (25 g) butter
1 tbsp oil
1 large onion, chopped
2 garlic cloves, crushed
1 green pepper, deseeded and chopped
4 tomatoes, chopped
8 slices ham
4 oz (110 g) Gruyére cheese
¼ pt (150 ml) single cream
freshly ground black pepper

Preheat the oven to 400°F/200°C/Gas Mk 6. Make the batter and cook eight pancakes. Heat the butter and oil and sauté the onion and garlic until soft. Add the green pepper and tomatoes and cook gently for 5 minutes. Place one slice of ham on each pancake. Add a little of the onion mixture and roll up. Place the pancakes in a shallow ovenproof dish and sprinkle with half the cheese. Pour over the cream and sprinkle with the remaining cheese and pepper to taste. Bake for 15 minutes and serve with a green salad.

GINGERED APRICOT CHOPS
Serves 2

1 tbsp plain flour
1 tsp ginger
salt and freshly ground black pepper
2 pork chops
1 tbsp oil
7 oz (200 g) can apricot halves
1 tbsp soy sauce
2 tsp vinegar

Mix the flour, ginger, salt and pepper together in a shallow dish and press the pork chops into it to cover both sides. Heat the oil and fry the chops for 3–4 minutes on each side until golden. Remove from the pan and keep hot. Sprinkle any remaining flour into the pan juices and gradually stir in the juice from the apricots, soy sauce and vinegar. Bring to the boil, stirring, then add the apricot halves with the chops and simmer for about 10 minutes or until the meat is cooked. Serve with plain boiled rice.

BACON SURPRISE
Serves 6

2–3 tbsp oil
2 lb (900 g) pork sausages
1 large onion, chopped
1 lb (450 g) bacon, diced
1 beef stock cube

15 oz (425 g) can baked beans
2 x 14 oz (400 g) cans tomatoes
salt and freshly ground black pepper
4 large potatoes, thinly sliced
1 oz (25 g) butter

Topping:
½ pt (300 ml) yoghurt
1 egg
chopped fresh parsley, to garnish

Preheat the oven to 350°F/180°C/Gas Mk 4. Heat the oil in a large frying pan and fry the sausages until brown all over. Remove from the pan, add the onion and bacon and cook gently for 5 minutes. Crumble in the beef stock cube and stir until mixed. Arrange in layers in an ovenproof dish with the sausages, beans and tomatoes. Season to taste. Put a layer of potato slices on top and dot with butter. Bake for 1 hour. Mix the yoghurt and egg; pour over the dish. Return to the oven for 20 minutes or until the top is set and golden.

POULTRY

LEMON AND LIME CHICKEN
Serves 6

6 chicken breasts
salt and freshly ground black pepper
lemon and lime wedges, to garnish

Sauce:
4 fl oz (125 ml) oil
4 fl oz (125 ml) fresh lime and lemon juice
1 onion, finely chopped
2 tsp dried tarragon
1 tsp salt
½ tsp Tabasco sauce

Mix together all the sauce ingredients and marinade the chicken for about 2 hours or overnight if you like a stronger flavour. Lightly oil a sheet of foil and place the chicken on it. Turn up the edges to catch the juices. Sprinkle with salt and pepper and brush with the sauce. Grill, skin side up, for 8 minutes to brown. Turn, baste again, then reduce the heat and cook for about another 5 minutes or until the skin is golden and crackling. Garnish with wedges of lemon and lime and serve with boiled rice and a green salad.

TURKEY FILLETS LIMONE
Serves 4

4 turkey escalopes
salt and freshly ground black pepper
3 oz (75 g) butter
2 onions, finely chopped
4 oz (110 g) button mushrooms, sliced

1½ oz (40 g) plain flour
¾ pt (450 ml) chicken stock
grated rind and juice of 1 lemon
2 tbsp fresh parsley, chopped
4 tbsp double cream

Season the turkey escalopes with salt and pepper. Heat the butter in a frying pan, and cook the onions until soft. Add the turkey and gently brown on both sides, then remove and set aside. Add the mushrooms to the pan and cook for 2 minutes. Stir in the flour and cook for 1 minute. Pour in the stock, stir in the lemon rind and juice and bring to the boil. Add the parsley and turkey and lower the heat. Cover and simmer for 30 minutes, stirring occasionally. Add more salt and pepper if required, then mix in the cream before serving.

MEDITERRANEAN CHICKEN
Serves 6

1 oz (25 g) butter
3 tbsp oil
6 chicken pieces
2 tsp tomato purée
4 tsp plain flour

3 tbsp Madeira or sherry
8 fl oz (250 ml) stock
1 tsp fresh tarragon
1 sprig fresh parsley
salt and freshly ground black pepper

Sauce:
3 tbsp olive oil
1 garlic clove, chopped
4 mushrooms, sliced

½ red and ½ green pepper, diced
2 tomatoes, skinned, seeded and diced
rind from 1 orange, cut into thin strips

Heat the butter and oil in a large saucepan and sauté the chicken for about 4 minutes, turning half way through. Remove and keep warm. Stir in the tomato purée, flour, Madeira and stock. Bring to the boil, stirring continuously. Return the chicken to the pan with the tarragon, parsley and a little salt and pepper. Cover and simmer gently for about 35 minutes. Meanwhile prepare the sauce by heating the oil in a saucepan, and cook the garlic and mushrooms for 1–2 minutes. Add the peppers and finally the tomatoes, use any liquid left in the chicken pan. Cook for about 10 minutes, then add the orange rind. Spoon the sauce over the chicken pieces and serve.

CHICKEN WITH OLIVES
Serves 4

2 oz (50 g) butter
3 lb (1.4 kg) chicken, skinned
  and cut into small pieces
1 onion, chopped
1 garlic clove, crushed

1 pt (600 ml) chicken stock
1 fresh thyme sprig
salt and freshly ground black pepper
2 tsp arrowroot
5 oz (150 g) stuffed green olives

Melt the butter in a saucepan and fry the chicken pieces, onion, and garlic until the chicken is lightly browned. Stir in the stock and bring to the boil. Skim. Add the thyme and salt and pepper to taste. Cover and simmer for 1 hour. Transfer the chicken pieces to a warmed serving dish and keep hot. Dissolve the arrowroot in 1½ tbsp water and add to the saucepan. Simmer, stirring, until thickened. Stir in the olives and heat through. Taste and adjust the seasoning. Pour the sauce over the chicken pieces and serve.

SPICED COCONUT CHICKEN
Serves 6

2 tbsp grated onion
1 red or green chilli pepper, seeded
3 garlic cloves
1 tbsp peanut butter
2 tsp grated lemon rind
1 tsp freshly ground black pepper
1 tsp ground cumin
½ tsp ground ginger
3 oz (75 g) creamed coconut, dissolved in 12 fl oz (350 ml) hot water
3–4lb (1.4–1.8 kg) chicken
4 fl oz (125 ml) single cream

Blend the onion, chilli, garlic, peanut butter, lemon rind and spices. Gradually stir in the coconut milk. Put the chicken in a large saucepan, pour over the sauce and bring to the boil. Reduce the heat, cover and simmer for 1–1½ hours, depending on the weight of the chicken, until the chicken is tender. Remove the chicken, allow to stand, and carve. Stir the cream into the sauce, heat gently and pour over the chicken.

GINGER CHICKEN WITH VEGETABLES
Serves 4

3½ lb (1.6 kg) chicken, cut into 8 pieces
salt and freshly ground black pepper
2 tbsp soy sauce
1½ in (4 cm) piece fresh ginger root, peeled and grated
1 medium onion, finely chopped
3 tbsp oil
2 green peppers, chopped
9 oz (250 g) mushrooms, chopped

Season the chicken to taste with salt and pepper. Heat the oil in a large casserole and add the chicken pieces. Fry for about 10 minutes, sprinkling with soy sauce. Add the ginger, onion, peppers and mushrooms, and enough water to cover the chicken. Cook on low heat for approximately 30 minutes or until tender.

CHICKEN IN CELERY SAUCE
Serves 4

4 oz (110 g) butter
4 chicken portions
1 small head of celery, diced
1 oz (25 g) plain flour
¾ pt (450 ml) milk
¼ cucumber, sliced
1 tbsp capers
salt and freshly ground black pepper

Heat 3 oz (75 g) of the butter in a saucepan and gently fry the chicken until tender. Keep hot. Cook the celery in salted water until tender, then rub through a sieve or purée in a blender. Melt the remaining butter in a pan, stir in the flour and cook gently for 1 minute, stirring. Remove the pan from the heat and gradually stir in the milk. Bring to the boil, add the celery and continue to cook, stirring, for 5 minutes. Add the cucumber, capers and seasoning to taste. Put the chicken in a hot serving dish and pour the sauce over.

CHICKEN CHASSEUR
Serves 4

2 oz (50 g) butter
3½ lb (1.6 kg) chicken, jointed
6 streaky bacon rashers, rinds removed, cut into 4 pieces
2 onions, finely chopped
2 oz (50 g) plain flour
¼ pt (150 ml) dry red wine
1 pt (600 ml) chicken stock
3 tomatoes, skinned and chopped
8 oz (225 g) mushrooms, sliced
2 bay leaves
1 tbsp soy sauce
salt and freshly ground black pepper

Melt the butter in a flameproof casserole and fry the chicken pieces with the bacon and onions until the chicken is browned. Sprinkle the flour into the casserole and cook, stirring for 1 minute. Stir in the wine and stock. Bring to the boil and skim. Add the tomatoes, mushrooms, bay leaves, soy sauce and salt and pepper to taste. Cover and simmer gently for 1 hour. Remove the bay leaves and adjust the seasoning before serving.

SPICED CHICKEN
Serves 8

8 chicken breasts or pieces,
  skinned and pricked with a fork
4 oz (110 g) butter
2 small onions, finely chopped

2 garlic cloves, crushed
8 whole cardamom pods
2 sticks cinnamon
8 fl oz (250 ml) water

Marinade:
¾ pt (450 ml) yoghurt
2 garlic cloves, crushed
1 onion, coarsely grated
2 tbsp ground coriander

2 tsp finely chopped fresh ginger root
2 tsp salt
2 tsp turmeric
½ tsp freshly ground black pepper

Mix together all the marinade ingredients and add the chicken pieces. Coat well with the marinade and leave for a few hours in the refrigerator. Preheat the oven to 400°F/200°C/Gas Mk 6. Melt half the butter and sauté the onions, garlic, cardamom pods and cinnamon sticks for 5 minutes. Add the water and stir. Drain as much marinade from the chicken as you can and reserve. Place the chicken pieces in a baking dish and spoon a little of the onion mixture on top of each one. Dot with the remaining butter. Bake for about 10 minutes, then spoon the reserved marinade over the meat. Cook until the chicken is tender; about 10–15 minutes. Place on a serving dish and keep warm. Remove the cardamom pods and cinnamon sticks from the sauce, bring to the boil and spoon over the chicken. Serve with plain boiled rice and raita (diced cucumber with yoghurt).

CHICKEN KIEV
Serves 4

4 oz (110 g) butter, softened
5 garlic cloves, crushed
1 tbsp chopped fresh parsley
freshly ground black pepper
4 chicken breasts, trimmed
2 oz (50 g) seasoned flour

2 eggs, beaten
4 oz (110 g) fresh white breadcrumbs
oil for deep-frying
tomato slices and watercress
  sprigs, to garnish

Mash the butter with the garlic and parsley. Season with pepper. Mould into four sausage shapes and chill until hard. Skin the chicken breasts and make a slit down one side of each. Insert the garlic butter. Secure the edges with cocktail sticks. Dip carefully in flour, then egg, then breadcrumbs to coat. Chill for 15 minutes. Deep-fry in a large pan of oil until golden brown and cooked through. Garnish with tomato and watercress.

CHICKEN WITH JUNIPER BERRIES
Serves 4

2½ oz (60 g) butter
2½ lb (1.1 kg) chicken, cut into 8 pieces
10 shallots, finely chopped
7 fl oz (200 ml) dry white wine
20 juniper berries
1 tsp cornflour
¼ pt (150 ml) low fat crème fraiche
salt and freshly ground black pepper

Heat the butter and fry the chicken pieces until lightly browned. Add
the shallots and cook until golden. Add the wine and juniper berries
and seasoning. Cover the pan and simmer for 35 minutes. Remove the
chicken and boil the cooking liquid until reduced to about 2 tbsp. Mix
the cornflour with 2 tbsp cold water and add to the cream. Pour into
the frying pan, boil for 2 minutes, then pour over the chicken pieces
and serve.

CHICKEN ARGENTEUIL
Serves 4

3 oz (75 g) butter
3 lb (1.4 kg) chicken, skinned and quartered, or 4 chicken portions
2 oz (50 g) plain flour
1 pt (600 ml) chicken stock
salt and freshly ground black pepper
¼ pt (150 ml) water
1 lb (450 g) fresh asparagus tips
2 tbsp double cream

Melt 1 oz (25 g) butter in a saucepan. Add the chicken pieces and fry
until lightly browned on all sides. Sprinkle half the flour into the pan
and cook, stirring, for 1 minute. Stir in the stock. Bring to the boil
and skim. Add salt and pepper to taste. Cover and simmer for 1 hour.
Transfer the chicken pieces to a warmed serving dish and keep hot.
Bring the water to the boil in a saucepan and add a pinch of salt. Add
the asparagus tips and poach until just tender. Strain the cooking
water into the sauce. Keep the asparagus tips hot. Mix the remaining
butter and flour together to make a paste. Add to the sauce in small
pieces and cook, stirring, until thickened. Stir in the cream; taste and
adjust the seasoning. Pour the sauce over the chicken and garnish the
dish with the asparagus tips.

CHICKEN VERONIQUE
Serves 4

4 chicken breasts, boned and skinned
¼ pt (150 ml) chicken stock
1 bay leaf
½ onion, stuck with 2 cloves
½ oz (15 g) butter

½ oz (10 g) plain flour
¼ pt (150 ml) milk
salt and white pepper
4 oz (110 g) seedless white grapes and
watercress, to garnish

Preheat the oven to 375°F/190°C/Gas Mk 5. Place the chicken in an ovenproof dish. Pour over the stock and add the bay leaf and onion. Cover and bake for 30 minutes until the chicken is cooked. Strain the juice into a jug, discarding the bay leaf and onion. Keep the chicken warm in the oven while making the sauce. Melt the butter, stir in the flour and cook for 1 minute. Remove from the heat and gradually add the reserved stock and milk. Return to heat and bring to the boil, stirring. Simmer for 3–4 minutes, then season to taste. Pour over the chicken and garnish with grapes and watercress.

CHICKEN MARENGO
Serves 6

4 oz (110 g) butter
3½ lb (1.6 kg) chicken,
    quartered, or 6 chicken portions
6 shallots, chopped
2 garlic cloves, crushed
4 oz (110 g) plain flour
6 tomatoes, peeled and quartered

6 oz (175 g) button mushrooms
1 bay leaf
1 tsp dried oregano
1 white truffle, chopped
    but kept in its juice (optional)
½ pt (300 ml) Marsala
3 fl oz (100 ml) brandy

Melt 3 oz (75 g) of the butter in a flameproof casserole. Fry the chicken pieces, shallots and garlic gently until the chicken is lightly browned on all sides. Sprinkle over half the flour and cook, stirring, for 1 minute. Add the tomatoes, mushrooms, bay leaf, oregano, truffle with its juice and Marsala. Bring to the boil and skim. Cover and simmer (add a little chicken stock if the chicken becomes dry) for 1 hour or until tender. Ten minutes before the chicken is ready, add the brandy and stir well. Mix together the remaining butter and flour to make a paste. Add to the sauce in small pieces, stirring, and simmer until thickened. Remove the bay leaf and adjust the seasoning before serving.

MOROCCAN CHICKEN AND PRUNE TAGINE
Serves 4

2 oz (50 g) butter
8 chicken drumsticks, or 4 breasts cut in half
2 garlic cloves, crushed
½ tsp each ground turmeric or saffron, coriander and cumin
¼ tsp ground ginger
salt, freshly ground black pepper and cayenne
2 medium onions, finely sliced
8 oz (225 g) dried prunes, soaked overnight (keep the water)
juice of 1 lemon

Melt the butter and sauté the chicken until browned. Stir in the garlic and spices and season with salt, pepper and cayenne. Cook for 5 minutes, then add half the onion, the water in which the prunes were soaked plus extra water if needed, to just cover the chicken. Bring to the boil, cover and simmer for 30 minutes or until the chicken is tender. Add the remaining onion, the prunes and lemon juice and continue to cook gently until the fruit is soft. Serve with couscous and salad.

HONEY-ROASTED CHICKEN
Serves 4–6

3–4 lb (1.4–1.8 kg) chicken
1 lemon
salt
2 oz (50 g) butter
4 tbsp clear honey
preserved ginger and chopped toasted almonds, to garnish

Preheat the oven to 450°F/230°C/Gas Mk 8. Clean the chicken and rub inside and out with half the lemon. Sprinkle with salt. Melt the butter and whisk it into the honey along with juice of the lemon. Brush chicken inside and out with this mixture. Place in an oiled roasting dish and bake for 10 minutes, then reduce the heat to 350 °F/180°C/Gas Mk 4 and cook for about 20 minutes per lb (450 g) plus an extra 20 minutes, basting occasionally. Serve garnished with preserved ginger and chopped almonds.

CHICKEN WITH CHICK PEAS
Serves 4–6

4 oz (110 g) oil
3 medium onions, finely chopped
¼ tsp cayenne pepper
1 tsp turmeric
3 lb (1.4 kg) chicken
4 garlic cloves, crushed

juice of 2 lemons
8 oz (225 g) chick peas, soaked
   overnight and drained
stock or water
salt and freshly ground black pepper
1 tbsp raisins

Heat the oil in a large, deep, flameproof casserole or saucepan. Add the onions, cayenne and turmeric and fry gently. Add the chicken and fry it on all sides until golden all over. Add the garlic, lemon juice, chick peas and enough liquid to cover. Season to taste and bring to the boil. Cover and simmer for about 30 minutes, then sprinkle in the raisins and continue simmering for another 30 minutes or until the chicken is tender. If you find the chick peas are not cooked through in this time, remove the chicken and keep warm while continuing to cook. If the cooking liquid is very thin, boil to reduce it. Cut the chicken into portions and pour the chick pea sauce over.

CHICKEN WITH MUSHROOMS AND RED WINE
Serves 6

2 tbsp oil
1 oz (25 g) butter
6 chicken portions
1 onion, sliced
2 garlic clove, crushed
1 oz (25 g) plain flour
½ pt (300 ml) red wine

¼ pt (150 ml) chicken stock
1 bay leaf
1 bouquet garni
salt and freshly ground black pepper
4 oz (110 g) button mushrooms
chopped fresh parsley, to garnish

Preheat the oven to 350°F/180°C/Gas Mk 4. Heat the oil and butter and fry the chicken pieces until browned. Remove and place in a casserole. Add the onion and garlic to the pan and fry until soft. Stir in the flour and gradually add the wine and stock. Pour over the chicken, add the bay leaf and bouquet garni and season with salt and pepper. Cover and cook in the oven for 1¼ hours. Add the mushrooms and cook for a further 15 minutes. Discard the bay leaf and bouquet garni and garnish with parsley.

CHICKEN STUFFED WITH MANGO AND GINGER
Serves 6

6 chicken breasts, boned and skinned
salt and freshly ground black pepper
1 ripe mango, sliced
1 tsp finely grated fresh ginger root
juice of 1 lime
2 shallots, finely chopped
1 oz (25 g) butter
1 small carrot, finely chopped
1 garlic clove, crushed

1 tsp coriander seeds
3 cardamom pods
½ tsp cumin seeds
6 cloves
1 tsp ground cinnamon
8 oz (225 g) fromage frais
lime slices and fresh
 coriander leaves, to garnish

Preheat the oven to 375°F/190°C/Gas Mk 5. Slice the pockets of the chicken breasts to enlarge the cavities for stuffing and season with salt and pepper. Fill the cavities with slices of mango and half the ginger. Sprinkle with lime juice. Place the breasts on separate pieces of buttered foil and make into parcels. Bake for 20 minutes. Meanwhile sauté the shallots in the butter, add the carrot and garlic, then remove from the heat. Crush the coriander, cardamom and cumin seeds with the cloves. Add this mixture to the cinnamon and remaining ginger. Stir into the shallot mixture, then liquidise with the fromage frais. Return to the pan to reheat gently. Add water if too thick. To serve, unwrap the cooked chicken breasts and spoon the sauce over the pieces. Garnish with slices of lime and coriander leaves.

CELTIC CHICKEN
Serves 4

3 lb (1.4 kg) chicken, cut into portions
seasoned flour
4 tbsp oil
1 onion, finely chopped

½ pt (300 ml) chicken stock
¼ pt (150 ml) dry white wine
3 leeks, trimmed and chopped
4 oz (110 g) button mushrooms

Preheat the oven to 375°F/190°C/Gas Mk 5. Dip the chicken portions in seasoned flour to coat. Heat the oil in an ovenproof casserole and fry the chicken portions until lightly browned on all sides. Remove with a slotted spoon and reserve. Add the onion to the pan and fry until softened. Return the chicken, pour over the stock and wine and add the leeks. Bake for 1 hour, adding the mushrooms after 45 minutes.

GARLIC CHICKEN
Serves 4

1 tbsp oil
2 oz (50 g) butter
2½ lb (1.1 kg) chicken, cut into 8 pieces
salt and white pepper
1 whole garlic bulb, cloves
  finely chopped

3½ fl oz (100 ml) dry white wine
1 pt (600 ml) warm milk
1 tsp cornflour
4 tbsp single cream

Heat the oil and half the butter in a large casserole and brown the chicken pieces. Season, then remove and reserve. Pour off the cooking fat from the casserole and put in remaining butter and the garlic. Stir continuously until it has a creamy consistency. Add wine and replace the chicken pieces in the casserole. Stir well until the wine has evaporated. Pour in the milk, cover and simmer for 30 minutes. Remove the chicken, place on a serving dish and keep warm. Mix the cornflour with 2 tbsp cold water, mix with the cream and pour into the casserole. Boil the sauce for 2 minutes over a high heat, stirring continuously, then strain through a sieve and pour over the chicken.

CHICKEN WITH SCONE TOPPING
Serves 4

2 tbsp oil
1 small onion, chopped
½ green pepper, finely chopped
4 oz (110 g) mushrooms, sliced

1 tbsp cornflour
½ pt (300 ml) milk
1 lb (450 g) cooked chicken, cut into
  small pieces

Scones:
8 oz (225 g) plain flour
1 tsp salt milk to mix

2 oz butter or margarine
2 tsp baking powder

Heat the oil and sauté the onion, pepper and mushrooms. Add the cornflour and cook for 1 minute, stirring constantly. Gradually stir in the milk and cook, stirring continuously, until thickened. Add the chicken and season. Place in a deep 8–9 in (20–23 cm) pie plate. Preheat the oven to 450°F/230°C/Gas Mk 8. Make the scones: sift the flour, salt and baking powder into a bowl. Rub in the fat until the mixture looks like coarse breadcrumbs. Stir in enough milk to make a soft dough. Knead lightly on a floured board, roll out to about ½ in (1 cm) thick and cut into 1½ in (4 cm) rounds. Place the rounds on top of the chicken mixture, overlapping each other, brush with milk and bake for 10–15 minutes.

POULET EN COCOTTE
Serves 6

1 x 3 lb (1.4 kg) chicken
1½ oz (40 g) butter
2 oz (50 g) streaky bacon,
  derinded and diced
12 button mushrooms, quartered
12 small onions

3 tbsp plain flour
¾ pt (450 ml) chicken stock
salt and freshly ground black pepper
bouquet garni
2 potatoes, chopped
chopped fresh parsley, to garnish

Preheat the oven to 350°F/180°C/Gas Mk 4. Clean the chicken and remove the giblets. Truss with string, so that the chicken keeps its shape. Melt the butter in a large, heatproof casserole and brown the chicken all over. Remove from the casserole and keep warm. Sauté the bacon, mushrooms and onions in the pan until golden. Remove and keep warm. Add the flour to the casserole and cook, stirring, for a minute, then add the stock. Season to taste and bring to the boil, stirring continuously. Add the bouquet garni. Return all the other ingredients to the casserole, cover and cook in the oven for about 1 hour, or until tender. Add the potatoes to the casserole 20 minutes before the end of the cooking time. Take the casserole out of the oven and remove the bouquet garni. Sprinkle with parsley and serve.

RIESLING CHICKEN
Serves 6

20 shallots, chopped
2 tbsp oil
2 oz (50 g) butter
4 lb (1.8 kg) chicken, jointed
  into 12 pieces

salt and white pepper
3½ fl oz (100 ml) brandy
¾ pt (450 ml) Riesling
4 fl oz (125 ml) single cream

Peel and finely chop the shallots. Heat the oil in a flameproof casserole and add the butter and chicken pieces. Add seasoning to taste and brown on all sides. Remove the chicken and put on one side. Pour away half the cooking fat, then add the shallots and fry over a very low heat. Return the chicken to the casserole, pour in the brandy and stir well until it has evaporated. Pour in the Riesling and simmer, uncovered, for 45 minutes. Remove the chicken to a heated serving dish. Boil the sauce until reduced to ¼ pt (150 ml), stir in the cream and simmer for about 2 minutes. Season to taste, then pour over the chicken.

CHICKEN BREASTS IN PORT WINE
Serves 4

6 chicken breasts	2 oz (50 g) butter
2 tbsp plain flour	½ pt (300 ml) chicken stock
salt and freshly black ground pepper	¼ pt (150 ml) port wine
1 clove garlic, crushed	4 oz (125 g) mushrooms, sliced
2 small onions, finely sliced	chopped fresh parsley, to garnish

Slice the chicken breasts into ½ in (1 cm) thick slices and lightly dust them with seasoned flour. Gently sauté the onion and garlic in the melted butter until golden brown. Remove with a slotted spoon, drain and keep warm. Fry the chicken breasts on both sides until lightly browned and then return the onion and garlic to the pan. Add the chicken stock, port wine and mushrooms. Bring to the boil, then lower the heat, cover the pan and simmer very gently for 15 minutes. Check the seasoning, adding more salt and pepper if necessary, and serve garnished with chopped parsley.

CHICKEN À L'ORANGE
Serves 6

2 lbs (900 g) chicken pieces	½ tsp dried thyme
2 tbsp olive oil	½ tsp ground ginger
1 large onion, sliced	1 rounded tbsp plain flour
½ pt (300 ml) chicken stock	3 tsp grated orange rind
½ pt (300 ml) fresh orange juice	1 tbsp orange rind, cut into very
1½ tbsp honey	thin strips

Preheat the oven to 325°F/170°C/Gas Mk 3. Skin the chicken pieces and sauté them in a little hot oil until golden brown all over. Remove from the pan and put in an ovenproof casserole dish. Sauté the onion slices and add to the chicken. Whisk together the remaining ingredients, adding salt and pepper to taste, and pour over the chicken. Cook, uncovered, for 45 minutes, then turn up the heat to 350°F/180°C/Gas Mk 4 and cook for another 30 minutes. Pour off any excess fat, and pour the remaining gravy into a saucepan. Bring to the boil and cook rapidly until the gravy has reduced by about half. Pour the gravy over the chicken. Blanch the strips of orange rind in boiling water for about 5 minutes, and then sprinkle the orange strips over the chicken. Serve with wild rice.

CHICKEN AND CASHEW NUT GRATIN
Serves 4

6 chicken leg joints
salt and freshly ground black pepper
12 oz (350 g) broccoli, chopped
   into florets
2 oz (50 g) butter or margarine
2 oz (50 g) plain flour
5 fl oz (150 ml) milk

1 oz (25 g) toasted unsalted
   cashew nuts, chopped
4 level tbsp grated Parmesan cheese
grated nutmeg
2 eggs, separated
4 oz (125 g) low-fat Cheddar
   cheese, grated

Preheat the oven to 400°F/200°C/Gas Mk 6. Put the chicken joints in a saucepan, just cover with water, season to taste and bring to the boil. Cover, lower the heat and poach for about 20 minutes until tender. Drain, reserving liquid, and cool. Divide the chicken flesh into bite-sized pieces, discarding the skin and bone. Cook the broccoli in boiling salted water for 3–4 minutes or until just tender. Drain well and place in a greased, shallow ovenproof dish with the chicken. To make the sauce, melt the butter or margarine, stir in the flour and cook for 30 seconds, then blend in the milk and ½ pt (300 ml) reserved stock. Slowly bring the mixture to the boil, stirring constantly, to make a smooth, fairly thick sauce. Stir in the nuts, Parmesan cheese, a pinch of nutmeg and the beaten egg yolks. Season to taste with salt and pepper. Whisk the egg whites until stiff and carefully fold into the sauce. Spoon this over the chicken, sprinkle with the grated Cheddar and bake for about 20 minutes, until golden.

CHICKEN WITH GARLIC CREAM
Serves 4

4 chicken breasts, skinned and boned
4 oz (110 g) garlic-flavoured soft cheese
2 oz (50 g) unsalted butter
4 tbsp dry white wine
2 tbsp double cream

Flatten the chicken breasts gently with a meat hammer or rolling pin and spread with the cheese. Fold up to enclose the cheese completely and secure with wooden cocktail sticks. Melt the butter in a saucepan and brown the chicken on all sides, then add the wine and cream. Cover and simmer gently for 15 minutes. Pour the sauce over the chicken to serve. This dish is good served on a bed of rice with sweetcorn or green beans.

DUCK ROUENNAIS
Serves 8

1 x 6 lb (2.7 kg) duck, with giblets
1 onion, quartered
2 carrots, halved
2 celery sticks, sliced
2 bay leaves
1 tbsp tomato purée

½ pt (300 ml) dry red wine
½ pt (300 ml) water
salt and freshly ground black pepper
1½ oz (40 g) butter
1 oz (25 g) plain flour
3 fl oz (75 ml) port wine

Preheat the oven to 425°F/220°C/Gas Mk 7. Place the giblets (reserving the liver), onion, carrots, celery, bay leaves, tomatoe purée, wine and water in a saucepan and bring to the boil. Simmer for 1 hour, skimming off any foam. Add salt and pepper to taste, then strain. Place the duck on a rack in a roasting tin. Prick all over. Cook in the oven for 45 minutes. Remove from the oven and keep warm. Melt the butter in a small saucepan and gradually add the flour. Cook, stirring, for one minute, then gradually stir in the strained stock. Simmer, stirring, until the sauce is thick and smooth. Place the sauce, raw duck liver and port wine in a blender and blend until smooth. Add salt and pepper to taste. Slice the duck as thinly as possible. Arrange the duck slices in a serving dish and pour over the sauce.

CHICKEN KORMA
Serves 4

2 onions, chopped
1 in (2.5 cm) piece fresh ginger root
1½ oz (35 g) blanched almonds
2 garlic cloves
6 tbsp water
1 tsp each ground cardamom,
    cloves, cinnamon and coriander

¼ tsp cayenne pepper
3 tbsp vegetable oil or ghee
4 chicken breasts, skinned and cubed
½ pt (300 ml) yoghurt
salt and freshly ground black pepper

Blend the onions, ginger, almonds, garlic and water to a smooth paste. Add the spices and mix well. Heat the oil or ghee in a heavy-based saucepan and brown the chicken breasts. Add the paste mixture and fry again for about 10 minutes, stirring. Blend in the yoghurt (retain 2 tbsp) a little at a time and season. Cover, reduce the heat and simmer for about 1 hour or until the chicken is really tender. Serve on a bed of rice with the remaining yoghurt trickled over the chicken.

DUCK AUX PRUNEAUX
Serves 4–6

1 x 4 lb (1.8 kg) duck
salt and freshly ground black pepper
5 apples, peeled, cored and cut into
*   small pieces*
15 prunes, chopped

Sauce:
3 tbsp plain flour
5 fl oz (150 ml) double cream
dash of blackcurrant juice

Preheat the oven to 350°F/180°C/Gas Mk 4. Wipe the duck and remove the giblets. Prick the skin all over with a fork and rub with salt and pepper. Mix the apples with the prunes and stuff the duck with this mixture. Truss the duck and place on a rack in a roasting tin with 2 tbsp cold water in the tin. Roast in a preheated oven for 30 minutes per lb. Skim the fat from the gravy which forms in the tin and pour the gravy into a measuring jug. Make up to 15 fl oz (450 ml) with water. Pour the gravy into a saucepan. Mix the flour with a little cold water and blend in with the gravy. Bring to the boil, stirring, then lower the heat and simmer until a smooth sauce is obtained. Stir in the cream off the heat and add a dash of blackcurrant juice. Carve the duck to serve and serve the sauce separately.

CHICKEN CELESTINE
Serves 4

4 chicken breasts
2 tbsp plain flour
salt and freshly ground black pepper
2 oz (50 g) butter
1½ tbsp Grand Marnier or brandy

¼ pt (150 ml) chicken stock
7 fl oz (200 ml) double cream
1 oz (25 g) flaked almonds, toasted
2 Cox's apples, peeled and cubed
2 oz (50 g) sultanas

Flour and season the chicken pieces. Heat the butter and fry the chicken pieces on both sides. When the chicken is a golden brown colour, sprinkle over the Grand Marnier, add the stock, cover and simmer for 30 minutes. Remove the chicken to a serving dish. To make the sauce, thin down the stock in the pan with a little water or liqueur, if necessary, and then gently stir in the cream. Add the apples and almonds to the sauce and pour the sauce over the chicken. Cook in the oven for 15 minutes, then sprinkle the sultanas on top just before serving.

CHICKEN NORMANDY WITH WALNUT SAUCE
Serves 4–6

4–6 chicken breasts
2 tbsp seasoned flour
2 oz (50 g) butter
1 tbsp oil
salt and freshly ground black pepper

4 tbsp Calvados or brandy
12 fl oz (350 ml) dry cider
8 fl oz (250 ml) single cream
2 tbsp chopped walnuts
2 large green apples, to garnish

Halve the chicken breasts and dust with seasoned flour. Heat the butter and oil in a large pan with a tight-fitting lid. Brown the chicken pieces on each side, and season to taste with salt and pepper. Meanwhile heat the Calvados or brandy in a small pan, set it alight and pour it over the chicken. Shake the pan until the flames subside and then pour in the cider. Cover and simmer gently for 15 minutes, or until the breasts are cooked and tender. Remove the chicken and keep warm. Boil the liquid in the pan over a high heat to reduce it by half. Taste and adjust the seasoning if necessary, then stir in the cream and walnuts. Peel and core the apples and cut into wedges. Gently sauté the apple wedges in butter for 3–4 minutes. Arrange the chicken on a serving plate, coat with the walnut sauce and garnish with the apple wedges.

TURKEY WITH CAPERS
Serves 4

2 turkey breast steaks,
    cut in half lengthwise
salt and freshly ground black pepper
4 tbsp olive oil
1½ oz (35 g) plain flour
½ pt (300 ml) single cream
¼ pt (150 ml) white wine

1 tbsp lemon rind, finely grated
½ tsp dried thyme
¼ tsp dried marjoram
2 tbsp capers
few thin strips of lemon rind
    and watercress, to garnish

Preheat the oven to 350°F/180°C/Gas Mk 4. Rub salt and pepper on the turkey steaks. In a pan, heat the oil, add the turkey and cook for 4 minutes on each side until golden brown. Transfer to an ovenproof dish. Stir the flour into the pan and cook for 1 minute. Gradually add the cream and wine, stirring all the time. Bring to the boil, stirring continuously, then lower the heat and simmer for 2 minutes. Stir in the lemon rind, herbs and capers. Pour the mixture over the turkey in the ovenproof dish. Cover and cook in the oven for 15 minutes until the turkey is tender. To serve, garnish with lemon rind and watercress.

ITALIAN ROAST TURKEY
Serves 10

1 x 9 lb (4 kg) turkey
1 oz (25 g) butter

Stuffing: *2 oz (50 g) canned stoned prunes, roughly chopped*
1 large can of chestnuts, drained and chopped
8 oz (225 g) sausage meat
1 large onion, chopped
1 tbsp olive oil
3–4 tbsp white wine
6 tbsp stock
salt and freshly ground black pepper

Braise: *1½ oz (35 g) butter*
2 onions, sliced
2 carrots, sliced
3 sticks celery, chopped
3 rashers bacon, chopped
2 cloves garlic, crushed
¾ pt (450 ml) red wine
½ pt (300 ml) turkey stock
6 peppercorns
1 sprig fresh rosemary
2 bay leaves

Preheat the oven to 350°F/180°C/Gas Mk 4. To make the stuffing:
mix the sausage meat with the prunes and chestnuts. Heat the oil in a
frying pan and fry the onion over a low heat for 2–3 minutes. Mix the
onion into the sausagemeat mixture. Add the white wine and the
stock to the mixture, season to taste with salt and pepper and mix
well. Leave aside to cool and then stuff the turkey with this mixture.
For the braise, melt the butter in a large flameproof casserole dish and
add the onions, carrots, celery, bacon and garlic. Fry for 2 minutes,
then add the red wine, stock, peppercorns, rosemary and bay leaves.
Rub the turkey with butter, put it in the casserole, cover and cook in
the oven for about 3½ hours until the turkey is tender. When it is
ready, place the turkey on a serving dish surrounded by the braised
vegetables.

CHICKEN IN AVOCADO SAUCE
Serves 4–6

8 chicken breasts
salt and freshly ground black pepper
1 tbsp powdered ginger
1 oz (25 g) butter
2 medium onions, chopped
1 tbsp mild curry powder
8 fl oz (250 ml) chicken stock
4 small ripe avocados
2 tbsp thick cream
pinch of cayenne pepper
fresh parsley, to garnish

Rub the ginger and some salt and pepper into the chicken breasts. Melt half the butter in a heavy frying pan over medium heat and add the onions. Cook until soft. Add the chicken pieces and cook, turning them, until lightly browned on all sides. Sprinkle over the curry powder and stir for a few minutes, then pour in the stock. Cover and cook over low heat for 40–45 minutes until the chicken is tender. Set aside the ripest avocado. Halve the others and remove the stones. Using a melon baller, scoop out the flesh into balls. Whatever flesh remains, mash this together with the flesh from the reserved ripest avocado. When the chicken is almost ready, melt the remaining butter in another frying pan, add the avocado balls and cook gently over very low heat. Shake the pan from time to time until the balls are heated through, but do not stir. Keep warm. When the chicken is cooked, remove from the stock with a slotted spoon and place on a warmed serving dish. Add the mashed avocado flesh, the cream and the cayenne pepper to the stock remaining in the pan. Heat thoroughly but do not boil. Then pour this sauce over the chicken, add the avocado balls, sprinkle with the parsley and serve immediately.

STUFFED CHICKEN BREASTS
Serves 4

4 chicken breasts
salt and freshly ground black pepper
4 thin slices ham
4 thin slices Bel Paese cheese
4 asparagus spears, cooked

plain flour
1½ oz (35 g) butter
1 tbsp olive oil
6 tbsp Marsala
2 tbsp chicken stock

Place the chicken breasts between two sheets of damp greaseproof paper and, using a rolling pin, beat well until thin. Sprinkle the chicken with salt and pepper to taste and place a slice of ham on each breast. Add a slice of cheese and one asparagus spear on top of the ham. Roll up the chicken breasts and tie them with cotton so that they retain their shape. Dust the chicken pieces with flour. In a frying pan, heat the oil and 1 oz (25 g) of the butter and fry the chicken rolls on a very low heat, turning frequently. Fry for 15 minutes until the chicken is tender and golden. Transfer the chicken rolls to a warm serving dish and remove the cotton. Add the Marsala, stock and remaining butter to the frying pan, bring to the boil, lower the heat and simmer for 4 minutes, stirring constantly. Pour the sauce over the chicken rolls and serve immediately.

CHICKEN TETRAZZINI
Serves 4

1 lb (450 g) cold cooked chicken
8 oz (225 g) tagliatelle
8 oz (225 g) button mushrooms, sliced
2 oz (50 g) butter
squeeze of lemon juice
1 oz (25 g) plain flour

1 pt (600 ml) chicken stock
salt and freshly ground black pepper
¼ pt (150 ml) double cream
2 tbsp dry sherry
1 oz (25 g) breadcrumbs
1 oz (25 g) Parmesan cheese, grated

Cook the tagliatelle in boiling salted water for 8 minutes, or until just tender. Cut the chicken into bite-sized pieces and set aside. Lightly fry the mushrooms in half the butter, then add the lemon juice. Melt the remaining butter in a pan over a low heat, stir in the flour and cook gently for a minute. Gradually stir in the hot stock. Bring to the boil, stirring continuously, then reduce the heat and simmer for 2–3 minutes. Remove from the heat, season to taste and add the cream, sherry and chicken pieces. Drain the tagliatelle and stir in the chicken mixture. Heat through gently and then place in a greased heatproof dish. Sprinkle the breadcrumbs and cheese over the top and brown under the grill. Serve with a crisp salad.

CHICKEN AND APRICOT CASSEROLE
Serves 6

6–8 chicken joints
2 oz (50 g) butter or margarine
1 large onion, sliced
1 yellow pepper, seeded and
   cut into strips
1 large tin apricots in juice

1 tbsp cornflour
1 tbsp soy sauce
3 tbsp white wine vinegar
2 tomatoes, peeled and thickly sliced
salt and freshly ground black pepper

Preheat the oven to 375°F/190°C/Gas Mk 4. Brown the chicken in half the fat and then place in a large casserole. Sauté the onion and pepper in the remaining fat until soft. Drain the apricots, reserving the juice. Mix the cornflour with the soy sauce and vinegar, and ½ pt (300 ml) of the apricot juice and pour into the pan. Stir until boiling and boil until clear. Pour over the chicken. Add the tomatoes and the apricots to the casserole and stir to mix all the ingredients. Cover and cook for about an hour, removing the lid for the last 10 minutes of cooking time. Season to taste with salt and pepper. Serve with saffron rice.

TURKEY SALTIMBOCCA
Serves 4

4 turkey breast fillets
plain flour
4 slices lean ham
2 oz (50 g) Cheddar cheese, grated
2 oz (50 g) Parmesan cheese, grated

2 tbsp oil
3 tomatoes, skinned and finely chopped
2 oz (50 g) walnuts, roughly chopped
chopped fresh parsley, to garnish

Place the turkey breasts on a well floured surface and, using a wooden rolling pin, beat until they are very thin and about twice their original size. Place a slice of ham on each turkey breast. Mix together the Cheddar and Parmesan cheeses and divide half of this mixture equally between the 4 turkey breasts on top of the ham. Roll up the stuffed turkey breasts and tie with cotton. Heat the oil in a frying pan and fry the turkey rolls for about 20 minutes until they are cooked through and golden brown. Transfer to a grill tray, sprinkle over the chopped tomato and walnuts and top with the remaining cheese. Grill until the cheese melts. Sprinkle over the chopped parsley and serve.

CHICKEN TONNATO
Serves 4

4 chicken breasts
1 pt (600 ml) chicken stock
1 onion, halved
1 stick celery, chopped
salt and freshly ground black pepper
pinch of dried thyme
few parsley stalks
1 bay leaf
¼ pt (150 ml) white wine

¾ pt (450 ml) thick mayonnaise
1 x 7 oz (200 g) can tuna fish, drained
6 anchovy fillets, drained
2 tbsp lemon juice
3 tbsp capers, drained
anchovy fillets
capers
4 tomatoes, sliced

Place the chicken, stock, onion and celery in a large saucepan, and season to taste with salt and pepper. Add the thyme, parsley stalks and bay leaf. Pour in the wine and add enough water to cover the ingredients. Bring to the boil, then lower heat and simmer for 20–30 minutes until the chicken is tender. Using a slotted spoon, remove the chicken and set aside to cool. Mix the mayonnaise, tuna, anchovy fillets, lemon juice and capers in a blender until smooth. Arrange the cooled chicken on a serving dish and spoon over the sauce. Garnish with anchovy fillets, capers and tomato slices.

TANDOORI CHICKEN
Serves 3–4

6–8 chicken pieces (breasts or thighs)

Yoghurt masala:
3 cloves garlic, peeled
    and finely chopped
1 in (2.5 cm) piece fresh ginger,
    peeled and finely chopped
1 tsp cumin seeds
pinch nutmeg

6 fl oz (175 ml) natural yoghurt
1 tbsp oil
4 tsp tomato ketchup
2 tsp lemon juice
2–3 drops red food colouring (optional)
salt and freshly ground black pepper

Lemon spice sauce:
½ tsp freshly ground pepper
¼ tsp ground cardamom

1 tbsp oil
2 tbsp lemon juice

Preheat the oven to 350°F/180°C/Gas Mk 4. Purée all the ingredients for the yoghurt masala in a blender, adding salt and pepper to taste. Skin the chicken pieces and cut two ½ in (1 cm) slits deep in each piece. Spread the yoghurt masala mixture over the chicken and marinate overnight in the fridge. Place the chicken on a rack over a shallow, lightly oiled roasting pan. Spoon over any remaining marinade. Roast for 30–40 minutes, basting frequently. Mix the remaining ingredients together to make the lemon spice sauce. Sprinkle this over the chicken and return to the oven at 400°F/ 200°C/Gas Mk 6 for 10–15 minutes until the chicken is a dark reddish-brown colour.

VALENCIA CHICKEN
Serves 6

6 large chicken breasts, boned
1 oz (25 g) plain flour
1 tsp paprika
½ tsp garlic salt
2 oz (50 g) lard
juice of 1 large orange

½ pt (300 ml) chicken stock
1 small onion, finely chopped
2 in (5 cm) stick cinnamon
salt and freshly ground black pepper
1 tsp cornflour
6 slices orange

Stuffing:
3 oz (75 g) seedless raisins
2 tbsp sherry
3 oz (75 g) diced ham
1 oz (25 g) butter, softened

1 tbsp chopped fresh parsley
grated rind of ½ orange
1 oz (25 g) fine breadcrumbs

To make the stuffing: soak the raisins in sherry for ½ hour. Chop one third of them and mix thoroughly with the other stuffing ingredients. Divide the stuffing equally between the chicken breasts. Fold over the chicken to enclose the stuffing and secure with cocktail sticks. Coat each piece of chicken in the flour mixed with the paprika and garlic salt. Melt the lard in a pan, and fry the chicken breasts, turning to brown all sides. Drain off the excess fat and pour the orange juice and stock over the chicken. Add the onion and cinnamon, and season to taste with salt and pepper. Cover and simmer for about 40 minutes or until the chicken is tender. Remove the cinnamon stick, add the remaining raisins, mix the cornflour with a little cold water and stir into the sauce. Simmer for a few minutes more, stirring frequently. Arrange the orange slices on a serving plate and put one breast on each slice. Pour the sauce over the top.

DUCK ALSACE
Serves 4

2 tbsp oil
1 oz (25 g) butter
1 x 3½ lb (1.4 kg) duck
salt and freshly ground black pepper

½ bottle dry white wine
1¼ lb (550 g) tin of sauerkraut
4 thick slices of streaky bacon
4 oz (110 g) sliced ham, finely chopped

Heat the oil in a large, flameproof casserole dish. Add the butter, then the duck. Brown on both sides. Skim off three-quarters of the cooking fat. Add salt and pepper to taste, then pour in the wine. Simmer for 1¼ hours over a low heat, turning the duck from time to time; 15 minutes before the end of the cooking time, add the sauerkraut to the pan to warm through. Cook the bacon under a hot grill, and then place it on top of the sauerkraut in the saucepan and cover. Add the ham to the casserole dish 10 minutes before the duck is ready. Remove the duck from the casserole dish and place on a serving dish. Arrange the sauerkraut, ham and bacon around the duck. Bring to the boil the cooking juice remaining in the casserole dish and boil until the liquid has reduced to 4 fl oz (125 ml). Pour over the duck and sauerkraut and serve immediately.

GAME

PIGEON AND CHESTNUT CASSEROLE
Serves 2

2 pigeons
1 tbsp seasoned plain flour
fat for frying
1 large onion, sliced
1 pt (600 ml) hot beef stock

8 oz (225 g) chestnuts,
  roasted and peeled
4 chipolata sausages
salt and freshly ground black pepper

Cut the pigeons in two, remove the feet and wash and dry the birds. Dip them in the seasoned flour. Heat the fat in a large frying pan and fry the birds until golden brown, then place them in a flameproof casserole. Sauté the onion until the slices are golden brown and arrange around the pigeons. Pour in the stock, cover and simmer very slowly for about 2 hours. Fry the chipolatas and add to the casserole, together with the chestnuts, 15 minutes before serving. Check the seasoning.

PHEASANT AND APPLES
Serves 2–3

1 tbsp cooking oil
1 oz (25 g) butter
1 pheasant
1 small onion, finely chopped
2 tbsp brandy

¼ pt (150 ml) chicken stock
2 dessert apples, sliced
¼ pt (150 ml) double cream
salt and freshly ground black pepper

Melt the oil and butter in a flameproof casserole. Add the pheasant and brown gently, then remove. Add the onion to the casserole and fry until softened but not brown. Drain off any surplus fat and replace the bird in the casserole. Pour the brandy over the bird, set alight and when the flames have died away, add the stock and apples. Cover and simmer over a low heat for 45 minutes until tender, then remove and place on a serving dish. Strain the cooking liquid into a bowl, stir in the cream, return to the casserole and reheat. Add salt and pepper to taste and pour over the pheasant.

PIQUANT RABBIT
Serves 4

1 rabbit, cut into four
bacon for larding
½ bottle dry white wine
4 fl oz (125 ml) wine vinegar
2–3 carrots, sliced
2–3 small onions, sliced
1 bay leaf
fresh parsley and thyme sprigs
tarragon leaves

coarsely ground black pepper
olive oil for frying
2 tsp dry mustard
2 tsp tomato purée
2 tbsp plain flour
a little single cream
chopped fresh parsley
croûtons

Cut the bacon into strips about ½ in (1 cm) wide. Wipe the rabbit joints and lard them with the bacon – push the strips through the flesh at 1 in (2.5 cm) intervals using a larding needle or sharp-pointed knife Lay them in a shallow dish. Put the wine, vinegar, carrots, onions, herbs and pepper in a bowl and stir well, then pour over the rabbit pieces and marinate for 2 hours. Drain well, reserving the marinade. Heat the oil in a heavy-based pan and brown the joints on all sides. Add half the marinade liquor, the mustard and tomato purée and cook gently for 1 hour or until the joints are cooked and tender. Remove from the pan, put in a warmed serving dish and keep hot. Blend the flour with a little stock or water and stir into the gravy. Bring to the boil and simmer, stirring, until a smooth gravy is obtained. Stir in the cream and strain over the rabbit joints. Garnish with parsley and croûtons.

MADEIRA PHEASANT
Serves 4

1 oz (25 g) butter
1 pheasant
4 slices fat bacon, chopped
2 slices ham, chopped
1 medium onion, finely chopped
1 celery stalk, finely chopped

1 carrot, finely diced
1 tbsp chopped fresh parsley
salt and freshly ground black pepper
¼ pt (150 ml) chicken stock
¼ pt (150 ml) Madeira

Melt the butter in a flameproof casserole. Gently fry the pheasant, bacon and ham until lightly browned. Transfer to a plate. Cook the onion, celery and carrot in the casserole until soft. Return the meat to the casserole, and add the parsley, salt and pepper to taste, stock and Madeira. Cover and cook over low heat for 1 hour or until the pheasant is tender. Remove to a heated serving dish. Liquidise or sieve the cooking liquid and pour over the carved bird.

STUFFED PHEASANT
Serves 4

1 pheasant
fat bacon rashers
1 glass sherry

2 tsp tomato purée
grated nutmeg
fried croûtons

Stuffing:
4 oz (110 g) pork sausage meat
2 oz (50 g) mushrooms, finely chopped
salt and freshly ground black pepper

chopped fresh parsley
1 egg yolk
a little single cream

Preheat the oven to 350°F/180°C/Gas Mk 4. Combine the sausage
meat, mushrooms, plenty of seasoning and the chopped parsley, in a
large bowl. Bind with the egg yolk and enough cream to make a fairly
stiff stuffing. Spoon the stuffing into the body of the bird, cover with
the fat bacon and roast for 45 minutes, or until nearly but not
completely cooked. Add the sherry, tomato purée and a little grated
nutmeg. Check the seasoning and add hot water if it is too dry. Cook
for about another 20 minutes, basting the bird often with the juices.
When cooked, remove the bacon and place the bird on a warmed
serving dish. Garnish with croûtons and strain the sauce over.

MARINADED ROAST VENISON
Serves 6–8

4 lb (1.8 kg) venison joint
2 oz butter or margarine, for spreading
6 slices of streaky bacon

Marinade:
½ pt (300 ml) red wine vinegar
½ pt (300 ml) red wine
3 carrots, roughly chopped
1 onion, sliced

3 bay leaves
1 thyme sprig
salt and freshly ground black pepper

Spread the venison with butter or margarine and place in a deep dish.
Heat the marinade ingredients, pour over the joint and leave in a cool
place for 2 days. Preheat the oven to 450°F/230°C/Gas Mk 8. After
marinating take the meat out and place in a roasting tin. Cover with
the bacon and roast for 1½ hours or until well cooked, basting
frequently.

PHEASANT AND ORANGE CASSEROLE
Serves 4

1 tbsp cooking oil
1 oz (25 g) butter
1 pheasant, jointed
8 oz (225 g) button mushrooms
1 tbsp plain flour

½ pt (300 ml) chicken stock
¼ pt (150 ml) orange juice
¼ pt (150 ml) dry white wine
salt and freshly ground black pepper

Preheat the oven to 350°F/180°C/Gas Mk 4. Melt the oil and butter in a frying pan, add the pheasant joints and fry until browned on all sides. Transfer to a flameproof casserole. Fry the mushrooms for 4–5 minutes, then add to the casserole. Sprinkle the flour into the frying pan and cook, stirring, for 2–3 minutes. Mix together the stock, orange juice and wine and gradually pour into the frying pan. Bring slowly to the boil, stirring constantly. Add salt and pepper to taste, then pour into the casserole. Cover and cook in the oven for 1 hour until the meat is tender.

ROMANY PHEASANT
Serves 3–4

1 oz (25 g) butter
1 garlic clove, crushed
1 large pheasant, jointed
12 oz (350 g) piece of bacon, cubed
2 large onions, sliced

4 tomatoes, peeled and sliced
¼ pt (150 ml) sherry
salt and freshly ground black pepper
pinch of cayenne pepper

Melt the butter in a flameproof casserole and fry the garlic. Add the pheasant joints and bacon and fry until golden brown. Remove and place on a warm plate. Fry the onions gently in the casserole until soft. Add the tomatoes and cook for 2–3 minutes. Return the pheasant, pour in the sherry and add salt and pepper to taste. Cover tightly and simmer over a low heat for 1 hour or until the meat is tender. Add the cayenne pepper just before serving,

ROAST GROUSE
Serves 4

2 oz (50 g) butter
juice of ½ lemon
salt and freshly ground black pepper

2 young grouse
2 rashers streaky bacon
2 tbsp olive oil

Preheat the oven to 425°F/220°C/Gas Mk 7. Mix together the butter and lemon juice in a small bowl, adding salt and pepper to taste. Place the mixture inside the birds. Cover the breasts with the bacon. Place in a roasting tin and cook in the oven for 25–30 minutes, basting from time to time with the oil.

PIGEON AND STEAK CASSEROLE
Serves 4

2 pigeons
1 oz (25 g) butter
1 tbsp oil
8 oz (225 g) chuck steak, cubed
2 rashers streaky bacon, diced
½ pt (300 ml) chicken stock

4 oz (110 g) mushrooms, sliced
salt and freshly ground black pepper
1 tbsp lemon juice
1 tbsp redcurrant jelly
1 tbsp plain flour

Cut the pigeons in half. Melt the butter and oil in a flameproof casserole. Cook the pigeons, steak and bacon and cook until lightly browned. Add the stock, mushrooms and season to taste. Cover and simmer over a low heat for 1½ hours until the birds are tender. Stir in the lemon juice and redcurrant jelly. Mix the flour with 1 tbsp water, stir into the casserole, bring to the boil and cook for 2 minutes.

PIGEONS IN WINE
Serves 2–3

1 tbsp plain flour
2 tsp paprika
salt
2 pigeons
2 oz (50 g) dripping
1 onion, sliced

1 garlic clove, crushed
¼ pt (150 ml) dry white wine
½ pt (300 ml) chicken stock
1 bouquet garni
2–3 tbsp yoghurt

Preheat the oven to 325°F/170°C/Gas Mk 3. Season the flour with the paprika and a little salt. Chop the pigeons in half and toss them in the flour. Melt the dripping in a flameproof casserole and cook the pigeons until golden brown. Transfer to a plate. Add the onion and garlic and cook for 5 minutes. Gradually stir in the wine and chicken stock, then add the bouquet garni. Return the pigeons to the casserole and bring the liquid to the boil. Cover and cook in oven for 1½–2 hours until the birds are tender. Just before serving remove the bouquet garni and stir in the yoghurt.

PHEASANT WITH ALMONDS
Serves 2–3

1 pheasant	1 small onion, chopped
2 oz (50 g) butter	2 oz (50 g) piece fat bacon
1 tsp freshly ground black pepper	2 oz (50 g) flaked almonds

Preheat the oven to 325°F/170°C/Gas Mk 3. In a bowl mix together the butter and pepper; spread over the pheasant. Place the onion and bacon inside the bird. Lay on a sheet of foil, cover the breast with the almond flakes and seal well. Place in roasting tin and bake for 1½–2 hours. Open the foil about 15 minutes before the end of the cooking time to allow the almonds to brown.

PHEASANT EN COCOTTE
Serves 4

2 oz (50 g) margarine or butter	½ pt (300 ml) chicken stock
1 pheasant	¼ pt (150 ml) dry white wine
4 oz (110 g) chopped ham or bacon	6 oz (175 g) button mushrooms

Melt the margarine in a flameproof casserole, put in the pheasant and brown all over. Season well, then add the ham or bacon, stock and wine. Cover and simmer very gently for 1½ hours, then add the button mushrooms, replace the lid and cook gently for a further 30 minutes.

PHEASANT WITH CELERY
Serves 4

2 oz (50 g) butter	7 fl oz (200 ml) stock
1 pheasant	7 fl oz (200 ml) single cream
2 medium onions, chopped	salt and freshly ground black pepper
1 head of celery, chopped	

Melt the butter in a large saucepan and cook the bird until brown on all sides. Add the onions. Cover the saucepan very tightly and simmer over a low heat for 45 minutes. Remove from the heat. Boil the celery in salted water for 8 minutes and drain. Add the stock, celery and cream to the pheasant and season to taste. Cover and simmer for a further 45 minutes until the meat is tender. Place pheasant on a heated dish, pour over the vegetables and stock and serve at once.

JUGGED HARE
Serves 4

2 oz (50 g) dripping or 4 tbsp oil
1 oven-ready hare, jointed
1 bacon rasher, diced
1½ pt (900 ml) stock
1½ oz (35 g) plain flour
1 onion, stuck with 2 cloves
1 bouquet garni
small bay leaf

4 peppercorns
small blade of mace
salt and freshly ground black pepper
½ tsp vinegar
1 tsp red currant jelly
1 glass red wine
forcemeat balls

Preheat the oven to 350°F/180°C/Gas Mk 4. Heat the dripping and fry the hare joints with the bacon. When browned, put into a casserole and pour the stock over. Blend the flour with a little stock and add to the casserole together with the onion and herbs; season well. Cover and cook in the oven for 3 hours or until the meat is tender. Stir the vinegar, redcurrant jelly and wine into the gravy, garnish the dish with forcemeat balls and serve with a separate dish of red currant jelly.

PARTRIDGE À L'ORANGE
Serves 4–6

2–3 oven-ready partridges
2 oz (50 g) butter, softened
2 oz (50 g) margarine
2 oz (50 g) plain flour
½ pt (300 ml) veal or chicken stock
¼ pt (150 ml) dry white wine

1 bouquet garni
salt and freshly ground black pepper
1 orange
chopped fresh parsley, to garnish
croûtons, to garnish

Preheat the oven to 450°F/230°F/Gas Mk 8. Spread the partridges with the butter and roast until not quite cooked through; about 40 minutes, but test with a skewer. Remove from the oven and separate into joints. Place in a serving dish and keep hot. Melt the margarine in a small pan and stir in the flour. Cook for a few minutes without browning, then gradually stir in the stock until smooth. Add the juices from the birds, the wine, bouquet garni and seasoning to taste. Bring to the boil, simmer until reduced by a quarter, then strain into a clean saucepan. Add the juice of half the orange, check the seasoning and reheat gently. Cut the orange skin into julienne strips and boil for a few minutes to soften. Pour the sauce over the joints and allow to heat in a moderate oven for a few minutes. Scatter the orange strips on top and garnish with parsley and croûtons.

BOOZY HARE
Serves 6

1 tbsp plain flour
1 tsp paprika
1 small hare, jointed
2 oz (50 g) lard
1 garlic clove, crushed with salt

2 medium onions, each
   studded with 2 cloves
1 pt (600 ml) brown ale
4 fl oz (125 ml) port
salt and freshly ground black pepper

Preheat the oven to 300°F/150°C/Gas Mk 2. Mix the flour and paprika together and coat the hare joints. Melt the lard in a flameproof casserole and fry the joints until browned on all sides. Add the garlic, onions and ale. Bring to the boil, cover and cook in the oven for 3–4 hours until the meat comes off the bone. Remove the onions with the cloves using a slotted spoon and discard. If the hare blood is available mix it with a little of the cooking liquid and stir into the casserole. Place on top of the cooker over a low heat, pour in the port and heat gently but do not boil. Add salt and pepper to taste.

RABBIT AND CIDER CASSEROLE
Serves 4

4 tbsp oil
12–18 baby onions
1 rabbit, jointed
1 oz (25 g) plain flour

salt and freshly ground black pepper
2 tsp French mustard
½ pt (300 ml) dry cider
¾ pt (450 ml) chicken stock

Preheat the oven to 325°F/170°C/Gas Mk 3. Heat the oil in a frying pan and cook the onions for 5 minutes, tossing to brown lightly all over. Remove with a slotted spoon and place in a casserole. Season the flour with salt and pepper, toss the rabbit joints in it and cook in the frying pan for 8 minutes until golden. Transfer to the casserole. Stir the mustard and any remaining flour into the frying pan and slowly pour in the cider and stock. Bring to the boil, then pour into the casserole. Cover and cook in the oven for 2 hours until the meat is tender.

STUFFED PHEASANT BREASTS
Serves 4

8 oz (225 g) smoked streaky bacon
4 oz (110 g) lamb liver,
  finely chopped

1 small onion, finely chopped
4 breasts of pheasant, boned
1 oz (25 g) butter

Preheat the oven to 300°F/150°C/Gas Mk 2. Finely chop 2 oz (50 g) of the bacon. Mix with the liver and onion and spread on two of the breasts, leaving the edges clear. Place the other two breasts on top as if making sandwiches. Wrap the remaining bacon rashers tightly around the breasts, reserving four to place down the centre of the meat. Put the pheasant parcels into a casserole, dot with butter and cover tightly. Bake for 1¼–1½ hours until the bacon is well browned. Carve into thick slices to serve.

PHEASANT AND CHESTNUT CASSEROLE
Serves 4–6

1 tbsp oil
1 oz (25 g) butter
1 pheasant
8 oz (225 g) button onions
8 oz (225 g) fresh chestnuts,
  peeled and skinned
1 oz (25 g) plain flour

¾ pt (450 ml) stock
4 fl oz (125 ml) red wine
juice and grated rind of 1 orange
2 tbsp redcurrant jelly
1 bay leaf
salt and freshly ground black pepper
chopped fresh parsley, to garnish

Preheat the oven to 325°F/170°C/Gas Mk 3. Melt the oil and butter in a frying pan and brown the pheasant on all sides. Chop into pieces and place in a casserole. Cook the onions and chestnuts in the frying pan until golden brown and add to the casserole. Stir the flour into the frying pan and cook for 1 minute before stirring in the stock, wine, orange juice, redcurrant jelly and rind. Bring to the boil, add the bay leaf and season to taste. Pour the liquid over the pheasant, cover the casserole and cook in the oven for 1½–2 hours until the meat is tender. Skim off any fat, remove the bay leaf and sprinkle with parsley.

POT-ROASTED PHEASANT
Serves 4

1 pheasant
2 carrots, sliced
2 shallots
4 oz (110 g) mushrooms, sliced

1 tbsp mixed dried herbs
¾ pt (450 ml) stock
¼ pt (150 ml) cider
salt and freshly ground black pepper

Preheat the oven to 325°F/170°C/Gas Mk 3. Put the pheasant in a large casserole with the vegetables and herbs. Pour in the stock and cider and season to taste with salt and pepper. Cover the casserole and cook in the oven for 2–2½ hours until the meat is tender. Place the pheasant on a serving dish and pour over the vegetables and stock.

RABBIT IN BEER
Serves 4

1 tbsp plain flour
salt and freshly ground black pepper
2 lb (900 g) rabbit, jointed
1 oz (25 g) lard
4 oz (110 g) streaky bacon, chopped
1 medium onion, sliced
½ pt (300 ml) pale ale

½ pt (300 ml) stock
1 tsp sugar
1 tbsp vinegar
1 bay leaf
2 tsp French mustard
12 prunes, soaked

Season the flour with salt and pepper and toss the rabbit joints in it.
Heat the lard in a flameproof casserole and fry the rabbit until brown.
Remove to a plate. Fry the bacon and onion in the casserole until the
onion is soft. Pour off any excess fat and replace the rabbit. Add the
ale, stock, sugar, vinegar, bay leaf and mustard and bring to the boil.
Cover and simmer over a low heat for 1–1½ hours or until almost
cooked. Add the prunes and cook for a further 20 minutes.

VENISON STEW
Serves 4–6

2 lb (900 g) shoulder of venison, cubed
½ pt (300 ml) red wine
1 large carrot, sliced
1 onion, sliced
1 garlic clove, crushed
2 tbsp olive oil
bouquet garni

salt and freshly ground black pepper
1 oz (25 g) butter
8 oz (225 g) bacon, diced
8 oz (225 g) baby onions
2 tbsp plain flour
1 bay leaf

Place the venison cubes in a shallow dish. Mix together the wine,
carrot, onion, garlic, oil, bouquet garni and seasoning to taste. Pour
over the meat and leave for 12 hours. Preheat the oven to 325°F/
170°C/Gas Mk 3. Dry the meat and reserve the liquid. Melt the butter
in a flameproof casserole and sauté the bacon and baby onions.
Remove with a slotted spoon. Add the meat and brown over a high
heat. Lower the heat, stir in the flour and cook for 1 minute. Strain
the wine and carrot marinade, discarding the vegetables, and pour
over the meat. Add water to cover if needed. Bring to the boil, stirring
continuously, then lower the heat. Stir in the bacon, onions and bay
leaf; add more seasoning if required. Cover and cook in the oven for
1½–2 hours.

RED WINE RABBIT WITH GRAPES
Serves 4

1 rabbit, jointed
¼ pt (150 ml) red wine
1 oz (25 g) plain flour
1 tbsp mixed herbs
salt and freshly ground black pepper
1 oz (25 g) butter
1 garlic clove, crushed
½ pt (300 ml) stock
8 baby onions
2 celery stalks, finely chopped
4 oz (110 g) black grapes, halved and deseeded

Place the rabbit in a deep dish and pour over the red wine. Leave for 24 hours, turning from time to time. Preheat the oven to 350°F/180°C/ Gas Mk 4. Mix together the flour, herbs and seasoning to taste. Remove the rabbit from the wine, pat dry and dip in the seasoned flour. Melt the butter in a flameproof casserole and stir in the garlic. Add the rabbit and cook until brown on all sides. Add the stock, wine, onions and celery. Cover and cook in the oven for 1 hour. Add the grapes, replace the lid and cook for a further 30 minutes.

RABBIT AND OLIVES
Serves 4

1 rabbit, jointed
¼ pt (150 ml) red wine
1 tbsp oil
1 onion, chopped
4 oz (110 g) bacon, chopped
1 green pepper, halved,
* deseeded and diced*

1 tsp dried basil
14 oz (400 g) can tomatoes
1 tbsp tomato purée
salt and freshly ground black pepper
4 oz (110 g) stuffed olives

Place the rabbit in a deep bowl, pour in the red wine and leave for 24 hours. Preheat the oven to 350°F/180°C/Gas Mk 4. Heat the oil in a flameproof casserole, add the onion, bacon, green pepper and basil; stir well. Cover and cook for 5 minutes. Remove the rabbit from wine and add to the casserole. Cook for a few minutes until lightly browned. Pour in the wine and add the tomatoes and tomato purée. Season to taste, cover and cook in the oven for 1¼ hours. Stir in the olives and cook for a further 15 minutes.

BRAISED VENISON
Serves 4–6

joint of venison from the haunch
oil for frying
2 lb (900 g) root vegetables
  of choice, diced

2 bacon rashers, derinded
a little stock
1 tbsp cornflour
redcurrant jelly

Marinade:
3 fl oz (75 ml) oil
4 oz (110 g) carrots, sliced
4 oz (110 g) onions, sliced
2 oz (50 g) celery, sliced
¾ pt (450 ml) red wine vinegar
1 bouquet garni

6 juniper berries, crushed
1 rosemary sprig
1 garlic clove, crushed
6 peppercorns, crushed
1 pt (600 ml) red wine,
  wine and water mixed, or cider

Heat the oil in a large pan and brown the carrots and onions. Add the remaining marinade ingredients. Bring to the boil, lower the heat and simmer for 30 minutes. Leave until cold. Put the joint in a deep bowl and pour over the cold marinade. Leave for at least 24 hours, basting twice a day. Remove, drain on a rack, then pat dry. Preheat the oven to 350°F/180°C/Gas Mk 4. Heat some oil in a flameproof casserole, add the joint and brown lightly all over. Remove the joint and keep warm. Add the diced vegetables to the casserole and sauté in the hot fat until softened, keeping the lid on. Pour off any excess oil and put in the bacon rashers, followed by a 1 in (2.5 cm) layer of the diced vegetables. Lay the browned meat on top and pour in enough stock and marinade combined to come half way up the side of the joint. Put in the oven for 2–3 hours or until tender. Slice the meat and arrange on a warmed serving dish. Strain the gravy and bring to the boil in a small pan, skimming if necessary. Thicken if necessary with a little arrowroot mixed with cold water and add 2 tsp of redcurrant jelly. Check the seasoning and pour over the meat. Serve with redcurrant jelly.

BRAISED PARTRIDGE
Serves 4

2 oz (50 g) dripping
2 large carrots, finely diced
1 turnip, finely diced
2 onions, chopped
1 leek, well washed and sliced
1 bacon rasher, diced

salt and freshly ground black pepper
1 bouquet garni
2 partridges, prepared and trussed
1 pt (600 ml) stock
1 oz (25 g) plain flour
cooked mushrooms, to garnish

Preheat the oven to 190°C/375°F/Gas Mk 5. Heat the dripping in a large frying pan. Reserving some of the carrot and turnip for garnishing, place the remainder in the pan together with the onions, leek and bacon and fry until golden brown. Lift out with a slotted spoon and put in a large casserole. Season well and add the bouquet garni. Fry the partridges until brown on all sides and place on top of the vegetables. Pour in the stock, cover and cook for 30 minutes or until the birds are cooked. Meanwhile cook the reserved carrot and turnip in salted water until softened, then mix with the cooked mushrooms. Lift the birds out of the casserole, place on a warmed serving dish and keep hot. Strain the gravy into a clean saucepan. Mix the flour with a little water, stir into the gravy, bring to the boil and simmer, stirring, until thickened. Pour over the birds and garnish with the vegetable mixture.

PHEASANT WITH LENTILS
Serves 8

8 oz (225 g) red lentils
1 brace pheasant
1 oz (25 g) butter
1 onion, finely chopped
2 garlic cloves, crushed
8 oz (225 g) smoked streaky
  bacon, chopped

2 celery stalks, finely chopped
2 large carrots, diced
1 small leek, chopped
7 fl oz (200 ml) stock
salt and freshly ground black pepper

Preheat the oven to 350°F/180°C/Gas Mk 4. Put the lentils in cold water and bring to the boil. Boil for 10 minutes, then drain. Roast the pheasant for 30 minutes, remove from the roasting tin and keep warm. Reserve the meat juices. Lower the oven temperature to 300°F/150°C/ Gas Mk 2. Melt the butter in a flameproof casserole and sauté the onion, garlic and bacon for about 5 minutes. Add the remaining vegetables and cook for another 5 minutes, stirring constantly. Add the lentils, stock and meat juices and season well. Bring to the boil, reduce the heat and simmer for about 3 minutes. Add the birds, cover and return to the oven for 40–50 minutes. If the sauce gets too thick add a little more stock or red wine. When cooked, cut each bird into quarters and pour the vegetable and lentil gravy over.

DUCHY RABBIT
Serves 4

1 rabbit, jointed
½ pt (300 ml) dry cider
1 tbsp oil
1 onion, chopped

2 celery stalks, chopped
1 lb (450 g) cooking apples, chopped
salt and freshly ground black pepper
¼ pt (150 ml) double cream

Place the rabbit in a deep bowl, pour in the cider and leave for 12 hours. Preheat the oven to 325°F/170°C/Gas Mk 3. Heat the oil in a flameproof casserole, add the onions and celery and cook over a low heat for 3–4 minutes. Add the apples and mix well. Add the rabbit and cider and season with salt and pepper to taste. Cover and cook in the oven for 2 hours, stirring occasionally. More cider can be added if necessary. Remove the rabbit joints to a warm serving dish. Place the casserole over a low heat and gradually stir in the cream. Heat gently without boiling, then pour over the rabbit.

PARTRIDGE BOURGUIGNONNE
Serves 4

2 oz (50 g) butter
2 partridges
6 oz (175 g) lean bacon, cut into strips
¼ pt (150 ml) red wine
½ pt (300 ml) chicken stock
1 tsp tomato purée

1 bouquet garni
salt and freshly ground black pepper
12 oz (350 g) baby onions
1 garlic clove, crushed
6 oz (175 g) button mushrooms, sliced
1 tbsp chopped fresh parsley

Preheat the oven to 350°F/180°C/Gas Mk 4. Heat half of the butter in a frying pan, and brown the partridges on all sides. Add the bacon and brown lightly. Stir in the wine, stock and tomato purée and bring to the boil. Transfer to a casserole, add the bouquet garni and season to taste. Cover and cook in the oven for 1 hour. Meanwhile heat the remaining butter in the frying pan and brown the onions and garlic. Stir in the mushrooms. About 30 minutes before end of the cooking time stir the mushroom mixture and parsley into the dish. To serve, cut each bird in half. Remove the backbone, trim the wing and leg bones and place in a deep warmed serving dish. Spoon the sauce over.

INDEX